WALKING WASHINGTON'S HISTORY

WALKING
WASHINGTON'S
HISTORY

Ten Cities

JUDY BENTLEY

A Ruth Kirk Book

UNIVERSITY OF WASHINGTON PRESS
Seattle and London

Walking Washington's History is published with the assistance of a grant from the Ruth Kirk Book Fund, which supports publications that inform the general public on the history, natural history, archaeology, and Native cultures of the Pacific Northwest.

Copyright © 2016
by the University of Washington Press
Printed and bound in the United States
of America
Composed in Adobe Garamond, Whitney,
and Helvetica Neue Condensed

20 19 18 17 16   5 4 3 2 1

Cover and frontispiece photo:
Smith Tower, by David Glass
Maps: Matt Stevenson of CORE-GIS

Quotation on page xiii from *Wanderlust:
A History of Walking*, by Rebecca Solnit,
copyright © 2000 by Rebecca Solnit. Used
by permission of Viking Books, an imprint
of Penguin Publishing Group, a division of
Penguin Random House LLC.

UNIVERSITY OF WASHINGTON PRESS
www.washington.edu/uwpress

LIBRARY OF CONGRESS
CATALOGING-IN-PUBLICATION DATA
Bentley, Judy.
    Walking Washington's history : ten cities
/ Judy Bentley.
        pages   cm
    Includes bibliographical references and
index.
    ISBN 978-0-295-99668-4 (paperback :
alkaline paper)
    1. Washington (State)—Guidebooks.
    2. Cities and towns—Washington (State)—
Guidebooks.   3. Historic sites—Washington
(State)—Guidebooks.   4. Walking—
Washington (State)—Guidebooks.
    5. Washington (State)—History, Local.
I. Bentley, Judy. Hiking Washington's
history.   II. Title.
    F889.3.B46   2016
    979.7—dc23   2015035913

Contents

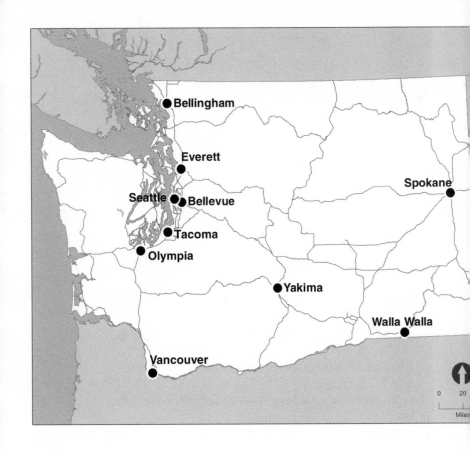

Bellingham

Everett

Spokane

Seattle ● Bellevue

Tacoma

Olympia

Yakima

Walla Walla

Vancouver

0   20

Miles

Introduction

All people have sought to manifest in lasting form their pride,
their loyalty and their faith.

Virgil G. Bogue, city engineer, 1911

Cities are meant to be walked.

Wayne Curtis, *The Last Great Walk*

I n teaching Pacific Northwest history, I have often asked students
to research one square block of a city or one square mile of the
country to uncover layers of history. Students discover that even
a limited space reveals amazing richness. They find, for instance,
that a stretch of the Duwamish Waterway in Seattle was destined to
become a port terminal until Duwamish chairwoman Cecile Hansen
made a few persistent phone calls. She knew of a village named hah-
AH-poos—Herrings House—on its banks. Later, Croatian fishing
families lived on the river's banks in a community called Riverside.
A mill provided lumber for Scandinavian shipbuilders but left a
"brownfield" of cement chunks, oil patches, and creosote. Now a trail
winds through a park along the only natural stretch of the river left
in the city.

History students throughout the state find coal mines in Bellevue, ghost signs in Spokane, treaty sites in Walla Walla. A few blocks from Seattle's Elliott Bay, they find Schmitz Park—once an old-growth forest, then an Olmsted-designed park, a source of firewood for neighbors during the Great Depression, and briefly a skateboard park known only to local teens. They uncover these layers in libraries but most directly on foot. To know a city's history, we must walk its sidewalks, trails, and streets; feel the land underfoot; and see the built environment, the succession of buildings, from cedar planks to brick to rusticated stone and steel. We will find Washington's history by walking Washington's cities.

Although the urge to gather and settle in groups is ancient, this state's urban history is relatively short. Native people in the Northwest lived dispersed along the rivers, coast, and plateaus, but thousands gathered during the height of the salmon runs to fish, socialize, and trade at Celilo Falls, Kettle Falls, and the confluence of the Snake and Columbia Rivers. Washington's cities also began on waterways—along the lower Columbia River, the Yakima River, and the falls of the Spokane River; on Elliott Bay, Commencement Bay, and Bellingham Bay, the inlets of Puget Sound named by European and American explorers. Fur companies set up trading posts on prairies. American settlers cleared land, built sawmills, and constructed docks to export logs. Mining rushes, farming, and ranching boosted Walla Walla, Spokane, and Seattle as both supply points and markets. Railroad surveyors determined the destiny of Tacoma and forced Yakima to move. These boomtowns anchored the territory as immigrants poured in from the East, from the Midwest, and even from Europe and Asia. In the 1880s, Washington grew faster than any other area of the nation.

In less than a hundred years from its founding, the nation of small farmers that Thomas Jefferson envisioned had been eclipsed. Instead, energy and talent went into building towns, according to historian J. William T. Youngs. Western cities wanted to be the next New York or Chicago. Urban real estate was a source of wealth. By statehood in 1889, more Washingtonians lived in cities than on farms, nearly one-third of them in Tacoma, Spokane, or Seattle. By choice or destiny, we became urban people.

Urban history is not a romantic history but a story of real conflict—whether to use space for private gain or common good and how to define the common good. Railroads have dominated waterfronts. Landfill and regrades have altered shorelines and displaced residents. Power companies have usurped rivers. Ethnic groups have competed for jobs. Owners and workers have clashed. Highways and freeways have bullied their way through cities, separating neighborhoods and destroying walkability. Landmarks, those markers of place that guided travelers and focused memories, have disappeared in parking lots and office towers.

Rebecca Solnit points out in her book *Wanderlust* that public space is being abandoned and eroded in older cites: "malls replace main streets; streets have no sidewalks; buildings are entered through their garages," and technology brings services to the home. The virtual marketplace replaces the real centers of human interaction.

Despite these forces, Washington cities are alive and well. In world's fairs and expositions, Seattle and Spokane have flaunted their identities. Slogans have boasted of prosperity: "Hear Everett Hum," "Bellingham's Better," and "The Valleys of the Yakima Beat the World." In the words of Virgil Bogue, who developed a grand plan for the city of Seattle, citizens have invested their pride, loyalty, and faith in civic centers. Women have fought for basic rights and founded civic institutions that enhanced community life. A new generation has moved back downtown from the suburbs. Visionaries have developed trails that lead along riverfronts or railroad grades, providing paths through each city's history. Walking carries us through the public spaces that have been shared for decades, preserving those spaces.

No city that remains vibrant is stuck in history, but many cities are best known for the periods when they first flourished—Vancouver as a fur-trading post in the 1820s, 1830s, and 1840s; Olympia as the fledgling territory's capital in the 1850s; Walla Walla as a crossroads of travois poles and mule trains in the 1860s; Tacoma as the first western terminus of the transcontinental railroad in the 1870s and 1880s; Spokane as a railroad hub and center of mining wealth during the late 1800s; Seattle as the jump-off point for the Klondike gold rush in the 1890s; Everett as a blue-collar mill town in the early 1900s; Bellingham as a series of boomtowns through the 1920s; Yakima as a transport center for the lush, irrigated Yakima Valley throughout the 1900s; and Bellevue as a bedroom community turned edge city in the late 1900s.

Each city has aspired to greatness. This book highlights those moments of aspiration. Taken as a whole, the moments trace the state's history. By walking each city, you will find its place in Washington history and its heart.

Legend

Walk Starting Points

- - - Featured Walks

• • • • Other Walks

Streets

Highway Markers

~~~ Creeks

Rivers & Lakes

College Campuses

Historic Sites and Other Features

■ Historic Site

□ Ghost Site

▲ Statue

Museum

Parking

Restrooms

Library

Visitor Center

Steps

Train

How to Use This Book

[Walking] is about being outside in public space.

Rebecca Solnit, *Wanderlust*

This book offers a sampling of the most historically important cities in Washington. They were chosen based on several factors: significance, size, geographical diversity, and walking appeal. In terms of population, the top ten cities in the state are Seattle, Spokane, Tacoma, Vancouver, Bellevue, Everett, Kent, Yakima, Renton, and Spokane Valley. Spokane Valley is much more populous than Olympia, but Olympia has been the capital since 1853, and so Olympia is included here. Kent is bigger than Walla Walla, but Walla Walla was the largest city in the territory in the 1860s, dominating inland Washington, Oregon, and Idaho. Ellensburg and Wenatchee are important to Central Washington, but so is Yakima, which is larger. The Tri-Cities have ballooned since World War II as the nerve center of the nuclear industry, but they present a walking and weather challenge. The fastest-growing urban centers today—

Kent, Federal Way, and Spokane Valley—were suburbs and farms less than a hundred years ago; Bellevue represents that change in this book. Victorian Port Townsend claims an early niche in Puget Sound history as the first port of call for ships and crews in the mid-1800s; Port Angeles along with Longview, Aberdeen, Hoquiam, and Bremerton could also claim fame, but this is a tale of only ten cities, leaving other urban treasures for further exploration.

Within each of these ten, the book emphasizes one period of its history—a moment of aspiration; other significant events may be mentioned only lightly. The order of chapters is roughly chronological, according to the time when each city first flourished, with some exceptions. Vancouver comes first, as the earliest large permanent gathering on the frontier, but it also boomed with shipbuilding during World War II, so that history is described, too. Spokane dominated the Inland Empire from the late 1800s on, but that chapter focuses on the revitalization of downtown and the riverfront during Expo '74, so it comes later in the book. Chapter introductions explain each city's niche in Washington history and preview the focus of each walk.

Each chapter features a central loop that starts and ends at the same place, all of those places with parking access, most with public restrooms, and most served by public transportation. Basic directions are provided to the start from major highways (recognizing the automobile's dominance even in historic districts), and addresses are provided for use with electronic locating tools. Each chapter map shows important streets. Words, devices, maps—use all three to navigate routes that may change with seasonal roadwork or transportation policies.

Each central loop is from two to seven miles long. Options for extensions or shortcuts are noted along the way. Don't hesitate to go off-route. Follow the advice of John R. Stilgoe in *Outside Lies Magic*: become an explorer. Several cities have what I call "pioneer walks" through early settlements on the periphery of the cities they foreshadowed: Old Town in Tacoma, Alki in Seattle, Tumwater south of Olympia, Lowell in Everett, Mercer Slough in Bellevue. Although the word *pioneer* has lost some of its luster, those who moved here early left their names and still capture our imagination.

In each chapter, a map shows the route, some amenities such as parking and restrooms, attractions such as history museums and libraries, and the most significant historical sites. Public restrooms are essential to the walker, and cities vary in their accommodations. Visitors' centers, firehouses, and libraries usually offer restrooms, as do museums, with donations appreciated.

Cities vary in the extent to which they have preserved the landmarks of their history. The larger cities have preservation and walking movements—organizations like Feet First, Historic Seattle, Historic Spokane, and Historic Tacoma. The oldest structure in Washington State on its original foundation is a mere 160 years old; you can still see it in Bellingham. Some cities have preserved their historic cores more effectively than others. These include Pioneer Square in Seattle, Fairhaven in Bellingham, historic districts in Tacoma and Spokane, and streets and avenues in Everett and Yakima. Lacking a nineteenth-century streetscape, some cities have incorporated historic interpretation into kiosks, sidewalks, plaques, history spots, and works of public art. Other cities, like Tacoma, Bellingham, and Vancouver, have seized on the aftermath of deindustrialization and Superfund cleanups to create new public space.

Still, heritage succumbs to growth, and development alters historic sites. Even as I was writing this book, the Philbrook House, the oldest remaining building in old Bellevue, was demolished. A vestige of the southern approach to the Alaska-Yukon-Pacific Exposition on the University of Washington campus was scheduled for obliteration. Expect some changes as you walk past bulldozers, cranes, and construction fences.

Since the 1920s, automobiles have won the streets in American cities, but this book utilizes whatever pedestrian-friendly facilities cities have retained: sidewalks, railroad grades, parks, biking and walking trails, and esplanades. Vancouver and Bellingham have constructed waterfront walking trails for both recreation and historic interpretation. Seattle has outlined a walking trail around Lake Union in its center. Spokane has uncovered the powerful river and falls in its midst and built a park for strolling. Olympia has constructed a trail from Tukwila around Capitol Lake to Budd Inlet. Tacoma features a waterfront esplanade. Cities have taken to heart the admonition by Jane Jacobs in her 1961 book, *The Death and Life of Great American Cities*, that "an unwalked city is a dead city; arguably it is no city at all."

Since the walking route and sites have been selected to showcase a particular theme in each city, the narrative doesn't mention every important building or point out every significant site. The chapters are a sampling of history, a story of people and events more than of architecture, yet each city has at least one edifice that evokes permanence and wealth, which I have included. The social and political history of a city is less visible than its economic history. Old meeting halls, stores, churches, hotels, train stations, and town squares speak of public life. For the grand campaigns, the visiting presidents, and the free speech fights, only street corners remain. The book uses boldface to indicate that something historic is visible. Photographs recall a few features long gone. Maps indicate sites of ghosts—structures that were important historically but no longer exist. The rest is up to your imagination.

Lastly, walking is about extending yourself into shared public space. Along the way, you will encounter all sorts of people: commuters and construction workers, protesters and tourists, dog walkers and street people, sketchers and cyclists, runners and free spirits. Approach these walks as an adventure into both history and city life.

WALKING WASHINGTON'S HISTORY

CHAPTER ONE

Vancouver

The First City

The towns were the spearheads of the frontier. Planted far
in advance of the line of settlement, they held the West for
the approaching population.

Richard C. Wade, *The Urban Frontier: The Rise of Western Cities, 1790–1830*

Vancouver was Washington's first city, a grand emporium
on a plain above the lower Columbia River where Chinook
traders, British and American explorers, fur company agents,
voyageurs, Kanakas, missionaries, and settlers converged. The river
made the plain an ideal location for a trading post and—in the next
century—a good place to build ships during two world wars.

In the late 1700s, European and American explorers and traders
sailed up and down the Northwest coast, searching for an entrance to
a water route across North America. There were rumors of a mighty
river of the West that led into the continent and might short-cut the
long journey around Cape Horn from Europe and Boston. The offshore grayness of fog and mist made the river's wide mouth hard
to find. In April 1792, English captain George Vancouver sailed right
past it. He noted in his journal a change in the sea to "river coloured
water" but didn't consider the opening "worthy of more attention"
at that time.

When he returned a few weeks later, he was too late. American trader Robert Gray had noticed the outflow "of some great river" and named it after his ship, the *Columbia Rediviva*. Unlike Gray, however, Vancouver sent a tender—a smaller ship—over the treacherous sandbar at the river's mouth. Under Lieutenant William Broughton, the *Chatham* sailed a hundred miles upstream to a point Broughton named for his captain, Vancouver Point. These explorations opened the vast watershed of the Columbia River to European trade and American settlement.

Intrigued by Gray's discovery and still hoping for a water passage across the continent, President Thomas Jefferson sent William Clark and Meriwether Lewis overland in 1805. They followed the Missouri River west but found no easy water route until they could paddle down the Snake and Columbia Rivers to the Pacific Ocean. Returning east up the Columbia in 1806, they passed islands that obscured the Multnomah (Willamette) River coming in from the south but noticed a large plain on the north bank, a spot Lewis declared could maintain "40 or 50 thousand souls if properly cultivated." More than a million people live on this plain today, first named Fort Plain and eventually Vancouver.

The Columbia River at Fort Plain was a confluence of cultures. Canoeing up and down the river to fish, trade, and socialize, some 16,000 Chinook-speaking Indians controlled the lower Columbia from its mouth at the Pacific Ocean to the rapids where the river flowed through the Cascade Mountains. Columbia Plateau tribes from the east followed the Klickitat Trail west over the Cascades to *Alaek-ae*, or "turtle place," on the plain above the river. Long before Americans arrived, tribes had been trading with Europeans, adding scarlet and blue blankets, sailor jackets, overalls, shirts, and hats to their wardrobes.

Despite the ventures of Americans Gray, Lewis, and Clark, it was the British who first named and claimed Vancouver. The king of England had granted the Hudson's Bay Company a monopoly on the fur trade of North America. That exclusive right had been challenged in the Oregon Country by the Northwest Company, owned by a collection of Scots without royal sanction. In 1825 the HBC merged with its rival and moved its headquarters from Hudson's Bay 2,000 miles closer to the Pacific Ocean. Vancouver's journal and the map Lieutenant Broughton had made when he sailed up the Columbia guided the location of the trading post. Fort Vancouver became the hub of a vast trade network that covered 700,000 square miles, from Russian Alaska to Spanish California.

Chief factor John McLoughlin, the company's agent, ruled the empire and its web of relationships with the Indians who supplied the furs. When the fur brigades plunged down the river, bringing beaver pelts from the hinterland to be packed and shipped to markets in China and London, the fort's population swelled to a thousand.

Chinook people benefited from the trade until epidemics of fever and ague, probably malaria, broke out from contact with foreigners in 1829 and 1830. What began as a lively interaction of cultures ended with the death of up to 90 percent of the Indian population along the river. McLoughlin wrote that "the intermittent fever is making a dreadful havoc among the natives and at this place half our people are laid up with it." He estimated that three-quarters of the Indians in the fort's vicinity had been "carried off." The Chinook would never rebound to their strength and numbers at the time of contact.

A progression of missionaries made Fort Vancouver their first stop in the Pacific Northwest and found a thriving metropolis. Reverend Herbert Beaver, clergyman of the Church of England, served for two years as chaplain, but he was often at odds with McLoughlin on issues of morality and propriety. Fathers Francis Norbert Blanchet and Modeste Demers came to serve the French-Canadian Catholics who had been voyageurs for the fur company. Reverend Samuel Parker came to scout mission sites for Protestant couples who would follow.

Arriving in 1836, Narcissa Whitman described the fort as "the New

York of the Pacific." By the 1840s, however, the Hudson Bay Company's dominance had waned. Beavers throughout the Northwest had been depleted and American settlers were moving in, attracted by a series of government land acts that promised 640 acres to those willing to build homes, plant crops, and stay. McLoughlin regularly sent HBC boats up the river to assist exhausted and hungry immigrants approaching the fort. He generously offered them food for the winter and seeds for spring planting on credit as long as they settled south of the Columbia River. Most were headed for the fertile Willamette Valley.

The United States and Great Britain had jointly occupied the Oregon Country since 1818, but the Willamette Valley was filling up, and Americans wanted the land north of the Columbia River and the ports on Puget Sound, too. In James Polk's jingoistic 1844 presidential campaign, expansionists adopted the slogan "54–40 or fight," referring to the 54th parallel at the southern border of present-day Alaska. After the election, Americans decided not to fight and negotiated the boundary at the 49th parallel, placing the Columbia River and Puget Sound within U.S. territory. McLoughlin moved to a homestead across the river in the Willamette Valley, and the Hudson's Bay Company moved north across the international border. Fort Vancouver became the Vancouver Barracks, a U.S. military post. In 1851, settlers north of the Columbia met at Cowlitz Landing, on the Cowlitz River north of Vancouver, and petitioned the United States Congress to become a territory separate from Oregon. Washington Territory was created two years later, encompassing a large area that stretched to present-day Idaho and part of western Montana.

When the British left, there was hardly a town of Vancouver, just disintegrating HBC structures and a pesky potato farm. Amos and Esther Short and their eight children had migrated from Pennsylvania in 1845 and claimed land on the Columbia on the fort's western boundary. The HBC was much annoyed by having American settlers north of the river and close to its own property. Company men tried to evict the family, harrowed their potato fields, destroyed their fences, and refused to sell them supplies, but Amos held on to plat the town he named, somewhat defiantly, Columbia City. Other settlers trickled in, and by 1857, the town incorporated as Vancouver, its name changed by the territorial legislature, with 250 people and a similar number of cows. For a brief time, Vancouver vied with Olympia to be the territorial capital, but Vancouver was deemed too close to Oregon.

As the town grew, its location on the river remained important. In 1908 the Northern Pacific Railway reached Vancouver from Pasco, and a railroad bridge crossed the Columbia River to Portland. That placed Vancouver at the intersection of both north–south and east–west transportation routes. Soon railroads dominated the waterfronts in many Puget Sound cities, and in 1911 the state authorized municipalities to create public port districts. A year later, Vancouver voters established the Port of Vancouver, continuing the tradition of international trade started by the Hudson's Bay Company. During World War I, the port leased land to Standifer shipyards, which turned out ten merchant ships. Spruce production on the plain above the river brought thousands of soldiers to town to work as lumbermen in the U.S. Army's Spruce Production Division.

More growth came during World War II. In 1940, the first aluminum plant in the West was opened by Alcoa in Vancouver. It benefited from the hydropower of the Bonneville and Grand Coulee Dams, completed on the Columbia in 1937 and 1941, respectively. The aluminum, in turn, supported the manufacture of airplanes and ships during World War II. Thousands of workers streamed to work in shipyards built by industrialist Henry Kaiser on both sides of the Columbia River.

In Vancouver, Kaiser dredged and built up land on the waterfront on the southern edge of Fort Plain. The Vancouver shipyard—or

"Vanship"—produced more than 140 "Victory Ships" during the war. Of the 38,000 workers, more than half were women. The population of Clark County grew from 18,000 people in 1941 to more than 95,000 in January 1944. Workers first lived in a 7,000-bed dormitory, then in temporary housing constructed in McLoughlin Heights just north of the shipyards. After the war, wartime housing was removed, but many of the newcomers stayed. Family housing continued to fan out beyond the city's core and away from the river. Vancouver is now the fourth-largest city in Washington, after Seattle, Tacoma, and Spokane.

As the city grew, the mighty river at its doorstep was tamed. In its natural state, the Columbia flooded often, surging across the west side of town in 1894 during its highest recorded crest, 34.4 feet above flood stage. On May 30, 1948, a flood wiped out Vanport, a wartime city just across the river in Oregon, resulting in the death of twenty Vancouver residents. That disaster led to the construction of new dams; now engineers at computers control water levels for both transport and flood control.

The Columbia bar, however, continued to impede commerce. Despite the use of pilots and the construction of jetties at the mouth of the river as early as the 1880s, the bar remains treacherous to cross and notorious for shipwrecks. Puget Sound ports eventually provided more placid access to the ocean, but Vancouver is still the third-largest port in Washington. A proposal to build a major terminal for the transfer of oil from railroad cars to barges would greatly increase the port's capacity for oil storage, but opposition to increasing the number of coal and oil trains rumbling along the banks of the Columbia River is strong.

The river separates Washington from Oregon but also connects the two states in joint use and management. The first trains crossed the Columbia River on a bridge in 1908, replacing the ferries that had carried railcars. Automobiles crossed in 1917 on the last link in the Pacific Highway from Canada to Mexico. In 1958, another span was built alongside the original bridge; both remain today, one for northbound traffic and one for southbound, with vertical lifts and humpbacks to accommodate shipping traffic. A new bridge opened on Vancouver's east side in 1982 to carry I-205 to Portland. Washington, Oregon, and the federal government have considered constructing a new bridge to replace the spans that carry I-5 over the river.

As Washington's first city, Vancouver claims many firsts: first town square, first civilian hospital, and first homes for orphans, the homeless, the aged, and the insane. A walk through Vancouver begins on the river, ascends a land bridge over Highway 14, wanders through the old fur trade fort and army housing, crosses the town square and shipyard sites, and passes a commemorative boat of discovery on its return to the river, the ancient avenue of commerce. An extended walk, the Columbia River Renaissance Trail, follows the riverfront east along the water routes traveled by traders, explorers, settlers, and ships launched from the shipyards.

Cathlapotle

When Lewis and Clark canoed downriver in 1805, they saw a large village called Cathlapotle at the confluence of the Lake and Lewis Rivers with the Columbia. Fourteen houses and an estimated 900 inhabitants were spread out northwest of what is now Vancouver. Salmon, steelhead, and wapato root were plentiful; Chinook women would loosen the wapato roots underwater with their feet to harvest the nutritious tubers. On their return trip in 1806, the Corps of Discovery camped about a mile upstream from the village at a site known today as Wapato Portage.

As epidemics decimated the Chinook, interior tribes such as the Cowlitz and Klickitat moved onto the river, but houses at Cathlapotle stood empty by the mid-1850s. In 2005, a plankhouse was replicated in the Carty Unit of the Ridgefield National Wildlife Refuge. The plankhouse is usually open on weekend afternoons except in the winter (see www.ridgefieldfriends.org to confirm hours).

Vancouver Loop

START: Waterfront Park, 115 Columbia Way

DIRECTIONS: From I-5 north, take exit 1B toward City Center and onto 6th Street. From I-5 south, take exit 1C toward City Center and onto E 15th Street. From either direction, turn left (south) on Columbia Street, and follow Columbia as it curves east under the I-5 bridge and along the river. Park

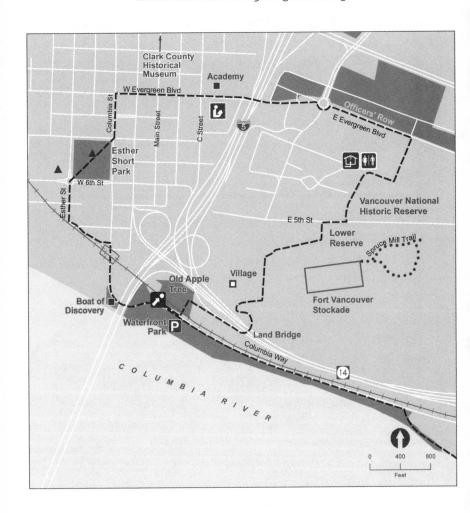

at Waterfront Park on the south side of Columbia Way, east of the bridge and just east of restaurant parking lots. Look for brown signs for the Riverfront Trail.

DISTANCE: About 3 miles round-trip (with an optional 3.5-mile one-way extension)

AMENITIES: Parking at Waterfront Park; restrooms at Vancouver National Historic Reserve, the Vancouver Public Library, and Esther Short Park

The earliest history of Vancouver is found in several places: in the replica of a plankhouse, in the statue of a chief's daughter, and most of all in a land bridge, a high paved path that leads to Vancouver National Historic Reserve. The walls of the bridge describe the confluence of cultures on the Columbia River. For walkers, the bridge restores the river's connection to the prairie, known successively as Turtle Place, Jolie Prairie, and Fort Plain.

Start at Waterfront Park, *and cross Columbia Way on a crosswalk, following signs* to the **land bridge**. At significant places along the lower Columbia River, artist Maya Lin has redesigned landmarks at the confluence of Native American, European, and American cultures (see www.confluenceproject.org). In Vancouver, the river, trails from the mountains, and cultures converged on Fort Plain. "Here I landed and walked on shore about three miles," wrote William Clark in 1805, "a fine open prairie for about one mile back of which the country rises gradually and woodland commences." After two centuries of human use, such a ramble was no longer possible; the riverfront and prairie had been cut off from each other by highways, railroad tracks, and streets. The land bridge over Highway 14, dedicated in 2008, completes a circle that's been broken, according to site architect Johnpaul Jones.

The path to the land bridge crosses under the raised berm for the transcontinental railroad, which first separated the plain from the river in 1901. *Pass the* **oldest apple tree** in the state, which first bore fruit in 1830. This tree is not native; its seeds came from England. From such trees, Hudson's Bay Company factor John McLoughlin handed out apples as a treat; many settler children had never tasted one. Vancouverites have carefully preserved this living remnant of the British presence.

Walk through the **Welcome Gate** to the right, an archway of canoe paddles designed by artist Lillian Pitt. A cast-glass image of a Chinook woman's face captures light at the top of a paddle. *Ascend the paved trail* through the **Entry Grove**. The concrete land bridge is covered with earth that supports native plants on both sides of the path. Several interpretive plaques note the natural history of this land's original prairies, oak savannahs, and conifer forests.

The trail pauses at a **River Overlook** and a **Prairie Overlook**, recognizing the many people who lived along the river and the many more who came from the higher prairies to fish and trade in season. Words for *river* and *land* are carved in nine native languages. Chinook basketry patterns line the path, and petroglyph images decorate benches. At its highest point on a clear day, the bridge has views of Mount Hood, Mount St. Helens, Mount Adams, and Mount Jefferson, as well as the river.

Stop at the **Village Overlook,** on the north side of the land bridge. Below you, 600 people lived in a multicultural village outside the fort's walls in the 1820s and 1830s, the largest settlement in the West at the time except for Sitka, Alaska. When the fur brigade paddled down the Columbia and resupply ships arrived from England, the fort came alive. The furs were transferred to ships for transport to California, the Hawaiian Islands, China, and Alaska, along with lumber, pickled salmon, and dairy products processed at the post. Traders and sailors replenished their stocks from the produce of the HBC's farm before heading upriver or out to sea for the next season.

Coming down from the land bridge, follow the paved trail to the **village site.** Only twenty-five people lived within the stockade at Fort

O.Sohon Del.   Sarony Major & Knapp Lith' 449 Broadway N.Y.

FORT VANCOUVER, W. T.

Gustavus Sohon drew Fort Vancouver—the orchard, village, stockade, farm, and residences—
when he visited as part of the U.S. Pacific Railroad Expedition and Survey team in the 1850s.
Sohon had left East Prussia as a teenager to avoid conscription and joined the U.S. Army,
where he was valued for his communication and artistic skills. Courtesy National Park Service.

Vancouver; everyone else resided in the village. The workers were
trappers, blacksmiths, coopers, carpenters, tinsmiths, dairy workers,
millwrights, and farm laborers from many countries of the world.
Some women accompanied men on the fur brigades, cleaning skins,
cooking, and making clothing. Others stayed in the village and
worked in fields or salted and packed salmon.

The broad lanes are bordered by split-rail fences and two recon-
structed cabins. A large entrance gate separated the village from the
fort proper. Archaeological excavations have uncovered objects from
around the world, including stoneware jars from England and China;
decorative tableware manufactured in England, France, China, and

Japan; English brick; and Hawaiian coral. Conversation took place mostly in French or Chinook, not English. In the words of the company's governor, George Simpson, an HBC boat was "the prettiest congregation of nations, the nicest confusion of tongues, that has ever taken place since the days of the tower of Babel." A jargon, called the Chinook jargon, developed to facilitate trade, drawing words from many sources.

Walk from the village, past an orchard, to a replica of the **Fort Vancouver Stockade**, which has a modest admission fee for adults. The stockade protected the company's store and furs. Buildings within it include a jail, an iron house, a well, numerous outhouses, a chapel, a clerk's office, a kitchen, and cannon used only to salute arriving British ships. Inside these walls, John McLoughlin presided as chief factor or business agent. His job was to keep the economic engine moving and to keep peace among the people at the post. He was well suited to the task; he came from Irish, Scottish, and French-Canadian stock, and he married a métis woman, Marguerite Wadin, whose father had been one of the original partners of the Northwest Company and whose mother was part Cree and part Swiss. Outside the stockade walls is the **garden**. By 1840, this garden in the wilderness had eight acres of strawberry vines; beds of carrots, turnips, cabbage, potatoes, squash, parsnips, cucumbers, peas, tomatoes, and beets; and a variety of fruits and flowers. The HBC employed more people in agriculture, including large farms at Cowlitz and on prairies near today's Olympia, than in the fur trade. Volunteers keep a much smaller garden growing at the site today.

The Hudson's Bay Company agreed to leave Fort Vancouver when the international border was settled in 1848. A year later, several hundred U.S. Army troops traveled around Cape Horn to take possession of what they would call Vancouver Barracks. By the 1860s, the unused stockade had fallen into disrepair and burned.

Vancouver Barracks was the first U.S. Army post in the Pacific

Northwest, the headquarters and supply depot during the Indian wars of the 1850s and the American Civil War of the 1860s. Soldiers heading for the Spanish–American War in 1898 and the subsequent Philippine–American War received training here.

From the eastern end of the stockade, you may walk a short loop, the **Spruce Mill trail.** During World War I, the field hosted the largest spruce sawmill in the world. Soldiers in the U.S. Army's Spruce Production Division produced more than a million board feet of lightweight lumber each day for use in aircraft. The soldiers worked eight hours per day instead of ten hours or more, a standard unions had been advocating without success.

At the far end of the loop is the **Pearson Air Museum,** and to the south is the **Pearson Air Field,** where the wind blows through the grasses at the end of the runway, reminiscent of the ancient prairie. The field has a long history. During Portland's world's fair in 1905, eighteen-year-old Lincoln Beachey flew a dirigible across the Columbia River to Vancouver Barracks to deliver a letter. In 1937, three Russian aviators landed on the field after flying nonstop over the North Pole from Moscow.

The U.S. Army stayed at Fort Vancouver for 150 years, leaving behind the barracks when the last reserve and national guard units moved out in 2011. Conversion of Vancouver Barracks into a national historic site run by the National Park Service started in 1948. In 1996, Congress created the **Vancouver National Historic Reserve**.

From the lower part of the reserve, cross E 5th Street into the Great Meadow, and *ramble at will. Beyond the meadow, to the north,* enjoy a visit to the **Fort Vancouver Visitor Center**. *North of the visitor center,* the houses on **Officers' Row** date from the 1850s. Ulysses S. Grant, who became the Union's victorious general in the Civil War, was a quartermaster on the base during that decade, and a **plaque** just outside the northeast corner of the reserve states that he planted potatoes to reduce the expense of the officers' mess. During the 1930s, the fort served as the district headquarters for the Civilian Conservation Corps, supervised by George Marshall, who lived in the **Marshall House** at *1301 Officers' Row*. Marshall became the nation's top-ranking military leader in World War II.

The destiny of lesser-known residents was also shaped at the reserve. In 1851, an African American woman named Monimia Travers arrived as a slave in the household of U.S. Army officer Llewellyn Jones. Jones freed her when he was transferred to the Southwest. Her life after that is unknown.

W Reserve Street divided the military reserve from its neighbors, a function served today by I-5, the main north–south arterial on the West Coast. *After the traffic circle at the northwestern corner of the reserve (E Evergreen Boulevard and Fort Vancouver Way), continue west on Evergreen Boulevard to cross over eight lanes of I-5 to C Street.*

On the north side of Evergreen at C Street is the **Academy,** a three-story brick building with a cupola on top. Built in 1873 with bricks supplied by Vancouver's Hidden Brick Company, the academy was the House of Providence, the headquarters for the Sisters of Providence in the Pacific Northwest. Mother Joseph (Esther Pariseau) and four sisters arrived from Montreal in 1856, when disputed land claims led to shootings and good water from wells attracted breweries. "Here the devil is so enraged he frightens me," Mother Joseph declared.

Trained as a carpenter and an architect, Mother Joseph immediately started work building hospitals, schools, and orphanages, which eventually numbered twenty-nine in the territory. Sister Stanislaus remembered many years later that Mother Joseph would stride through the construction "complete with saw and hammer at her girth . . . praying aloud while she worked." Needing funds for her enterprise, she embarked on "begging trips" to the mining camps. In 1858, the sisters opened St. Joseph Hospital, the first hospital in Washington Territory.

The Sisters of Providence sold the House of Providence to the

Hidden family of Vancouver in 1966, and the Academy is now occupied by offices and businesses. The legacy of St. Joseph's continues as a PeaceHealth hospital. You will find a statue of Mother Joseph in a prayerful mode with her tools at her side at the PeaceHealth Southwest Medical Center, at Mother Joseph Place and Mill Plain Boulevard, which is not in easy walking distance. She also represents the state in the National Statuary Hall in Washington, D.C., along with the Protestant missionary Marcus Whitman.

On the south side of Evergreen Boulevard at C Street is the new **Vancouver Public Library**. Climb to the top floor and visit the Vancouver Room for a panoramic view of this prime location on the Columbia River. Clark County was named in 1849, honoring the explorer William Clark, who had walked the "fine open prairie" in 1805.

Walk west on Evergreen, crossing Main and Washington. You may take a side trip three blocks north on Main to the **Hidden House** at 100 W 13th Street, home to the family that manufactured most of the brick used in Vancouver from 1871 on. From there, *continue on to 16th Street* for the **Clark County Historical Museum** *and return on Washington Street, past* **St. James Cathedral**, the oldest Catholic church in the state, *at 12th between Washington and Columbia*. Completed in 1885, the cathedral was the headquarters of the Catholic Church in western Washington until a new St. James Cathedral was built in Seattle in 1907.

Back at Evergreen and Columbia, turn south and walk two blocks to **Esther Short Park**, the first public square in Washington. Early history is memorialized in the **Pioneer Mother**, a heroic statue of a woman, flintlock in hand, with three children clinging to her skirt.

Esther Short

Esther Short was such a mother. She and her husband, Amos, tangled repeatedly with the Hudson's Bay Company about the land they claimed on Fort Vancouver's western boundary. Once, when Amos was away, company agents forcibly rowed Esther and her ten children across the Columbia to Oregon, but the family returned. Another time, while Amos was away on trial for killing two HBC employees who had approached the Shorts' cabin, other HBC men tried to destroy fences around the cabin, but Esther knocked one of them down. Amos was acquitted on the grounds that he was defending his home. Shortly after that, in 1853, Amos drowned in a boat at the mouth of the Columbia River, returning from selling his potatoes in California, but Esther hung on. She opened one hotel and then another and prospered enough to donate one section of her land for a town square and other land for a wharf.

Vancouver acknowledges its British heritage in the **statue of George Vancouver** at the *corner of 6th and Esther Streets.* The young captain holds a map of North America over a globe of the world showing his route along the Pacific coast.

Continue south on Esther Street to Phil Arnold Way, where the railroad lines head northwest. The railroad depot, several blocks west at 1301 W 11th Street, has served four railroad lines—the Northern Pacific, Great Northern, Union Pacific, and the Spokane, Portland & Seattle Railway—and remains the fourth-busiest Amtrak station in the state. The tracks also carry an increasing number of coal cars and oil tankers from the Midwest. A **wall of murals** below the tracks memorializes veterans who served in the two world wars, and in the Korean, Vietnam, and Gulf wars.

Walk southeast on Phil Arnold Way, and then south (right) on Columbia Street to cross under the railroad tracks. (A major waterfront park and pier is planned in this vicinity, and streets may have changed, but head southeast toward the riverfront.) Esther Short gave the valuable waterfront part of her claim for a public wharf, which became the Port of Vancouver in 1912. The first terminal was built here, at the foot of Columbia Street. During World War I, the port contracted with

Standifer shipyards to build both wooden and steel-hulled ships for the war effort. For many years after that, the site was a paper mill. The port expanded along the waterfront to the west, with a second terminal completed in 1936. In the future, the Port of Vancouver may include a major terminal facility to store crude oil for transfer to barges, a controversial proposal opposed by many civic leaders.

At the foot of Columbia Street, pass through a small park with a red metal "**Boat of Discovery**" held aloft by concrete pillars. This boat commemorates not just one great voyage by George Vancouver and his ship *Discovery*, says the plaque, but "the hundreds of lesser voyages made by the small boats and unfailing courage by which these tasks were carried out through the long years of exploration of the Great River of the West."

Continue along the sidewalk as Columbia curves under the I-5 bridges. Land claims were shooting matters in the young territory. A **bronze marker** in the ground just east of the bridge, on the north side of Columbia Way, marks the site of the balm of Gilead tree. Amos Short carved his initials on the cottonwood, marking it as a witness tree on the eastern corner of his land claim. All of the land boundaries in downtown Vancouver were measured from this tree, which stood where Main Street began. The tree was too close to the river, which undercut it in 1909.

The lower Columbia today is controlled by many dams upriver. Fishing boats crowd its relatively placid waters in season, and bridges carry heavy traffic—an average of 127,000 cars—daily. These looming structures darken the waterfront trail underneath. Jetliners from Portland International Airport soar overhead, and the constant whir of car traffic echoes the vital trade network of earlier centuries. Vancouver is now allied closely to Portland. For the travelers on these bridges, the river is merely an obstacle to be crossed, no longer the mighty river of the West carrying the people to a Grand Emporium.

Extended Walk: Columbia River Renaissance Trail

START: Waterfront Park, 115 Columbia Way

DIRECTIONS: See Vancouver Loop.

DISTANCE: 3.5 miles one-way to the Kaiser Viewing Tower

AMENITIES: Parking at Waterfront Park, Ilchee Plaza, and the Kaiser Viewing Tower; restrooms at the Kaiser Viewing Tower

For a richer sense of human history along the river, *walk the Columbia River Renaissance Trail east from Waterfront Park.* The trail follows sidewalks and paved trails for more than three miles through parks, along beaches, and between housing developments and the water. It passes through many periods of Vancouver history: the Chinook trade period, exploration, fur trading, and shipyards.

After about one mile, you will encounter a seven-foot-tall, 700-pound bronze statue of **Ilchee**, created by Eric Jensen in 1994. Ilchee,

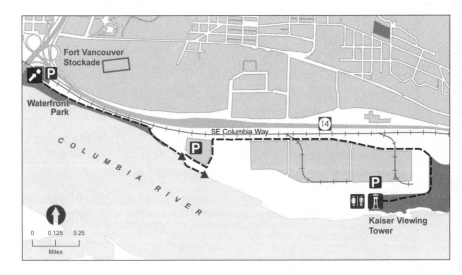

Workers at the Kaiser shipyard in Vancouver watch the launch of a ship during World War II. Photograph is by Louis Lee, a Kaiser photographer. Courtesy National Park Service.

or Moon Girl, was born along the Columbia River around 1800, the daughter of a powerful Chinook chief named Comcomly. Fur traders commonly sought liaisons with Indian women to increase their trade networks, and in 1811 Ilchee was married to Duncan McDougall, the chief factor at Fort Astoria, the American fur post at the mouth of the Columbia. (Read her story at www.trailtribes.org/fortclatsop/celiast-and-ilchee.htm.) However, McDougall left her after a few years and returned to a Hudson's Bay Company fort on Lake Superior. Ilchee then married Casino, who was a rival chief to her father. She was said to be a remarkable woman who had the power of a shaman and paddled her own canoe.

A short distance beyond, on the waterfront, find the **Wendy Rose** monument, which honors women who worked in the shipyards during World War II. The stainless steel sculpture designed and created by a local artist group called Women Who Weld portrays "Wendy the Welder" striding into her new job sporting a jaunty red glass polka-dot bandanna on her head.

At about three miles, follow a 0.5-mile side trail to the **Kaiser Viewing Tower**, which recalls the period during World War II when Vancouver was heavily industrialized. The first ship produced by the Kaiser shipyards here was named the S.S. *George Vancouver*—what else?—and launched on July 4, 1942. In early 1943, a crowd of 75,000 gathered on the riverfront to watch Eleanor Roosevelt christen the first aircraft escort carrier. North of the shipyards, 5,500 units of temporary housing were constructed to house workers. The shipyard site was closed at the end of the war and later sold to Gilmore Steel. The trail continues another 1.5 miles to Marine Park, taking detours away from the riverfront because of flood damage in 2011.

Resources   City of Vancouver Parks and Recreation,
            www.cityofvancouver.us/parksrec

            Clark County Historical Museum, 1511 Main Street

            Vancouver Public Library, 901 C Street

            Visitor Center, Vancouver National Historic Reserve,
            1501 E Evergreen Boulevard

CHAPTER TWO

Olympia

The Birthplace of Washington

Glorious news for Washington! Arrival of Governor Stevens!
Complete success of the Expedition! Entire practicability of the
Northern Pacific Route.

Washington Pioneer, December 3, 1853

Isaac Stevens arrived in Olympia in 1853 on a November night drenched with rain, a traditional Northwest weather welcome. Right away, the new governor declared that the wet hamlet would be the temporary capital of Washington Territory, newly separated from Oregon Territory. Then he set to work reporting on his survey for a transcontinental railroad, convening a legislature, and planning treaty councils.

Margaret Stevens followed her husband west a year later, approaching the hamlet with their four children after a bone-shaking trek on the Cowlitz Trail. "At night we were told, on ascending a hill, 'There is Olympia.' Below us, in the deep mud, were a few low, wooden houses, at the head of Puget Sound," she wrote. "My heart sank, for the first time in my life, at the prospect."

Despite her misgivings, the mud flats on Budd Inlet were a natural spot to set up government. An Indian trail and trade route led from the coast up the Chehalis River to the south end of Puget Sound. A primitive wagon road called the Cowlitz Trail led north from the water highway of the Columbia River and from Vancouver, the first fledgling city in the territory. From Budd Inlet, ships could sail or steam north into the Strait of Juan de Fuca, west into the Pacific Ocean, and south to San Francisco or more distant ports.

As emigrants poured over the Oregon Trail in the 1840s, they found that land in the fertile Willamette Valley on the south side of the Columbia River had already been claimed. Instead they turned north toward Puget Sound, even before the international border was negotiated with Great Britain in 1846. The first settlers—the Simmons, Bush, and McAllister party—had come in 1845 to the falls of the Deschutes River, which empties into Budd Inlet. They established a sawmill and store at the falls they called Tumwater and spread out to farm. In the late 1840s, partners Levi Lathrop Smith and Edmund Sylvester filed a joint land claim and built a log cabin on the peninsula that reaches into Budd Inlet. Both men were temporarily lured away by the California gold rush, and Smith suffered an epileptic fit and drowned as he was returning. Sylvester decided to gamble on their joint land claim rather than on finding gold. In 1850 he platted a tiny settlement with grand aspirations, as grand as the Olympic Mountains in full view to the west.

Named for those mountains, Olympia took hold when settlers south of the Columbia River wanted to become a state. They needed to shed some of what was then the huge Oregon Territory, which included present-day Oregon, Washington, Idaho, and parts of Montana and Wyoming. Olympia lawyer Daniel Bigelow and businessman William Winlock Miller had argued in letters and Fourth of July speeches that separation would be just fine for northern Oregonians, too. In 1853, Congress agreed to carve out a new territory and name it after the country's first president, George Washington.

Olympia already had a customs office, post office, and newspaper— the weekly *Columbian,* later renamed the *Washington Pioneer.* The newspaper gushed that the law creating the territory "has given a gallant, dashing, sparkling and ponderous momentum to the march and swagger of progress. . . . During our poor dependence upon the cold charity of Oregon, we must as weak and puny infants, creep. But now . . . we have become a people within ourselves." The swagger of progress would be slow. Oregon became a state just six years later, while Washington remained a territory for the next thirty years. Olympia's destiny was linked with that long road to statehood. The territorial legislature would decide the location of the permanent capital not once but several times, a deliberation that kept Olympia's citizens in perpetual suspense.

The most immediate task for Governor Stevens was convincing Native Americans to give up access to land all across the territory. The Donation Land Act of 1850 gave American men and their wives the right to claim 640 acres of land in the West, the impetus for a land rush. But settlers like Sylvester had no legal claim until a surveyor-general was appointed, a land office established, and treaties signed. President Franklin Pierce appointed James Tilton surveyor-general; Stevens appointed Tumwater settler Michael Simmons as Indian agent; and their campaign to secure the land began.

In the fall of 1854, Stevens met with Nisqually, Puyallup, Steh-chass, Squaxin, and other native people gathered east of Olympia at Medicine Creek, the site of Indian council grounds near the farm of James McAllister, who had come with the first wagon train. During a rainy three-day camp, many of the leaders identified by Stevens agreed to give up their lands in the Nisqually delta and on Budd Inlet. Stevens then embarked on a whirlwind tour of the territory, signing similar treaties with other tribes. The results were similar: Indians gave up land in return for fishing rights, promises of reserved land, education, and other benefits.

But Stevens had moved quickly, and resentment lingered. The treaties were particularly unpopular among Indians east of the Cascades. Although many of those living along Puget Sound found trade advantages with the newcomers, Chief Leschi of the Nisqually realized that his people had been relegated to a bluff separated from the river delta that had sustained them for hundreds of years. Under his leadership, the Nisqually joined with Yakama Indians east of the mountains to resist the terms of the treaties. A series of skirmishes followed; five settlers who had joined the local militia were killed while out on patrol. Passions ran high, and Olympians built a stockade and blockhouses. They feared an attack, which came on Seattle, not Olympia, in the so-called Battle of Seattle in January 1856. A year later, the war was over in western Washington, and the Medicine Creek treaty was modified to reserve more of the original land to the Nisqually.

With Indians confined to reservations, the property claims of the Hudson's Bay Company settled, and land claims legalized, Washington Territory looked ahead to the coming of the railroad, population growth, and amassing enough political clout to become a state. The decision to leave the permanent location of the capital in the hands of the legislature was a democratic but risky proposition. For the new cities of Washington Territory, the location of the capital, the territorial university, and the penitentiary were matters of pride and growth. The first round of vote swapping ended with the university in Seattle, the penitentiary in Vancouver, and the capital in Olympia. Then the 1857–58 legislature took the territorial university away from Seattle and gave it to Cowlitz Prairie, between Vancouver and Olympia. That unsettling move prompted a compromise to move the university back to Seattle, the capital to Vancouver, and the penitentiary to Port Townsend. The bill passed and the governor signed it, but there was no enacting clause and no date.

With the territory's capital still uncertain, the outbreak of the nation's Civil War revealed more divisions among its citizens. A slave boy belonging to James Tilton, the surveyor-general, had escaped to Victoria, causing some consternation in Olympia. Officials who had been comrades in the Mexican–American War and appointed to territorial positions in the West chose different sides in the war. Isaac

Stevens, who had been a delegate to Congress after his gubernatorial term, returned east to fight for the Union cause and was killed at the Battle of Chantilly. U.S. Army captain George Pickett resigned from his post at Whatcom to fight for the South. Washington's third governor, Richard Gholson, resigned to work for Kentucky's secession from the Union.

When a newly appointed governor arrived in 1861, he thought the capital was in Vancouver, but legislators were at work in Olympia. In the summer of 1862, they punted the capital location to the voters, who kept it in place. The university remained in Seattle and the penitentiary moved to Walla Walla, then the largest city in the territory.

After the war, Washington's cities competed to become the Puget Sound terminus of the transcontinental railroad. Governor Stevens had surveyed for the northern route as he crossed the continent in 1853, but the Northern Pacific Railway was not completed until 1873, with Tacoma as its terminus. Its arrival kick-started the territory's path to statehood, bringing thousands of immigrants and opening up new markets. From Walla Walla and Spokane in the east to Tacoma and Seattle in the west, the territory boomed.

With the push for statehood came a push for women's right to vote, a right they would gain first in western states. Daniel Bigelow, a member of the legislature, and his wife, Ann Elizabeth White Bigelow, advocated this cause. After a dinner at their home in 1871, suffragist Susan B. Anthony was invited to address the Washington legislature, the first time in national history that a woman had been allowed to address lawmakers in session. Many more speeches by women in cities all over the territory would follow.

By 1889, Washington Territory had 239,544 residents, more than enough to justify statehood. When a partisan logjam broke with the elections of 1888, the U.S. Congress admitted six western states within a year (Washington, Idaho, North Dakota, South Dakota, Montana, and Wyoming). Washington voters adopted a constitution and chose Elisha P. Ferry as their first elected governor, but in a referendum attached to the constitution, voters declined to give women the vote (Wyoming would be the first state to do so, in 1890). They also voted to keep the capital in Olympia, fending off contenders in Ellensburg and North Yakima who were arguing for a more central location.

With the capital firmly ensconced, Olympia led Washington's transition from a roughhewn territory to a state with a capitol worthy of its ambition. A national competition to create a suitable campus was initiated in 1911. It was won by architects Walter Wilder and Harry White; their design was later modified and redesigned by brothers John Charles Olmsted and Frederick Law Olmsted Jr. Buildings and landscaping were completed twenty years later, after much political and aesthetic wrangling. Architectural historians Henry-Russell Hitchcock and William Seale described the result as the climax of "the American renaissance in state capitol building," the embodiment of the Jeffersonian ideal of government on a hill.

To reach that hill, begin at Tumwater and trace the Cowlitz Trail into the heart of the town on Budd Inlet. The walk passes the sites of docks, sawmills, blockhouses, stores, churches, schools, and the still-vibrant town square. It follows legislators who met first on the second floor of a waterfront store, then marched to a truly grand statehouse on the top of Capitol Hill. The complete loop circles back to Olympia's origins at the northern terminus of the Oregon Trail.

Pioneer Walk: Tumwater

START:	Tumwater Falls Park, C Street and Deschutes Way, or Tumwater Historical Park, 777 Simmons Road, off Deschutes Parkway
DIRECTIONS:	From I-5 north or south, take exit 103 onto the Deschutes Parkway. Follow signs and park at Tumwater Falls Park or Tumwater Historical Park.
DISTANCES:	1 to 2 miles round trip, including both parks (with an

optional extension to downtown Olympia and back,
for a round trip of 7.4 miles)

AMENITIES: Parking, restrooms, and paved trails at Tumwater Falls
Park, a park operated by the Olympia Tumwater Foun-
dation; restrooms, parking, picnic tables, shelter,
playground, and paved trails at Tumwater Historical
Park, a municipal park; restrooms and parking at
Marathon Park

At Tumwater Falls Park, you are standing at the upper falls of the
Deschutes River as it descends to Puget Sound. The heartbeat sound
of the falls resonates in the name first given to this place—Tumchuck.
The **petroglyph** inside the park building, which was moved from
Harstine Island north of Olympia, displays the symbol of a bear, a
frequent visitor to the falls. Artifacts unearthed from a midden at the
river's mouth revealed the presence of a village known as Steh-chass.
Salish people had been gathering shellfish here for at least 500 years
when the first wagon train of Americans arrived in 1845.

The emigrant party of three families—Bush, McAllister, and
Simmons—had come up the Cowlitz River, hauling their lives' pos-
sessions. Where the river turns east, they blazed their way north
through the forests toward Puget Sound, creating a trail many others
would follow. Their names are engraved on a **stone** near the falls.

Settlers were lured west by promises of free land under various
acts passed by the United States Congress, which wanted to encourage settlement, but a leader of this party, George Bush, was a mulatto
and not eligible, so the wagon train had headed north of the Columbia River into territory still under British control. George and Isabella
settled on a prairie that soon provided food for the new settlers, as it
had for the Salish. One of the first acts of the territorial legislature
would be to request a special act of Congress to legitimize the Bush
claim. (The Olympia airport now occupies much of Bush Prairie.)

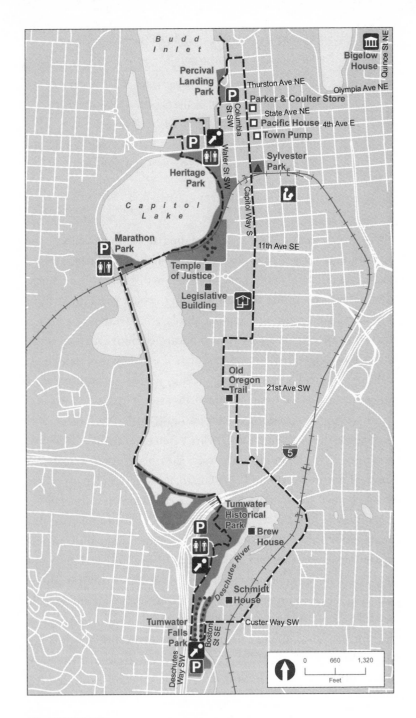

Budd
Inlet

Percival
Landing
Park

Thurston Ave NE

Parker & Coulter Store

State Ave NE

Pacific House   4th Ave E

Town Pump

Bigelow
House

Quince St NE

Olympia Ave NE

Columbia
St SW

Water St SW

Heritage
Park

Capitol
Lake

Sylvester
Park

Capitol Way S

Marathon
Park

Temple
of Justice

Legislative
Building

11th Ave SE

Old
Oregon
Trail

21st Ave SW

I-5

Tumwater
Historical
Park

Brew
House

Deschutes River

Schmidt
House

Tumwater
Falls
Park

Boston St SE

Custer Way SW

Deschutes Way SW

0   660   1,320

Feet

The McAllister family settled on Medicine Creek to the north, encouraged by Chief Leschi of the Nisqually, a decision that eventually resulted in the death of both men.

Michael Simmons claimed his site on the Deschutes, named it New Market, and competed for commerce with Hudson's Bay Company forts at Vancouver and Nisqually. Simmons bought wheat, potatoes, cattle, and peas on credit from the company and agreed to work off that debt by splitting cedar shingles, a ubiquitous building material on the frontier. The name New Market never caught on, and it reverted to Tumwater, a combination of the Chinook trade jargon word *tum* and the English *water*.

Walk the wide gravel trails along the banks of the river, crossing the water on bridges that once led to the larger town downriver. The trail on the west side follows the roadbed of the first railroad to come to Olympia, a line that connected Tumwater south to Tenino, where the Northern Pacific Railway had a depot, and north to saltwater. The **pedestrian bridge** in the park is a replica of a footbridge built in 1853. In 1916 the **Boston Street Bridge**, made of reinforced concrete with Luten arches, replaced an older wagon bridge at the upper falls.

Upper, middle, and lower falls still plummet through the canyon with great force in seasons of high water, drowning out the sound of traffic from I-5. Settlers built both a grist mill and a sawmill, powered by the falls, and nearly a dozen small factories developed—furniture companies, a tannery, a wooden pipe factory, a prune-drying company, and eventually a brewery using water from artesian wells. Little is left of these enterprises except the six-story **brew house**, built in 1906 for the Olympia Brewing Company, headed by German immigrant Leopold Schmidt. The company supplied beer in time for the Klondike gold rush in 1898 and stayed in business for almost a hundred years, with a juice break during Prohibition. Below the lower falls, see the **foundation of the power house and dam** of the first hydroelectric plant of the Olympia Light and Power Company. *Finish the loop on the eastern side of the river and return on the pedestrian bridge.*

Drive or walk to Tumwater Historical Park by following Deschutes Way at the west side of Tumwater Falls Park. (Try as you might, you can't walk through Falls Park to the Historical Park.) *Cross Boston Street, and continue on the sidewalk and side road, Grant Street, past* the **Henderson House**, built in 1905, and the **Crosby House**, dating from 1858. Captain Clanrick Crosby (great-grandfather of singer Bing Crosby) bought Michael Simmons's land claim, including the three waterfalls and his sawmill. Crosby promised the new Methodist minister in Olympia that he could have as much lumber as he could carry away from the sawmill, by himself, in one day. Reverend J. F. DeVore carried enough boards to build a whole church and rafted them downriver, into the west bay of Budd Inlet, around the tip of the peninsula, to the shore of the east bay, where First Methodist arose.

Continue down Grant Street to **Tumwater Historical Park**, created in 1980. The last mile of the Deschutes River below the falls was an estuary with water that rose and fell with the tide. Travelers arriving on the Cowlitz Trail hired Indians with canoes to carry themselves and their gear across the estuary or loaded their wagons onto boats and floated across at high tide. This was simplified in 1860, when the aptly named Long Bridge was built on wooden pilings, stretching from the northern edge of Tumwater to the southern edge of Olympia.

Today, the Deschutes flows into Capitol Lake, which was created when the river was dammed in 1951. Instead of a wagon road bridge, I-5 soars above the estuary, thanks to the 1956 Federal-Aid Highway Act, which offered states 90 percent of the cost of building interstate highways. With that funding, I-5 was constructed in western Washington in the 1960s, often going right through the middle of cities. Along Capitol Lake, large amounts of fill were added along the beaches to form a footing for the new bridge and entrance ramps, and a huge cut was blasted out of the ridge along the east bank to let the new highway through. In Tumwater, the interstate took over much of Deschutes Way, the main street, and about ninety buildings were moved or demolished, erasing downtown Tumwater.

Explore the trails in the park, reading signs interpreting its history. If you wish to continue one mile to downtown Olympia, follow the paved path edging the western side of the park. Pass an interpretive center and restrooms, then continue to Marathon Park. Continue along the west side of Capitol Lake or take the gravel path that cuts east on a railroad grade. Both ways lead to Heritage Park and the Olympia loop.

Olympia Loop

START: 4th Avenue W and Water Street

DIRECTIONS: From I-5 north or south, take exit 105 toward City Center. Turn right on Capitol Way. Turn left onto Amanda Smith Way SW, then right onto Columbia Street SW. Park on the street or at Percival Landing Park (405 Columbia Street NW) and walk to 4th Avenue W and Water Street.

DISTANCE: About 2.5 miles round trip to the capitol campus

AMENITIES: Metered parking on streets near the waterfront; restrooms in Heritage Park and in buildings on the capitol campus

Look down at the **inlaid map** of the historic shoreline *on 4th Avenue west of Water Street.* You are standing at the edge of Budd Inlet, named by Lieutenant Charles Wilkes, who headed a U.S. Navy exploring expedition in 1841. As he sailed down Puget Sound to its southern end, Wilkes sent Lieutenant Thomas Budd and Midshipman Henry Eld to take soundings of the water's depth in two inlets. Indian villages stood at the bottom of each inlet, and the canoes of the Coast Salish people lined the shores. They had camped and fished there for unknown thousands of years, harvesting salmon, clams, and oysters.

They called the area Steh-chass. Wilkes named the inlet to the west for Eld and the bigger inlet, with two channels surrounding a peninsula, for Budd. Olympia started on that peninsula between the channels of Budd Inlet.

The map stands on **Percival Landing**, a boardwalk that extends almost a mile in length around today's shoreline. Captain Sam Percival and his wife, Lurana Ware Percival, arrived in 1853, the same year as Governor Isaac Stevens. Captain Percival operated a store, a sawmill, and a steamship operation; built a dock here at the foot of Water Street; and became the town's harbor master. Boats from San Francisco loaded salmon, shingles, wood, and spars at his dock. Stern-wheel and side-wheel steamboats carried mail and passengers in and out of the coves around Puget Sound. Landfill has since altered the historic shoreline, which lapped as far east as the **marker** down the block at *204 4th Avenue W.*

Roam the boardwalk as you like, noticing the roster of Mosquito Fleet boats *at State and Water* on docks once loaded with bags of oysters. Oysters were a key part of the native diet, and women sold them from baskets on the streets of the town. Early residents served these small shellfish with pride at ceremonial dinners; they were described as a silent and succulent lobbyist in the battle to claim the capital.

A longhouse sat on the block between Columbia and Water Streets and between 4th and State. The Squaxin village on the shore was called Cheet-woot in the Chinook jargon, which meant place "frequented by black bears." The bears were still present when Edmund Sylvester hired a surveyor to plat the town site. The two bays of Budd Inlet circumscribed the heart of the early town, roughly between 1st and 4th Avenues running north and south and Columbia and Washington Streets running west and east. Sylvester reserved land for a Masonic temple to host the patriarchs of the town, a town square for common use, and land for schools and the hoped-for capitol.

Continue walking north along the waterfront to Thurston Avenue. Olympia avenues are nicely numbered, but some names have changed: 1st Avenue to Thurston, 2nd Avenue to Olympia, 3rd Avenue to State, and Main Street to Capitol Way. A **medallion** in the sidewalk next to the water sculpture at *Thurston and Columbia* marks the site of the U.S. customs house, which also housed the post office and a store set on pilings, all owned by Michael Simmons. High tides flooded the village twice a day.

The shoreline ended here in 1850. A long wharf, known as Giddings Wharf, extended from Main Street across the tideflats to reach deep water. In the first decades, and for many decades thereafter, the primary export was logs. As Olympia grew, the peninsula was gradually enlarged by dredging the inlets and dumping fill on all three sides. Much of the fill to the north grounded the Port of Olympia, created in 1922. For a view over the port, *walk north along the boardwalk to its end* at the Port Plaza Tower.

Bigelow House

For a 1.5-mile round-trip excursion to the oldest house still remaining in Olympia, go east on Thurston Avenue NE, which becomes Olympia Avenue, to East Bay Drive, which skirts the east bay of Budd Inlet. Walk north on East Bay Drive to Glass Avenue, the first street that it intersects. Go east on Glass Avenue to the **Bigelow House**, number 918. Daniel Richardson Bigelow came to Olympia in 1851 and served in the first legislature when the territory was created two years later. A year later he married Ann Elizabeth White, who taught school in the Nisqually Valley, and this house was built. Together they supported public education, temperance, civil rights for non-whites, and voting rights for women. The Bigelow land claim included a spring that still bubbles out of the ground in a park on the hillside above the house.

Continue east on Glass Avenue to Quince Street and south on Quince to Olympia Avenue, through the Bigelow Historic District, which features many houses built between 1866 and 1937. Some of the bungalows and cottages along Olympia Avenue were built for mill workers at the Olympia Veneer Company, a plywood cooperative that was owned by its workers and operated from 1921 until its sale in 1947. This area was known as Swanton, platted by John M. Swan on his donation land claim north and east of Sylvester's and south of Bigelow's. Swan eventually decamped for Walla Walla, where he was the founding spirit and superintendent of the Odd Fellows Home.

Priest Point Park

For an even longer walk back to 1840s history, hike northeast of downtown on East Bay Drive for 1.4 miles from its intersection with Olympia Avenue to Priest Point Park, which is bordered on the south by 26th Avenue. The Missionary Oblates of Mary Immaculate operated a school for Indian boys at this favorite gathering place for Coast Salish people, beginning in 1848. Chief Seattle of the Duwamish and Suquamish tribes was baptized here. Margaret Stevens visited the mission in the late 1850s, conversing in French with Father Pascal Ricard before the mission was abandoned in 1860, after treaties moved local tribes to reservations. The tidal shoreline Ellis Cove trail extends 2.4 miles in the park, passing through the site of ancient Squaxin villages.

From the boardwalk, return south on Capitol Way to its intersection with Olympia and the heart of the old village. Little remains of the original buildings except plaques on buildings and medallions on the sidewalk. An exception is the **Barnes Bank Building** *at 114 Capitol Way*, said to be the oldest brick building in Olympia, dating from 1869. *On the northeast corner of Olympia and Capitol Way* stood the Washington Hotel, where Isaac Stevens arrived in 1853.

On the night of November 26, 1853, the citizens of Olympia were preparing a great banquet at the Washington Hotel (featuring oysters, no doubt) to welcome the first governor of the territory. All the leading citizens of both Olympia and New Market, including Michael

Simmons, Daniel Bigelow, Sam Percival, and Clanrick Crosby, had gathered to meet him at the end of his long overland journey. Stevens was in a hurry to reach Olympia and had not stopped to clean up. Consequently, as historian Gordon Newell describes it, "When a swarthy, black-bearded little stranger in shabby frontier garb dismounted stiffly from his horse in the chill November rain, the citizens were too busy to notice him." The stranger strode into the dining room but was told to go to the kitchen for food as the dining room was reserved for the governor, expected momentarily. He was the governor! Once past that gaffe, Olympians greeted Stevens with great enthusiasm and optimism for the future.

Continue south on Capitol Way to the block between Olympia and State. Two days after Stevens arrived, he proclaimed Olympia the temporary capital and set up his own house and office on the west side of the street with two offices for the surveyors who would establish boundaries for settlers' land claims. At the rear of the house a large fenced yard extended to a gate that opened to the beach, where a boat was kept and a seasonal Indian camp began at the corner of the yard. Margaret Stevens swam daily in Puget Sound.

The legislature, Governor Stevens said, would meet for the first time in February 1854, and they did—on the east side of the street on the second floor of the Parker & Coulter store. The building fell into disrepair and was razed in the early 1900s. The location is marked by a **bronze tablet** *at 222 Capitol Way.*

During that very first session, the twenty-seven legislators denied women the right to vote in the territory by a margin of one vote, the vote of a man who voted no because his wife was Native American and would not have been included. The effort to give Washington women equal suffrage would continue for fifty-six more years, about as long as the struggle for the capital. The legislators put off the ultimate decision about the location of the capital but made Olympia oyster suppers the order of their evenings.

The first legislative ball was held at the Pacific House, on the *northeast corner of State and Capitol Way.* A parking lot dominates that corner, but a mural on the wall facing the lot depicts Rebecca Howard, who managed the hotel and restaurant in the early 1860s. Howard and her husband were two of the few African Americans in town, besides the Bush family on Bush Prairie. Another was Charles Mitchell, a thirteen-year-old boy of mixed race in the household of James Tilton, the surveyor-general. Mitchell stowed away on the steamer the *Eliza Anderson* from the dock on Budd Inlet and escaped to Victoria just before the Civil War began.

Louis Bettman came to Olympia in 1853 from Bavaria and opened a general merchandise store with his brothers. The successor **store**, built in 1891, remains at *316 Capitol Way.* Edmund Sylvester could be found playing checkers in his store *just north of 4th and Capitol Way.* Sylvester had expanded Smith's log cabin into a crude hotel and store and may have moved it a block south to this location.

Continue on Capitol Way to 4th Avenue. On the northeast corner is a **HistorySpot** in the sidewalk that marks a spring and the town pump, the town's first water source. Early Chinese residents clustered on 4th Avenue between Columbia and Capitol Way. They worked as contract laborers, cooks, house servants, launderers, and growers and peddlers of vegetables. Most were Lockes, from villages in Guangdong Province in southern China. Suey Gim Locke, grandfather of Washington governor Gary Locke, elected in 1996, came to Olympia in 1890 and worked as a house servant.

Railroads

What you will not find in downtown Olympia are railroad tracks separating the city from the waterfront. At one time, it was assumed that Olympia would be the terminus of the Northern Pacific Railway, but the Northern Pacific turned to cheaper land on Commencement Bay in Tacoma, much to the dismay of Olympia and every other would-be terminal on Puget Sound. Alarmed by this slight, Olympia citizens built their own fifteen-mile rail line to connect to the Northern Pacific in Tenino. When the transcontinental railroad finally decided to serve Olympia, citizens insisted the train not run on surface streets, especially near the homes of wealthy citizens on 7th Avenue. A **tunnel** under 7th Avenue between Adams and Columbia was opened in 1891 and is still used for freight traffic.

The southern boundary of the old village of Olympia is 4th Avenue, which also marks the line of a fifteen-foot-tall stockade, constructed in the fall of 1855. Besides surveying for the railroad, choosing the temporary capital, and convening the legislature, Isaac Stevens convened treaty councils. The Yakama east of the Cascades and the Nisqually west of the Cascades, under the leadership of Chief Leschi and his half-brother Quiemuth, were dissatisfied with the treaty results. Four members of a militia patrolling northeast of Olympia were ambushed and killed, and residents panicked. With lumber from Percival's mill, citizens built the stockade and a blockhouse on the *northeast corner of 4th and Main* to which they could come each night. In another year, the Indian wars in western Washington were over, after an unsuccessful attack on Seattle, not Olympia, but settlers wanted revenge.

Leschi

Chief Leschi and Quiemuth were blamed for the American deaths that resulted from the conflict. In November 1856, Quiemuth turned himself in. He was escorted to the governor's office on Main Street to await transfer to the U.S. Army post at Fort Steilacoom, but during the night he was killed by a settler, who was never prosecuted.

Leschi was arrested and tried twice for the murder of a militiaman; the first trial ended in a hung jury and the second in a conviction. He was hung on a knoll north of town when the military authorities at Fort

Steilacoom refused to participate in his execution. They questioned Leschi's involvement and called the militiaman's death a casualty of war, not murder. In 2004 a court of inquiry and retrial agreed with that determination and formally acquitted Leschi.

Walk out of the stockade village, south on Capitol Way, to the block between Legion Way and 7th Avenue. Once land claims were legal, residents continued cutting down the forest to expand the town south of the waterfront. Edmund Sylvester had set aside a block for a town square, which Margaret Stevens described as nothing but a "tangle of fallen timber." The tangle is today an urban common space, much like the town square of Vancouver. A Daughters of the American Revolution **plaque** identifies this spot as the end of the Oregon Trail. The turn north from the Columbia River to Puget Sound ended here. Livestock grazed in the square in its early days, as footloose youth graze today, seeking shelter from the rain under its cedar trees. U.S. presidents have made speeches and bands have played here, as befits a town square.

A second blockhouse was built in the *northwest corner of* **Sylvester Park** in April 1856, large enough to hold more of the townspeople. The blockhouse became the city jail for a few years, but in 1859, an inmate set fire to it and escaped, destroying the log building in the process. In 1905 schoolchildren's donations erected the **statue of Governor John Rogers**. He had been elected to the state legislature ten years earlier as a Populist. As legislator and governor from 1897 until his death in 1901, Rogers was instrumental in passing the Barefoot Schoolboy Law, which financed free public education for all children in Washington by providing for a consistent property tax.

Churches and schools spread out from this square. Like Vancouver, Olympia boasts many "firsts" in Washington: first post office, first newspaper, first public school, first Masonic lodge, first fire department. Northeast of Sylvester Park, on the southwest corner

A festive crowd gathers around the gazebo in Sylvester Park, between 1895 and 1904. Courtesy Washington State Archives.

of 4th and Adams, Reverend J. F. Devore built the town's first Methodist church in 1856 with planks from Crosby's sawmill in Tumwater. The building lasted almost a hundred years, until it was destroyed by fire in 1949. To the northwest of the square, the first Presbyterian church in Washington, built at 5th and Columbia, is now a parking lot.

The first school, a cabin of split lumber, opened in 1852 at about 6th and Franklin, northeast of the square. It was a "free school" to make children "good citizens, good Republicans, good Christians." Sylvester lived in a mansion on 8th Street between Main and Washington. He donated two lots just south of his home for the Masonic hall, which housed the 1854, 1855, and 1856 legislatures. The sidewalk from the hall to the town was an occasional winter boon for the youth of the village, who coasted down the steep grade on the few snowy days. Of these landmarks, only the steep grade remains.

For its first few years, the legislature moved up and down Olympia hills. Sylvester had donated ten acres for the capitol at 13th Avenue, overlooking Olympia, but construction was delayed by the Indian wars. In 1857, the legislature met for the first time on the hill in a white frame building. That lasted until Washington was admitted to statehood in 1889, when voters reaffirmed their choice of Olympia as the capital. Perhaps hoping to set that decision in stone, in 1905 the legislature moved downhill from the wooden capitol building to the imposing Romanesque **sandstone building** on the east side of Sylvester Park. Originally used as the county courthouse, the building has endured fire, earthquakes, and threat of sale but still serves as a state government building. During the renovations, the legislature moved again for one session to Adams between 7th and 8th Avenues, marked dutifully with a **plaque**.

On March 7, 1927, legislators left the old capitol on Sylvester Square and marched up the hill to a grand, new home. *To reach the capitol, follow in their footsteps, along the aptly named Capitol Way, to the state capitol campus at 11th Avenue.*

The west campus was designed on a north-south axis; diagonals were later added for those approaching from the east. The east campus spreads seven blocks to accommodate parking, memorials, and a **rock** marking the second Stevens home. Trees on the campus include Douglas firs, which typify the Evergreen State, the nation's largest English oak, and an American white elm allegedly grown from a cutting of the tree under which General Washington, the state's namesake, took command of the Continental Army.

On any given day when the legislature is in session, advocacy groups throng the campus, usually dressed alike in bright T-shirts. The **Legislative Building** and the **Insurance Building**, a general office building, are clumped on Sylvester's original donation. To enter the Legislative Building, with its impressive dome, climb

Elisha P. Ferry, the first elected governor, is inaugurated in 1889 in front of the territorial capitol building as Washington finally gains statehood. Courtesy Washington State Archives.

forty-two steps representing Washington's status as the forty-second state. Notice the symbols for logging, sheep grazing, shipping, the first capitol building, an early homestead, and Washington's scenic beauty on the heavy bronze doors. A **plaque** on the southeast corner marks the approximate location of the white frame building that was the territorial capitol. The current governor may be in residence at the **Governor's Mansion**, which is the oldest building on the campus, built in 1908. The **Newhouse and O'Brien** office buildings, named after legislators, were built in the 1930s in a spare modern design.

On the northern edge of the high bluff overlooking Olympia, find the **Temple of Justice**, the first of the Capitol Group buildings completed in 1920 in neoclassical style with sandstone from Wilkeson (near Mount Rainier) on its exterior, granite from Index as its foundation, and stone cut in Tacoma. Within the Temple of Justice, lawyers argue the issues of the state before the Supreme Court.

You have reached the apex of statehood building that began in 1853. From this eminence, Capitol Lake stretches north to Budd Inlet, reflecting the capitol's image; railroad tracks lead west across the lake; a remnant of the Oregon Trail arrives from the south; and the city of Olympia spreads in all directions, a view to lift the heart of contemporary travelers.

You have choices for the rest of the loop. To return downtown, take the 200-foot switchback trail from the top of the bluff at Law Enforcement Memorial Park north of the Temple of Justice to Heritage Park and walk north, counterclockwise, around the lake.

To return to Tumwater, you may also walk down the bluff and take the trail across the lake to Marathon Park, retracing your steps south along Capitol Lake.

To see a remnant of the Oregon Trail, the last part of the Stevens family's journey to Olympia, walk south from the capitol campus on Water Street through South Capitol Hill. As settlers arrived, this neighborhood was the site of logging operations and several homesteads, but as the capital was secured, the newer homes reflected—and still reflect—a sense of Olympia in its prime. *At 21st Avenue, venture a half block east to find a* street sign identifying the very last segment of the **Old Oregon Trail** to Puget Sound. Do not expect ruts or discarded wagon wheels; the street sign marks a driveway that leads to private homes.

To complete the long loop and return to Tumwater from here, *walk east to Capitol Way and follow it south for a little more than a mile to Custer Way,* passing the **Schmidt House**, built in 1904 for the founder of the Olympia Brewing Company, his wife, and their six children. *Turn left on Boston Street to return to Deschutes Way SW* and Tumwater Falls Park.

Resources   Bigelow House Museum, 918 Glass Avenue NE

Olympia-Lacey-Tumwater Visitor & Convention Bureau,
103 Sid Snyder Avenue SW

Olympia Timberland Library, 313 8th Avenue SE

CHAPTER THREE

Walla Walla

Frontier Town

In 1864, Walla Walla was "a semi-Godless city," as "lively and wide-open a town then as the frontier West has often produced."

Historian Thompson C. Elliott, writing in the *Washington Historical Quarterly*, April 1915

As Vancouver flourished on the lower Columbia River and Olympia claimed the south end of Puget Sound, Walla Walla centered the frontier east of the Cascade Mountains. In the 1860s and 1870s, Walla Walla was the largest city in Washington Territory, important enough to host a constitutional convention and contest Olympia for the capital.

The town grew at a convergence of trails, waterways, and people in the valley of the Walla Walla River, framed by the Blue Mountains on the south and the Snake River on the north. The Walla Walla and Touchet Rivers flow out of the Blue Mountains and converge with Mill and Dry Creeks on the way west to a confluence with the Columbia, giving the river, town, and native people the name "land of many waters."

Walla Walla, Nez Perce, and Cayuse people traveled freely through the Walla Walla Valley, making seasonal migrations along the Nez Perce Trail, the great intertribal highway between the Rocky

Mountains to the east and the Columbia River. On their journey of exploration in 1805, Lewis and Clark encountered tribes fishing at the confluence of the Snake and Columbia Rivers who advised them to return east overland, rather than attempting to canoe upriver. They could follow the trail made by the ruts of travois poles. The travois, a platform made of poles lashed together, hauled belongings, food, and even small children, pulled by people, dogs, or horses. Before there was a town of Walla Walla or even a mill, the trail crossed Mill Creek, and the poles carved a wide path, ideal for the main street.

In 1836, a missionary band of four couples from New England journeyed west across the continent under the sponsorship of the American Board of Commissioners for Foreign Missions. They were responding to an appeal from the Nez Perce for knowledge of "the black book," the Bible, which seemed to give power to the whites moving through their homeland. After visiting British fur trading posts at Wallula and Vancouver, the missionaries established missions among the Nez Perce, Spokane, and Cayuse Indians. Doctor Marcus Whitman and Narcissa Prentiss Whitman chose a site on the Walla Walla River at Waiilatpu, which means "place of the rye grass." For ten years they tried to convert the Cayuse to Christianity and to an agricultural way of life, but they did not succeed at either.

Instead, they became the vanguard of settlement. The missionaries had demonstrated that women and men could cross the vast middle of the continent on foot and horseback, hauling their belongings in wagons. In the 1840s more wagons streamed west across the country on what became known as the Oregon Trail. Most headed for the Willamette Valley near today's Portland, but after the exhausting journey across the plains, the Rocky Mountains, and the Blue Mountains, travelers often detoured to the Whitman mission for a rest.

Cayuse lifestyle and power were threatened by this influx of settlers. When an epidemic of measles swept the mission in 1847, killing many Indian children who had no resistance to it, hostile Cayuse massacred the Whitmans and twelve others. Their attack increased the American military presence as settlers called for the federal government to protect the growing number of immigrants traveling on the Oregon Trail. The massacre led to demands for the creation of Oregon Territory in 1848, followed by the separation of Washington Territory from Oregon in 1853. The new territory was huge, encompassing not only Washington but today's Idaho and parts of Montana and Wyoming.

The territorial governor, Isaac Stevens, met with the eastern tribes—Cayuse, Umatilla, Yakama, Nez Perce, and Walla Walla—on the banks of Mill Creek in June 1855, negotiating for control of most of the land. The tribes had always moved freely over the land, traveling great distances on horseback, and they resisted being confined to reservations. Three of the chiefs for the Yakama, Walla Walla, and Nez Perce people signed the treaty but soon regretted it. The treaties provoked more violence than they prevented, and war erupted in the Columbia Basin in the fall of 1855. Governor Stevens then convened another treaty council; those negotiations failed, and the U.S. Army established a cantonment on the banks of Mill Creek and made forays against the tribes as far north as the Spokane River. The tribes were defeated in 1858, with the Spokane consigned to a reservation along the Spokane and Columbia Rivers, the Cayuse and Walla Walla moved to the Umatilla reservation in eastern Oregon, and many Nez Perce confined to a reservation in Idaho.

With the conflict over, the land of many waters was declared open to settlement. Settlers claimed land, started farming, and sold products to one another and to the army. Walla Walla was incorporated in 1859. A year later, E. D. Pearce passed through town on his way to investigate a rumor he had heard in California about a glittering ball embedded in rock. Indeed, Pearce found gold in the Coeur d'Alene Mountains on the Nez Perce reservation. He came back to Walla

Walla with about $80 in gold, and the rush was on. The Nez Perce appealed to the U.S. government for protection from the invasion, as was their right by treaty, but heavy snowfall kept soldiers out of the mountains. In March 1861, a prospector came out with $800 in gold dust. Word traveled down the Columbia River, the great waterway of the interior, to Portland, and thousands started for the goldfields. Travelers and goods moved along the Columbia and landed at Wallula, at the mouth of the Walla Walla River, and then traveled overland to Walla Walla, where they stopped to provision up. The town became a hub for miners and mule trains passing through. The local newspaper reported that no fewer than 225 pack animals laden with provisions had left for the mines in a single week. Prospectors returned with a collectively huge fortune in gold dust, an amount equal to more than $100 million today.

A prospector passing through from the mines described the transformed town in 1862: "Walla Walla has grown . . . from a very ragged country village to the mature proportions of a respectable city. Wooden buildings begin to give place to brick and stone, the sidewalks and streets are swept clean and are kept well watered. . . . Stages arrive and leave almost every day; long trains of mules and horses may be seen constantly coming in and quietly emerging with well assorted cargoes, to the different mining camps. . . . The cheerful music of the anvil may be heard at all hours of the day from every part of the city."

The gold rush brought growth but also lawlessness to Walla Walla. It was a "roaring camp" such as Bret Harte would have delighted to describe, said historian W. D. Lyman. "Every species of vice flourished without restraint," wrote Lyman, "and horse racing and gambling were the principal amusements." Settlers fought over range and water rights, and vigilante groups arose to settle the disputes. In the winter of 1863–64, the Vigilance Committee hanged twenty-five men in the space of four months, trying to stop cattle thieves and robbers.

For three years Walla Walla boomed on gold, but the more lasting wealth was in cattle and wheat. Native grasslands had been building fertile soil for centuries on what had been called the Great American Desert. European settlers brought small grains such as drought-resistant wheat and barley that could grow using the available moisture, a process called dryland farming. Responding to the rush of immigrants who doubled the territory's population in the 1860s, ranchers and farmers around Walla Walla increased their harvests of grain and their cattle and sheep grazing on ryegrass. The first threshing machine arrived in 1863. Four years later, a thousand barrels of wheat flour were exported to San Francisco, followed by exports to New York and London. Wheat was milled into flour in Walla Walla mills and provisions stocked in the stores, spurring growth in eastern Washington just as lumber exports financed western Washington cities.

Although Walla Walla was a key crossroads of the interior, at first it did not have a railroad for transporting products such as wheat to distant markets. Supplies, passengers, and livestock were carted west by oxcart, wagon, and stagecoach to the Wallula landing on the Columbia River and then to The Dalles and Portland on steamers. The Northern Pacific Railway, the great hope of many city founders, had planned a route through town but was stalled by financial problems and its focus on a Puget Sound terminus. Like many city leaders in the late 1800s, Walla Walla doctor Dorsey Syng Baker knew his city needed a railroad if it was to thrive. He determined to build one connecting to the Columbia River.

With financial backing from a few partners but mainly his own money, Baker started building east from Wallula, the port on the Columbia. He got as far as Waiilatpu before running out of funds, then raised $25,000 from the citizens of Walla Walla to complete the last six miles into town in 1875. Because iron and steel rails were expensive and unavailable, the narrow-gauge Walla Walla and Columbia River Railroad Company ran on timbers made of fir and topped with strap iron. Although the train moved very slowly, the company was well managed, made money, and cut local farmers' shipping costs. Spokane eventually became railroad central for eastern Washington, but Walla Walla had enough lines and water routes to ship its products and feed at least part of the world. By 1880, the dryland region produced 1.5 million bushels of wheat every year, much of it around Walla Walla. "We will raise the Wheat, Grind the Flour, and Feed the World," read a banner above bags of flour stacked on Main Street.

Recognizing the city's prosperity and location on a main travel route, territorial delegates met in Walla Walla to draft a state constitution in 1878. In the first decades of the territory's history, more people lived in eastern Washington than on the coast, and city boosters suggested that Walla Walla should be the capital. Even into the early 1880s, Walla Walla was the largest city in the territory. In the sweepstakes for state-supported institutions and the commerce they bring, however, Walla Walla won the state penitentiary. It was built on a hill among the wheat fields north of town in 1886.

Throughout the late 1800s, Walla Walla's reputation as a godless frontier town and its twenty-six saloons were balanced by its godfearing residents and seven churches. A decade after the Whitman massacre, missionary Cushing Eells grieved at the Waiilatpu gravesites and vowed to erect a monument of education, a school "of high moral character," to honor the Whitmans. In 1859 he obtained a charter from the legislature for the first institution of higher learning in the territory, which he located in Walla Walla. Whitman Academy struggled for years, but in thirty years, with the support of Walla Walla businessmen and Congregational church leaders, it evolved into Whitman College, the first four-year college in the state and a civilizing force on the frontier.

By the end of the 1800s, the forces of stability dominated the roaring camp. "All the early settlers who have kept clear of gambling dens and saloons are rich," noted the new president of Whitman College, James F. Eaton, in 1891. Walla Walla remained the predominant city in Washington Territory until the Northern Pacific was constructed through Stampede Pass in 1887, making Tacoma and Seattle dominant in the western half of the state and Spokane in the east. For the next hundred years, Whitman College and agriculture sustained a city with the ambience of a large town. In the twenty-first century, a thriving wine industry brings tourists and concern that Walla Walla could become too attractive. Explosive growth and resort development would change the character of a frontier town deeply rooted in Native American, missionary, military, mining, and farming history.

This tour begins at the western end of town with the statue of Peo Peo Mox Mox, the Walla Walla chief who died defending his territory. It follows the Nez Perce Trail—Main Street—through the center of commerce, passes a statue of Marcus Whitman at the eastern end of Main Street, and reaches the missionary legacy at Whitman College. It returns past parks, homes, schools, and churches that stabilized the frontier town and ends at the most visible downtown landmark, "the Marc," an upscale hotel in the heart of southeast Washington named after the missionary.

Frenchtown

For a chronologically correct start, visit the Frenchtown Historic Site, between Lowden and College Place. A short trail leads to a cemetery and overlook interpreting early métis settlement.

British fur traders established a trading post at Wallula on the Columbia River in 1818, which they first called Fort Nez Perce and later Fort Walla Walla. French Canadian employees of the Hudson's Bay Company married native women, established farms, and settled down on the banks of the Walla Walla River, with the consent of local tribes, beginning in

1823–24. There were about a dozen cabins, including those of A. D. Pambrun and Joseph LaRocque and his Walla Walla wife, Lizette.

After the Whitman massacre, wars raged through the Walla Walla Valley, beginning with the Cayuse War. Then treaties took away Indian lands, and a thousand warriors fought 350 Oregon volunteers in the Battle of Walla Walla for four days in December 1855. When reinforcements arrived for the volunteers, the Indians withdrew, effectively ending the battle. Many Frenchtown residents who had left during the war returned, rebuilt a chapel that had burned, constructed a log schoolhouse, and built the St. Rose of Lima Mission Church in 1876. The settlement lasted into the 1880s, with the final burial in the cemetery in 1912.

Waiilatpu

To understand the missionary influence on Walla Walla, visit the Whitman Mission National Historic Site, 8.5 miles west of the city center. Before it was a mission, Waiilatpu was a favorite council ground and grazing land of the Nez Perce and Cayuse people. The park has an obelisk commemorating the site of the mission and interpreting the conflict that resulted in the killing of Marcus and Narcissa Whitman and twelve others in 1847.

Take a self-guided tour to see preserved remnants of the Emigrant House, the blacksmith shop, the gristmill, and the white granite marker atop a hill overlooking the mission grounds. Cushing Eells, who had been a missionary among the Spokane Indians, visited the Great Grave a few years after the massacre. He was so affected that he moved his family to the mission site, bought the land from the American Board of Commissioners for Foreign Missions, and vowed to found a school in the Whitmans' honor—Whitman College.

Listen for the sound of the wind in this Valley of the Ryegrass, the grassland that would make Walla Walla prosperous.

Walla Walla Loop

START: N 3rd Avenue and W Rose Street

DIRECTIONS: From Washington State Highway 12, the artery of southeastern Washington, take the exit for downtown Walla Walla to N 2nd Avenue south to Rose and west to N 3rd.

DISTANCE: About 2.5 miles round trip

AMENITIES: Parking on streets or in the community parking lot at W Main Street and N 4th Avenue (not available Saturdays and Sundays on farmers market days); restrooms at Heritage Park, Wildwood Park, and Pioneer Park

Begin the walk through early Walla Walla history *at N 3rd Avenue and W Rose Street*, at the statue of a Walla Walla chief with the hallmark double name Peo Peo Mox Mox, sometimes spelled Peu Peu Mox Mox. Called *Yellow Bird Returns*, the sculpture honors the legacy of this leader, using his English name. It towers above a plaza recalling the volatile intersection of cultures in the Walla Walla Valley.

Yellow Bird was a leader among the Walla Walla. Friendly toward the few settlers in the valley, he offered them land in exchange for a Catholic mission. But he became embittered when his son was murdered by a California settler during a trading trip for cattle. At first he refused to sign the treaties presented by Isaac Stevens, the territorial governor; he relented under pressure from other leaders but soon regretted the decision. During the hostilities a few months later, the chief carried a white flag into an army camp, where he was taken hostage and then killed during a skirmish.

To the west (left) of the plaza see **Mill Creek**, which curves through the center of town, its swiftly flowing waters now contained by concrete banks. The Walla Walla Indians, the U.S. cavalry, and the first

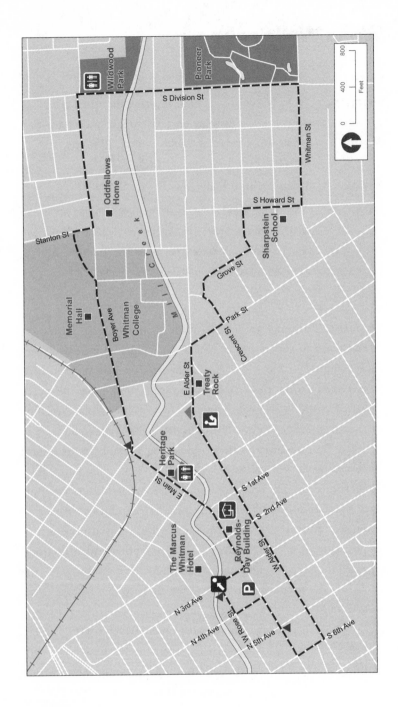

Fort Walla Walla

In the summer of 1858, the U.S. cavalry moved from its encampment on Mill Creek to this site they named Fort Walla Walla. The Indian wars had recently ended, and the soldiers at the fort had the job of keeping the peace. This meant protecting miners in their remote camps and immigrants on the Oregon Trail, as well as the Nez Perce, who were plagued by encroaching miners and whiskey peddlers. Soldiers also constructed new forts and in 1862 helped complete the Mullan Road, linking Walla Walla with Fort Benton on the Missouri River. The war chest of the fort supported the local economy; even officers from forts to the east, such as Fort Lapwai and Fort Boise, often purchased goods in Walla Walla.

The Fort Walla Walla military reservation is set on high ground above the surrounding plains, with the Blue Mountains visible in the distance. It includes the Veterans Administration Medical Center, a city park, a cemetery, and the **Fort Walla Walla Museum**, at 755 Myra Road. The museum interprets the military, agricultural, Native American, and pioneer heritage of the Walla Walla Valley, displaying a replica of thirty-three mules harnessed to a wheat combine.

A short trail connects to the medical center, whose grounds retain fifteen buildings from the 1858–1906 period. Officers' quarters in wooden frame buildings with long porches and bay and dormered windows line a driveway. An old stable with wooden siding, Building 31, is still in use, recalling the cavalry stationed here.

Most troops were removed from the fort in 1865, but some participated in the Bannock War in 1877 and the Nez Perce War in 1878. The fort was also a headquarters for troops returning from the Philippines during the Spanish-American War. A statue in the center of the oval drive commemorates General Jonathan M. Wainwright, who was born at the fort when his father was a cavalry officer. Wainwright commanded troops in the Philippines during World War II, surrendered Corregidor in 1942, and was a Japanese prisoner of war until 1945.

settlers were all drawn to the banks of the creek. The native people called the area Pashxa for the wild sunflowers or arrowleaf balsamroot that grew on its banks. From here the creek joins the Touchet and Walla Walla Rivers, rushing through the land of many waters from their origins in the Blue Mountains toward the Columbia.

In 1861, early settlers used the flow of Mill Creek to power a flour mill and a planing mill to convert logs into planks. Within a few years, there were six more flour mills on the creek. **The Whitehouse Crawford planing mill building**, constructed in 1904, now houses a restaurant at 3rd and Cherry, a block north.

Besides mills, the early town consisted of a few straggling tents, frame houses, and buildings that sprang up between the treaty grounds on the creek and Fort Walla Walla a mile to the southwest. A county government was formed in 1859, and the commissioners laid out a town site with east-west streets running a hundred feet wide, enough space to turn a wagon. The old Nez Perce Trail became **Main Street** just in time for an onslaught of miners and mules. When gold was found along the rivers of southern Idaho, long packtrains of mules and horses laden with supplies departed the boomtown every day, heading north on the Mullan Road. Even camels were used for a few years; they could carry twice as much weight as a mule and travel longer stretches without water. (A marker near the state penitentiary north of Highway 12 shows where that earlier highway headed north and east.)

Walk south on 3rd Avenue one block to W Main Street, then east on Main toward 2nd Avenue. Mule packers camped on Mill Creek, a water source, so the most successful stores developed there. The first tent store, run by William McWhirk, set up near the creek at *2nd and Main* in 1857, serving prospectors, emigrants, and soldiers. Once the gold rush started, eighty buildings were built along Main Street and secondary streets in 1860 and 1861. One, the **Schwabacher store**, housed the first department store in the territory, selling clothing, groceries, building materials, and hardware. The Schwabacher brothers—Abraham, Louis, and Sigmund—had fled anti-Semitic rule in Bavaria. They built a chain of stores with headquarters in San Francisco, including one in Seattle. The Walla Walla store operated as Schwabacher's until 1909 and then as Gardner's Department Store until 1980. The present building *on the north side of Main between 2nd and 3rd Avenues,* which now serves as a bank, replaced a series of earlier store buildings in 1910.

On the south side of Main between 2nd and 3rd is the **Brechtel Building**, built in 1869, making it the oldest commercial building in the city. The Brechtel Bakery specialized in crackers, which kept better than bread in the mining camps. The **Baumeister Building**, built by real estate brokers Baumeister and Reynolds in 1889, is *east of the bakery.* The first building on the site hosted the town's second newspaper, the *Walla Walla Union,* forerunner of today's *Walla Walla Union-Bulletin.*

Miners spent summers in the goldfields, then flocked to the boardinghouses and saloons of Walla Walla for the winter. Looking for a place to stash their bags of gold dust, they sought out the heavy iron safe in the back of the store owned by John Boyer and his brother-in-law, Dr. Dorsey Baker, the same man who had built a railroad. Their handshake deals evolved into the **Baker-Boyer Bank**, the first bank in the territory, established in 1869 and built in 1911 *on the southwest corner of 2nd and Main.* Main Street fairly bristles with stately bank buildings, including the **Paine Building** *on the southeast corner of 2nd and Main,* which housed the First National Bank beginning in 1878. By just one day, Levi Ankeny beat Boyer to the federal bank in Washington, D.C., to register his as the first national bank in Walla Walla in 1878. The newer **First National Bank Building**, a block south at 2nd and Alder, was built in 1921.

Continue east on Main. When Walla Walla's gold fortunes turned to wheat fortunes in the mid-1860s, Baker and Boyer became the

The Nez Perce arrive for the Walla Walla treaty council in May 1855. The dramatic drawing is by Gustavus Sohon, artist with the U.S. Army. Courtesy Washington State Historical Society.

bankers for farmers. As the central Idaho mines played out, the prospectors went elsewhere, but mining and farming brought enough prosperity to Walla Walla that the territory's first constitutional convention met in 1878 at *4 E Main between 1st and 2nd Avenues* in the **Reynolds-Day Building**, built in 1874. Fifteen delegates gathered in an upstairs room to hash out a proposed state constitution, which the United States Congress failed to act on. (The final draft was negotiated and penned in Olympia eleven years later.) The Reynolds-Day Building was one of the few to survive an 1887 fire that engulfed both sides of Main Street and destroyed City Hall, the engine house of the fire company, and all of Chinatown.

Despite the fire, Walla Walla's downtown continued to thrive into the 1890s. The **Barrett Building**, built in 1882 on the north side of the street, is now a delicatessen. The 1890 **Sayer Building** on the south side was the Bee Hive variety store until 1977. Along Main Street, saloons, gambling dens, outfitters, blacksmiths, wagon repair shops, and livery stables have given way to Macy's, Starbucks, and wine-tasting rooms.

Mill Creek flows under Main Street *at 1st Avenue* where the Nez Perce Trail once crossed it. The **Die Brucke Building**, dating from 1903, bridges it now. The land across the creek had long been a gathering place for native people—a tribal council ground. Some 5,000 Indians, including women and children, camped along the banks of the creek during the treaty talks of 1855. Governor Stevens and his staff sat at a table under an arbor of trees on the north bank of the creek with Indians arrayed in concentric semicircles before them. Exactly where the grove was or even where the creek flowed in 1855 is a matter of conjecture and debate. Two plaques on rocks farther along this route mark other sites, and the names of streets provide more clues.

Walla Walla Treaty Council

The treaty council convened in June 1855, with large delegations from the Nez Perce, Yakama, Cayuse, Walla Walla, Palouse, and Umatilla attending. According to a description provided by thirteen-year-old Hazard Stevens, son of the territorial governor, a thousand Nez Perce arrived first, with painted horses and painted faces, beads and fringes of gaudy colors, and plumes of eagle feathers interwoven with their horses' manes and tails. Negotiators sat for several days around a table under a small arbor. On nearly the last day of the encampment, Looking Glass of the Nez Perce returned from a three-year hunt in the Montana country. As recorded by army officer Lawrence Kip, without even getting off his horse, Looking Glass protested: "My people, what have you done? While I was gone you have sold my country. I have come home and there is not left to me a place on which to pitch my lodge." The next day Looking Glass made a strong speech against the treaty, and several chiefs recanted their agreement. However, Kamaiakin of the Yakama, Peo Peo Mox Mox of the Walla Walla, Lawyer of the Nez Perce, and Weyatenatemany of the Cayuse reluctantly agreed to the treaty.

A block beyond, the first decades of Walla Walla's history are portrayed in a charming pocket park called **Heritage Park** *on the south side of E Main Street between Colville and Spokane Streets.* Painted murals line the walls of buildings on two sides, visualizing Walla Walla as it was.

Continue a block east to the corner of Boyer, Palouse, and Main, still on the traditional council grounds. This curious three-way intersection resulted from a reorientation of city streets. Main Street followed the Nez Perce Trail in a predominantly east–west direction, but the streets leading off it were not always in a north–south orientation. As the city moved eastward, the streets were realigned with the compass to run north and south and east and west at right angles, a correction that begins where Palouse, Main, and Boyer intersect.

Here, on the tip of the triangle created by the intersection, stands a **statue** of missionary and pioneer doctor Marcus Whitman. With his wife Narcissa, Whitman served the mission at Waiilatpu west of Walla Walla from 1836 until their deaths at the hands of hostile Cayuse in 1847. This statue is a duplicate of the Whitman statue representing Washington State in the National Statuary Hall in Washington, DC. (The other statue there is of Mother Joseph, a Sister of Providence and builder of many schools and hospitals.) The Whitman statue anchors the eastern edge of downtown, marking the evolution of Walla Walla from a frontier town to a college town.

Cross **railroad tracks** at the tip of the triangle, a remainder from the decades when railroads shipped grain forty-six miles west to Wallula. Dr. Dorsey Baker's Walla Walla and Columbia River Railroad Company had a depot at 10th and Elm, now lost between a

Rose and a Cherry—you won't find it. In 1878, Baker sold most of his stock in the railroad to the Oregon Steam Navigation Company, which was eventually sold to the Northern Pacific Railway. A branch line of the Northern Pacific arrived in town in 1883. Its depot is now a restaurant several blocks away at 2nd and Pine. Union Pacific operates the current railroad line from Walla Walla to Wallula.

Continue on Boyer Avenue onto the campus of **Whitman College**. The statue of Marcus Whitman stands just off campus, but his name and status as a martyr were used for years to promote the college. Reverend Cushing Eells wanted to start the college on the Whitman Mission site, a safe distance from saloons and unsavory characters. Most supporters thought that was too far out of town, and Eells accepted a donation from Dorsey Baker of four acres on the eastern edge of town.

Because the college was poor, the first three buildings were made of wood. The oldest building on campus still standing—built of stone in 1889—is **Memorial Hall**, on the *north side of Boyer between Park and Otis Streets*. Its clock tower chimes the college's hard-won stability 180 times in a day. *At Boyer and Otis* is the **Baker Center**, built in 1904 as a home for Dr. Dorsey Baker's daughter Mabel, who married Louis Anderson, a classical languages professor and son of the first Whitman president.

Continuing east on Boyer, pass **Lakum Duckum**, which was created by a dam on College Creek and does have resident ducks but also hosted tugs-of-war until its muddy banks were concreted, *and continue* around Maxey Hall to the **amphitheater**, which hosted graduations until the student body grew too large.

Outside the amphitheater stands a **large rock** containing a plaque remembering Chief Lawyer of the Nez Perce. This is one of two markers for the site of the treaty council. Lawyer and the Nez Perce were friendly to incoming whites but ultimately unsuccessful in preserving their wealth and power. Streets and buildings on campus sport the names of other significant figures in Walla Walla history: John F. Boyer, Almos H. Reynolds, Narcissa Prentiss Whitman, and Stephen Penrose, long-serving president of Whitman.

As the college matured, so did the town. Wealth was channeled into homes, churches, and cultural institutions. *On the eastern edge of campus, return to Boyer along Stanton Street and continue* past the Washington **Odd Fellows Home**, a retirement center. Fraternal organizations like the Odd Fellows provided socializing opportunities for men and service for communities. Their three links symbolize friendship, love, and truth. The Walla Walla chapter had a temple downtown, built in 1902; its facade is now a wall in Heritage Park.

In 1897 the Odd Fellows erected this home for the aged on land donated by neighbor H. P. Isaacs. Isaacs was an early wheat farmer who demonstrated that the hills used for stock grazing would also grow wheat. He built many flour mills around the region and found markets for wheat in China, thereby starting the Asian trade for Walla Walla wheat. If you wish, take a short walk north on Brookside Drive to the **Isaacs home** at 100 Brookside Drive, built in 1886.

Helen Isaacs created a Walla Walla Woman's Club in 1886 for the purpose of self-improvement and the study of literature. The club's focus changed a year later, when a court decision deprived the women of Washington Territory of the right to vote that the territorial legislature had granted. The club transformed into the more activist Equal Suffrage League, which disbanded in 1889 when women were again denied the right to vote at statehood.

At **571 Boyer** *on the corner with Clinton*, notice an impressive neoclassical home built in 1909 for Oliver Cornwell. It stands on a lot that is small for the home's size, but farmers like Cornwell, who had 1,500 acres of land and another home outside of town, did not feel they needed large grounds for their town homes. Cornwell was a state legislator as well as a farmer.

At Division Street, turn south along **Wildwood Park**, site of the North Pacific Flour Mill started in 1862 by Isaacs. *Proceed two blocks* to **Pioneer Park**, the city's first park. The famous landscape architect John C. Olmsted planned its design with a characteristic curving road, a Victorian bandstand, trees that have grown tall and wide, and an aviary.

At Whitman Street, turn west (right) and walk three blocks to Howard Street to the three-storied **Sharpstein School**, built in 1898, expanded in good taste, and lovingly maintained. It is the oldest continuously operating elementary school in the state, named after Benjamin L. Sharpstein, a lawyer, state legislator, and member of the constitutional convention of 1889 and the Walla Walla school board. The school first opened in the winter of 1861–62 on land donated, of course, by Dorsey Baker.

Turn right on Howard Street and then left on Lincoln Street. Turn right on Grove Street and follow it two blocks to Crescent Street, which curves west to Park Street. According to local historian Daniel Clark, **Grove Street** takes its name from a grove of trees that lined Mill Creek and may be the site of the arbor under which treaty leaders sat to talk and make their marks. An early housing development in this area was called Council Grove Addition. The curiously curved Crescent Street may follow an earlier channel of Mill Creek so that the area now south of Mill Creek was north, matching the description given in historical records.

Turn right on Park, passing the **Drumheller home** at 233 S Park Street. Jesse Drumheller ran the first hardware store. The family also farmed wheat and raised cattle, profiting from Walla Walla's cowboy period, when thousands of cattle were driven to markets at the Idaho mines and to California. The cattle industry remained healthy even after mining declined, and, as late as the 1950s and 1960s, cattle drives still went through parts of town along the railroad tracks, moving from winter to summer range.

Cross Alder and turn left, noting a 1927 fire station, now the local Red Cross building. *Head west on Alder* past the original Carnegie library. In the triangle behind the building, look for a recent plaque and the **treaty rock** signifying the Treaty Council of 1855. This is another likely location for the negotiations since the encampment of Indians spread over several acres.

Religion battled with vice in the town's early decades. The Methodist Episcopalians organized a church in 1859. Reverend Cushing Eells preached a sermon for a competing denomination at a shack out on the plains in July 1860. Eells lamented that many of the settlers in the valley were gamblers, horse thieves, and Sabbath breakers. *Across the street* from the old library stand three church buildings, two for the First Congregational Church and one for the First Christian Church. The spire of St. Patrick's Catholic church is visible to the west on Alder Street.

Walk west to the southwest corner of 2nd and Alder and the restored 1904 **Drumheller Building**, which housed the hardware store. On the second floor of the adjacent building was a bordello run by the notorious Josephine Wolfe, the town's first madam, who arrived in 1860.

Bounded by 2nd and 3rd, Alder, and an alley south of Main was the half-block center of the Chinese community in Walla Walla. The Chinese came during gold rush days and stayed to become gardeners, merchants, launderers, cooks, and domestics in a city short of women who could do that work. The Chinese composed one-tenth of the population in 1898. Charles Tung came from San Francisco in 1880 and started the Kwong Chung Sing Company. He imported Chinese merchandise, such as chinaware, porcelains, bronzes, embroideries, silks, and teas. This area was destroyed by the fire of 1887, but the Chinese community rebounded by organizing the Pacific Enterprise Corporation and building a two-story structure at 5th and Rose Streets in 1911. The community contributed a slithering Chinese dragon to the town's Fourth of July parades, but the building was sold in the 1940s, dispersing about ninety Chinese residents, and it was razed in 1962.

At 6th Avenue, find **St. Patrick's Church**, built in 1881 at the western end of Alder, and notice the spire of the Congregational Church

A stagecoach rumbles down wide Main Street in a 1958 reenactment of frontier days by the Wagon Wheelers and the Walla Walla Fifty-Niners. Sears, the Liberty Theater, and the Book Nook are all visible. *Courtesy* The Walla Walla Union Bulletin.

visible to the east. These blocks once housed a boys' school, a parsonage, and St. Mary's Hospital, which remains a presence today as Providence St. Mary's Medical Center on Poplar, one block southeast.

Turn right on 6th and walk northwest to Main Street, passing the block where civic order began. The **Walla Walla County Courthouse**, facing Main Street, was built in 1916. Before that, the county rented the upper story of a saloon, which is no longer standing, on 5th Street between Alder and Main. In front of the courthouse stands a **statue of Christopher Columbus**. This one honors Italian immigrants who introduced the Walla Walla sweet onion to the market and started some of the early wineries.

Walk east on Main Street. The first public meetinghouse in Walla Walla was a small split-board shack about 300 yards *south of 4th and Main,* which residents called the schoolhouse. They cast their first votes there. *On the southwest corner of 4th and Main* stands the **Dacres Hotel**, built in 1873 and partially rebuilt after a fire in 1892. It housed visiting performers at the opera house a block south (part of which remains near 4th and Alder). Stagelines arrived regularly at the hotel, bringing passengers and mail. George Dacres's wealth came from farming and from packing into the mining camps with a team of forty-five to fifty mules.

Continue walking east on Main through what was once the red-light district. The upper floors of **202, 206, 208, and 210 W Main Street** have very small rooms, known colloquially as the Rose Rooms. The bordellos survived several decades beyond a 1913 law making prostitution a misdemeanor. In the 1950s, *Look* magazine infamously described Walla Walla as one of the "seediest" cities in America. More recently, at the other end of Main Street, the city won a Great American Main Street award in 2001 for renovating the Liberty Theater and the Die Brucke Building so as to keep the Bon Marche, now Macy's, downtown.

Walk north on 4th to Rose Street; turn east on Rose and return to the start, noticing ahead of you the **Marcus Whitman Hotel**, built in 1928. A dominant landmark on the city skyline, it has had extensive remodeling in recent years but is still known locally as "the Marc." Generations of college students have danced in its ballroom.

At the end of the walk, the statue of Peo Peo Mox Mox bookends downtown with the statue of Marcus Whitman at the other end, the two memorializing parallel sacrifices to differing visions of the Walla Walla Valley. Since their time, the city has flourished from mines, wheat, onions, and wine but remembers its frontier beginnings in street names, buildings, and statues.

Resources   Fort Walla Walla Museum, 755 Myra Road,
www.fortwallawallamuseum.org

Frenchtown Historic Site, www.frenchtownpartners.org

Tourist Information Center, 26 E Main Street

Walla Walla Public Library, 238 E Alder Street

Whitman Mission National Historic Site,
www.nps.gov/whmi/

CHAPTER FOUR

Tacoma

Boomtown on Commencement Bay

Make a note of it, readers, for from this day, you may date the rise
of the second (perhaps the first) city of the Pacific Coast—Tacoma.

Pacific Tribune, December 15, 1873

S
ettlers around Puget Sound waited breathlessly in the 1870s
for a decision that would be made by investors and capitalists
outside of the territory—where to put the terminus of the
northern transcontinental railroad. During the Civil War, the U.S.
Congress and President Abraham Lincoln had authorized the construction of a railroad, and in 1869 the Union Pacific reached San
Francisco, having crossed the middle of the country. Four years later,
it was the North's turn. Washington's territorial governor, Isaac Stevens, had surveyed routes for the Northern Pacific; his report recommended going along the Columbia River, then turning north to
Puget Sound, or going through the central Cascade Mountains.

Puget Sound was the prize, with its access to the Pacific Ocean
through the Strait of Juan de Fuca. An advance man for the railroad,
Sam Wilkeson, had heralded the sound's promise: "There is nothing
on the American continent equal to it. . . . Such timber—such soil—
such orchards—such fish—such climate—such coal—such harbors—
such rivers. . . . There is no end to the possibilities of wealth here."

Wilkeson also sounded a warning. The terminus would thrive on this wealth, but it would be the "chained slave of the Northern Pacific Railroad." Young settlements like Olympia, Steilacoom, Port Townsend, Seattle, and Mukilteo all wanted to be that wealthy slave. The question was which bay on Puget Sound would offer the deepest harbor and which town the most incentives and cheapest land.

Civil War veteran Job Carr thought he had found the perfect site for the terminus at a sheltered cove on Commencement Bay where the Puyallup Indians had beached their canoes, camped, and dug clams for centuries. He filed a land claim, cut down firs, and built a cabin on a bluff overlooking the wide expanse of the bay. Morton Matthew McCarver, a city promoter, liked the odds, too. He bought much of Carr's land and platted a town. He called the town Tacoma City after the Indian name, Tahoma, for the glacier-clad mountain looming to the east. (English explorer George Vancouver named it Mount Rainier.) Then he waited.

The railroad line crept across the continent and finally reached Kalama on the north side of the Columbia River, poised to plunge on to Puget Sound. A terse telegram from railroad executives to McCarver on July 14, 1873, carried spectacular news: "We have located terminus at Commencement Bay." But it would not be at Tacoma City. The Northern Pacific directors chose a site two miles east, where waterfront land was unclaimed and cheaper: a New Tacoma.

The tracks had advanced to Tenino and company engineers had six months to build the last forty miles of track across the prairies to the bay. If the railroad couldn't complete the line by the end of the year, it would forfeit forty million acres of public land promised by the federal government to finance construction. The company spun off a land company, bought up land along the waterfront, hired Chinese workers, and hastily laid track. Taking the shortest, most direct route from the southwest, the Prairie Line plunged diagonally down a steep hillside and reached the bay on a clear, cold day in December 1873. Job Carr and Matthew McCarver tapped a last ceremonial spike before the railroad's head spiker drove it home. At the end of the line, the iron rail met ocean sail.

"Make a note of it, readers," wrote a reporter for the *Pacific Tribune*, "for from this day, you may date the rise of the second (perhaps the first) city of the Pacific Coast—Tacoma." His prediction was premature. Just as the Prairie Line was completed, investors lost confidence in the railroads. Financial markets tanked, and the Northern Pacific declared bankruptcy. For the next decade, Tacoma grew slowly. Not until 1887 did tracks cross the Cascade Mountains through a tunnel at Stampede Pass, follow the Green River down the western slopes, pick up the Puyallup River, and arrive at Commencement Bay. With this shorter route bypassing Portland, and with a financial reorganization of the railroad company, Tacoma's "delirious decade" began.

From 1887 to 1897, the new city boomed. A thousand immigrants a month streamed through its portals looking for jobs in the western United States. For a time, Tacoma truly was the second city of the Pacific Coast behind San Francisco, which had a sizeable head start. An outbreak of civic optimism was expressed in the lyrics of a song weighted with superlatives: "Tacoma, the gem of the ocean, the pride of the North and the West, the grandest, the noblest—the Best."

The decade's prime instigator was Charles Wright, the Northern Pacific's main man in Tacoma. "I looked up at the sloping hills," he said, "and saw how Nature had done everything except build a city, and I said to myself—Here is the place." Wright began speculating in land and building a city high on the bluff above the bay. Northern Pacific moved its headquarters from Portland to New Tacoma. City hall, grand hotels, boardinghouses, and saloons clustered around it. Rail lines snaked along the waterfront carrying produce from the Inland Empire to loading docks on the bay.

Tacoma's delirium eased in the financial panic of 1893, when the Northern Pacific declared bankruptcy (again). Like the depression of 1873, the panic was caused by the cost of building railroads without revenue from freight and a consequent loss of investor confidence. This led to a run on the gold supply and on banks. Still a slave to the railroad's prosperity, Tacoma could no longer take pride in calling itself the "City of Destiny," a title promoted in the 1880s. One-third of its residents fled, and Tacoma's population lagged behind Seattle's for the first time. Waterfront businesses cut back, yet Tacoma found a new footing, anchored by trade built on coal, wheat, and lumber. The coal came in a steady supply from mines in Wilkeson, a station named after the man who had promoted Puget Sound. Some two hundred carloads of wheat arrived daily from eastern Washington during the harvest season, and three grain elevators rose on the south bay.

Lumber was the most significant cash crop of Puget Sound in the last half of the nineteenth century. In Seattle, Tacoma, Everett, and Bellingham, citizens cut down trees, built sawmills near water, filled the holds of sailing ships with lumber, and exported it to the world. The first large-scale sawmill in Tacoma, operated by Hanson & Company, stored logs in the sheltered cove Job Carr had found; as early as 1871, well before the railroads arrived, it was shipping lumber on French ships to Callao, the chief port of Peru.

Foreign trade accelerated when the Northern Pacific gained control of vast timberlands through the land grants given by Congress. In 1888, midwestern lumbermen, including Henry Hewitt and Chauncey Griggs, incorporated the St. Paul and Tacoma Lumber Company to harvest the trees of the Pacific Northwest. They bought 80,000 acres of timberland near Tacoma from the Northern Pacific. St. Paul, as it became known, built two large sawmills on the tide-flats. By 1929, twenty more sawmills dotted Commencement Bay, working around the clock seven days a week. Exporting to China, Australia, Chile, New York, and California, Tacoma could claim to be the "Lumber Capital of the World."

Tall-masted freighters wait to take up cargo from the mile-long warehouse around 1906. Rails from eastern Washington brought wheat to the sails of Commencement Bay. Courtesy Tacoma Public Library.

A rival company, Weyerhaeuser, started in 1895 when James J. Hill, the empire builder of the Great Northern Railway, took over the bankrupt Northern Pacific. He acquired the rest of the company's land grants and sold 900,000 acres to his neighbor in St. Paul, Frederick Weyerhaeuser. Although his company's largest mills would be built in Everett, their timberlands were administered from Tacoma.

In most Puget Sound cities, the railroads dominated the waterfronts, handing out land parcels to favored businesses, like the St. Paul, which would transport their products by rail. Corporations allied with the transcontinental railroads flourished, but individual entrepreneurs were often stifled. Such power alarmed the public, resulting in passage of the Sherman Antitrust Act of 1890, which required the federal government to investigate and pursue trusts. To protect their positions, the Northern Pacific, Great Northern, and Chicago, Burlington & Quincy formed a holding company, the Northern Securities Company. For a while, the company threatened to become the world's largest company and to monopolize all railroad traffic on the West Coast. President Theodore Roosevelt ordered the Department of Justice to "bust the trusts." Northern Securities was dissolved by a 1904 Supreme Court decision.

That decision signaled the end of Northern Pacific's unchallenged dominance in Tacoma. Other railroads sent lines into Tacoma, and in 1911 the Milwaukee Road, Union Pacific, and Great Northern built a shared depot, Union Station. Not until 1969, when railroad power was much less threatening, did the three original partners merge into a new company, the Burlington Northern.

In another reaction to monopolies, Progressive leaders in Seattle and Tacoma lobbied the state to allow cities and counties to create port districts that would manage the waterfronts for a broader public good. The railroads opposed such districts as socialistic, but in 1918, Tacoma citizens took control of the waterfront by voting to finance a port district. The port then engineered waterways where the Puyallup River flowed into Commencement Bay and created new fingers of land by filling the tideflats on the waterways' banks. With the head start the railroads provided, the Port of Tacoma now handles more than 40 percent of Washington's water-borne international trade.

Tacoma's trade-driven economy produced a succession of social ripples. First was the displacement of the Puyallup tribe, a sovereign nation owning land in the middle of the city. In 1857, in return for ceding thousands of acres, the Puyallup signed a treaty accepting 18,000 acres of reserved land on the tideflats, land that today includes much of the Port of Tacoma, part of downtown Tacoma, all of Fife, and a stretch of I-5. But gradually Puyallup claims to the tideflats were diminished. By 1886, Tacoma had grown to the edge of the Puyallup land, and Washington's congressional delegation complained that federal protection of tribes was hampering westward advancement.

In 1887, the Dawes Severalty Act provided that Native American land could be allotted to individuals, rather than held by the tribe as a whole, and individuals could eventually sell their allotments. The idea was to assimilate Indians by encouraging individual land ownership, but for the Puyallup, the period an allotment had to be held before sale was reduced from twenty-five years to only ten years, and real estate speculators managed to buy much of the land. By 1934 tribal members held only thirty-three acres on the outskirts of Tacoma. Successfully protesting the land grab in court, the tribe agreed in 1990 to give up claims to the original reservation in return for 900 acres along the northeastern edge of Commencement Bay extending east along the Puyallup River.

Also displaced were the Chinese. Laying track was labor intensive, and the railroad companies wanted cheap labor. In their rush to build the Prairie Line in the 1870s, the Northern Pacific had contracted with agents to hire 250 Chinese workers, who outnumbered white residents on Commencement Bay. After the railroads were completed, many of the Chinese stayed on to work as domestic servants, waiters, lumber mill workers, laundrymen, or merchants. The white community resented the importation of foreigners, and workers resented the competition for wages. Despite a city council draft resolution warning that any unlawful acts would damage Tacoma's reputation, a mob sanctioned by city officials rounded up 200 Chinese and forced them to leave town in 1885.

Tacoma was not alone in expelling the Chinese. A meeting in Seattle that formed the Puget Sound Anti-Chinese Congress had representatives from eight towns, including Tacoma, and seven labor unions. They set a date of November 1, 1885, for Chinese to leave.

Anti-Asian hostility all along the West Coast resulted in the federal Chinese Exclusion Acts of 1882 and 1892, outlawing Chinese immigration for sixty years. Not until the 1990s would Washington elect a governor of Chinese descent, Gary Locke, the same decade Tacoma citizens initiated reconciliation with the building of a park.

When Chinese immigration was restricted, more Japanese men came to work on the railroads, in canneries, and in agriculture. Barred from citizenship and owning land, many leased Puyallup land for farming; others leased property in the Nihonmachi business district of the city. Although Tacoma had the largest Japanese American community on the West Coast by percentage of total population, most lost their businesses during the forced internment of World War II and few returned to the city after the war.

African Americans found jobs around Tacoma as miners, longshoremen, farmers, and Pullman porters on the railroads. Many settled in the Hilltop neighborhood, above the eastern end of Commencement Bay, a plot of land bought in 1869 by an alliance of African American real estate investors. Many more came to work in war production during World War II. Decades later, in 1994, Tacoma elected its first African American mayor, Harold Moss.

The mills around the bay and the transfer of cargo from rails to ships created many jobs, and workers formed strong unions. During the Great Depression, Tacoma experienced both the West Coast longshoremen's strike, which lasted for eighty-three days in 1934, and the shorter 1935 lumber mill strike. The longshoremen's strike required federal intervention and mediation, which settled issues in the union's favor, including higher hourly pay and union control of hiring. The lumber mill strike resulted in recognition of the union and a forty-hour work week, gains achieved only after workers confronted civic authority on Tacoma's 11th Street Bridge.

Industrial jobs made Tacoma a "Gritty City" in both attitude and landscape and left a legacy of pollution on the waterfront. The Northern Pacific's fateful choice of Tacoma as its terminus determined the city's destiny at considerable cost to Commencement Bay. As is true of many Puget Sound cities, Tacoma now wrestles with protecting and cleaning up its shorelines. Commencement Bay was identified as a Superfund site in 1983, among the sites highest on the national priority list for cleanup.

The notorious aroma that plagued Tacoma for many years came from sulfides released by the St. Regis Paper Company, but the pulp mill was not the only source of the odor. Chemical factories, petroleum processors, and other industries on the tideflats contributed to the poor air quality. In the 1990s, Simpson Tacoma Kraft, successor to St. Regis, reduced sulfide emissions by 90 percent, greatly diluting the aroma.

The more deadly offender was a smelter operated by the American Smelting and Refining Company (Asarco) just northwest of the city at Point Ruston. For almost a hundred years, the smelter processed lead and then copper ore. Its smokestack was once the tallest in the world, blowing lead, arsenic, and other heavy metals over the surface soil of more than a thousand square miles. After spending millions on cleanup, Asarco declared bankruptcy, reorganized, and closed the smelter in 1985. Eight years later, the smokestack was blown up, as part of a massive cleanup.

In addition to cleaning up damaged areas, Tacoma has revitalized its downtown core with housing, art, museums, and a branch campus of the University of Washington. Running through the campus is a trail on the Prairie Line, which first brought prosperity to Tacoma.

The first trail here is a short loop in Old Town, where civic ambitions soared. The longer, central loop begins at Tollefson Plaza, where the Northern Pacific first came to town. It follows the Prairie Line rail grade to the waterfront, climbs to New Tacoma on the bluff above the bay, follows Pacific Avenue and the waterfront escalade downtown to the tideflats, and loops back to the warehouse district and to Union Station. The lone traveler sculpted on the sidewalk in front of the station recalls the adventure and promise of a railroad city.

A walkway along the waterfront north from Old Town leads two miles to a major reclamation of the land around the former Asarco smelter at Point Ruston. The site was cleaned up in stages: demolishing the smoke-stack and sixty-eight buildings, excavating soil and slag, disposing of the contaminates, addressing surface water drainage, capping the area, and protecting it from erosion. New housing, retail, and offices have been built on the site. The walk from Old Town along Ruston Way connects to a one-mile waterwalk at Point Ruston, which features mosaic center-pieces at intersections, trash cans wrapped with historic photographs, and benches shaped like mooring cleats, which were used to tie up the freighters bringing copper ore to the smelter. On its north end, the path-way connects to Point Defiance Park.

Pioneer Walk: Old Town

START: Old Town dock, 2200 Ruston Way

DIRECTIONS: From I-5, take I-705 north to exit 133, toward City Center; merge onto Schuster Parkway via the exit on the left; take Schuster Parkway, which becomes Ruston Way, for 2 miles.

DISTANCE: 1 mile round trip

AMENITIES: Free public parking across from the Old Town dock, at the foot of McCarver Street, on the bluff side; restrooms and drinking fountains at the Old Town dock

Begin at the **Old Town dock** stretching into Commencement Bay. The bay was named by Charles Wilkes, a U.S. Navy admiral, as he commenced an exploration of Puget Sound in 1841. At the end of the dock, look back at the gentle draw that leads to the top of a hill. The confluence of two creeks at the foot of the draw produced a small lagoon protected by a sandbar. The Puyallup called this **Shubahlup**, "the sheltered place." They camped here, found abundant clams, and rested, awaiting the tide that would carry them through the narrows farther south on the sound. Spying Shubahlup from his canoe offshore in 1864, Job Carr shouted "Eureka!" thinking he had found the perfect spot for the terminus of the transcontinental railroad.

Although the terminus landed farther east, it was here that Tacoma's maritime trade began. A Danish sea captain backed by California investors, Charles Hanson, built a sawmill and wharf in 1868. The lumber mill boasted the first electric lights on Puget Sound; a village of 200 grew around it, and the lagoon served as a holding pond for logs. Although the mill remained the largest in Tacoma for twenty years, the town moved east in 1873 when the Northern Pacific bought two miles of waterfront from here to the east end of the bay. The small medallions secreted in wooden railings and elsewhere on the dock—an art project called *Droplets*—evoke images of its past. The fish company on the dock has been in business since 1912, selling the day's catch.

Mill workers lived in modest homes on the hill above the waterfront. Near here, at the foot of the hill, was Little Canton, a community of Chinese who worked at the mills. Their houses were burned down in November 1885, when several hundred Chinese left or were forced onto trains for Portland or San Francisco. On the waterfront side of Schuster Parkway, you may walk southeast 0.5-mile to **Chinese Reconciliation Park,** which portrays that injustice.

Chinese Reconciliation Park

A paved trail runs along the waterfront side of Ruston Way from the Old Town dock to the park at *1741 Schuster Parkway.* In 1991 the park began as an "act of reconciliation and inclusivity toward appreciation of the people of diverse legacies and interests," according to its website (www.taco machinesepark.org). Several phases have been completed since groundbreaking in 2007, including Fuzhou Ting, a pavilion.

From the Old Town Dock, use the crosswalk over Ruston Way at the foot of McCarver Street, and walk uphill to the small community known as "the birthplace of Tacoma." The center of Job Carr's claim was *at 30th and McCarver Streets*. He had come west seeking land available to Civil War veterans. *Turn west on 30th and walk to a small park* where **Job Carr's cabin** carries his story.

On the way you will pass **Ribarski Pripovijest** (A Fish Story), a sculpture of a fisherman presenting a fat fish to his wife. It stands in front of the **Slavonian Hall**, marking what Old Tacoma became—not a terminus for the railroad but a flourishing fishing center worked by Scandinavians and Slavonians. Grocery stores on this street supplied fishermen with staples.

After visiting Carr's cabin and **canoe** and reading the **interpretive plaques**, *find steps at the back of the park leading up to 29th Street. Turn left to walk east on 29th to McCarver Street, and then walk south one block. On the southeast corner of 28th and McCarver* is a **rock with a plaque** marking the homesite of Morton Matthew McCarver, the man who bought most of Carr's claim. Once it was clear that the railroad would arrive two miles east, Job Carr sold off much of his remaining farm for homes. A building boom began on what was called **Job Carr's Hill** and is now called the **North Slope Historic District** (see the walking tour at tacomanorthslope.org).

Walk east one block and north one block to the corner of 29th and Starr Streets. One week after the Northern Pacific announced its terminus on Commencement Bay, an Episcopal bishop arrived from Portland to select a site for a new church. Within months, **St. Peter's Church** was built, with a bell tower perched on top of a very high stump. St. Peter's remains the oldest church in Tacoma, with the stump now ivy-covered, a reminder of the cash crop that came down on these hillsides (the trees, not the ivy).

Continue north on Starr Street to 30th, and turn left to return to the waterfront. You will pass the Spar, which claims status as Tacoma's oldest saloon, the last of eight that served workers in a two-block stretch. The Spar has many photographs of Old Tacoma and a large wall map echoing McCarver's promotion of the "terminus of the Northern Pacific Railroad." One photograph shows the Hanson mill at the foot of Starr Street.

This ends the Old Town loop. The city plans a Schuster Corridor multi-use trail that will eventually link Ruston Way, Old Town, and the north end of downtown Tacoma.

Stadium High School

Between Old Town and downtown, overlooking Commencement Bay, is **Stadium Bowl**, on E Street between Second and Third Streets, and **Stadium High School**, at 111 N E Street. The ravine holding this impressive stadium, first known as Hud-Hud-Gus, was a seasonal fishing camp for the Puyallup. It became "Old Woman's Gulch" when widows of fishermen and longshoremen lived in shanties there in the decades before workers' compensation and social security. On the bluff above the ravine, a grandiloquent hotel was planned to house railroad barons, industrialists, and investors who might come to town. Construction halted during the financial panic of 1893, and the would-be hotel caught fire a few years later. The exterior was repurposed into the city's first high school, a source of pride for its graduates to this day. The widows in the gulch were evicted and their shanties burned when an athletic field was built for the school in 1910.

Tacoma Loop

START: Tollefson Plaza, Pacific Avenue and S 17th Street

DIRECTIONS: From I-5, take I-705 north to exit 133 to City Center, then the Pacific Avenue exit on the left. Go north (right) to 17th Street.

DISTANCE: 5.8 miles round trip

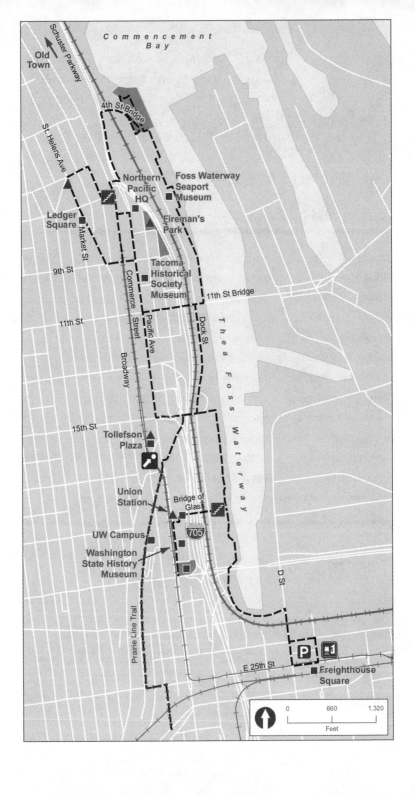

Commencement Bay

Schuster Parkway

Old Town

4th St Bridge

St. Helens Ave

Northern Pacific HQ

Foss Waterway Seaport Museum

Ledger Square

Fireman's Park

Market St

9th St

Commerce Street

Tacoma Historical Society Museum

11th St Bridge

11th St

Broadway

Pacific Ave

Dock St

Thea Foss Waterway

15th St

Tollefson Plaza

Union Station

Bridge of Glass

UW Campus

705

Washington State History Museum

Prairie Line Trail

D St

P

Freighthouse Square

E 25th St

0   660   1,320

Feet

AMENITIES: Free public parking at Freighthouse Square, where you can catch Tacoma Link (the city's light-rail line) downtown; paid parking lots and two-hour metered parking on the streets near Pacific and 17th

Begin high on the bluff above Commencement Bay below the open-palmed hands of a **Welcome Figure**, a traditional Coast Salish carving that greeted visitors. It was crafted by Puyallup artist Shaun Peterson and placed on **Tollefson Plaza** in 2010. Tollefson was Harold M. Tollefson, a 1950s and '60s mayor of Tacoma.

The Puyallup were still living along the bay in July 1873, when the Northern Pacific announced it would locate its Puget Sound terminus there. The so-called Prairie Line, the last segment of the route, would remain in service for 130 years until it became a trail.

Follow the Prairie Line trail downhill under I-705. Walk on the trail, if it is completed, or on the sidewalk parallel to it (on Hood Street) and cross an exit ramp from I-705 on a very faint crosswalk to the **15th Street Bridge**. *Walk over the bridge to the waterfront.* (The Prairie Line continues under the freeway, but the trail is not marked and ends a block or two west.)

Once across the bridge, you are standing by **Dock Street**, near the site of a major Puyallup village. Even after the Puyallup were consigned to a reservation by the Treaty of Medicine Creek, they returned often to this place where the Puyallup River flowed down from Tahoma (Mount Rainier) and into the bay.

For the promoters of a new Tacoma, this is where the rails met the sails, on the south side of Commencement Bay, where the water was deepest. The tideflats to the east were too shallow for navigation and too unstable for rail yards. The water in front of you was the mouth of an old channel of the Puyallup River. One of the major projects of Charles Wright, the driving force of the Tacoma Land Company, was to dredge this channel closest to the bluff supporting the new town.

Puyallup Indians gamble at a bone game near the foot of 15th Street, circa 1886. This was the site of a traditional village before the railroad arrived in Tacoma in 1873. Courtesy Tacoma Public Library.

A giant steam dredge dug through the tideflats to create the **City Waterway**, a project begun in 1889 and completed in 1905.

Walk north along the sidewalk on Dock Street. In the years after 1873, when the Prairie Line reached the waterfront, the Northern Pacific built a long, high trestle across the tideflats and the mouth of the Puyallup. It led to two large bunkers offshore used to store coal brought on a branch line from mines at Wilkeson. After the completion of the main Northern Pacific line through Stampede Pass in 1887, wheat from eastern Washington was freighted to the longest warehouse in the world, the so-called mile-long warehouse. The Northern Pacific built yards to maneuver engines and cars, a 350-foot loading dock to reach ships in the bay, and a hotel to lodge important visitors in a cluster once known as the town "On the Wharf." Little remains of this town except the four lines of active track still lining the shore and ships loading on the waterway.

Four blocks north, pass under the Murray Morgan Bridge, known

The Tacoma commanded the bluff above Commencement Bay between 9th and 10th Avenues in 1927, in an era when railroad travel had spurred the building of grand hotels. The Tacoma was destroyed by fire in October 1935. Courtesy Tacoma Public Library.

first as the **11th Street Bridge**. On its north side are the remnants of a municipal dock. Angelo Fawcett, mayor of Tacoma four times in the late 1800s and early 1900s, espoused populist principles. He persuaded the Northern Pacific to exchange some of its waterfront land for a dock and boathouse at the foot of 11th Street. Passengers walked down steps from the grand Tacoma Hotel on the bluff to catch the steamer ferries that plied Puget Sound.

Take the elevator up to the bridge to gaze across acres of filled land at the industries that would sustain Tacoma well beyond the Northern Pacific. The earliest, longest, and most significant of these was the St. Paul and Tacoma Lumber Company. The company built two huge sawmills on "the boot," an island between channels of the Puyallup River that were dredged to create waterways and to scoop up enough silt, sand, muck, and sawdust to bridge the island to the tideflats. St. Paul started supplying its mills with fifty carloads of logs a day from the forests bought from the Northern Pacific. By 1907, the two mills provided 500 to 600 jobs. You may still see lumber stacked on the distant docks for shipment or processing into wood chips, although the corporate name and ownership of the St. Paul has changed many times.

Return to waterfront level and continue walking north to the **Foss Waterway Seaport** in the Balfour Dock building and the **Eureka Dock warehouse**, both dating from the 1890s; these are the only remnants of the mile-long warehouse. Across the street is the **Half Moon Yard**, which was a swamp before it became a storage yard for railroad cars. Freight could be transferred directly from the cars to the warehouses and to the ships.

Continue past the Eureka Dock warehouse to the **4th Street Bridge** over the rail lines. Off to the right was the Blackwell Hotel and the first Northern Pacific depot, at the end of what was called Ocean Wharf. **Thea's Park** is named after Norwegian immigrant Thea Foss, who parlayed a rowboat rental service into a fleet of tugboats. Her life was the inspiration for a movie and television series, *Tugboat Annie*. The City Waterway became the **Thea Foss Waterway** in 1989, one hundred years after Thea first rented out a rowboat.

Ahead on the bay are the TEMCO (Tacoma Export Marketing Company) **grain elevators**, the functional descendant of the mile-long warehouse. The elevators can hold three million bushels of corn, soybeans, or other agricultural products coming along railroad lines from the upper Midwest.

Buried somewhere on the bluff above are petroglyphs, hieroglyphic images pecked into an eight-foot-tall signal rock that marked a place for Indians around Puget Sound to meet. The rock was considered too large to excavate and move when Pacific Avenue was graded in the 1870s.

Cross Schuster Parkway at the stoplight and head uphill on the sidewalk to New Tacoma on top of the bluff, the brain and money center of all the activity on the wharf. Everything important in the 1880s and 1890s happened on these blocks—capitalist dreams, city government, newspapers, and vaudevilles amid offices, hotels, saloons, and boardinghouses. Still looming over the waterfront is the heavy stone and turreted **Northern Pacific headquarters building** at *7th Avenue and Pacific*. When the Northern Pacific route through Stampede Pass was completed in 1887, the railroad's western headquarters moved here from Portland. For the next thirty years, all the important economic decisions were made in this impressive building, including the sale of 900,000 acres of timber to Frederick Weyerhaeuser. The Weyerhaeuser Company rented rooms in the building because the railroad had the only maps of the timberland.

Next door to the headquarters is the **Fawcett Fountain**, a pillar given to the city in 1908 by Angelo Fawcett, the Tacoma mayor who championed public improvements such as the municipal dock. He wanted to ensure that anyone walking along the street could get a cool drink of water, but its four faucets are now dry. (The fountain first stood at the intersection of Broadway, St. Helens, and 9th.) **City Hall**, Fawcett's office and the seat of political power from 1893 until 1959, was located at *625 Commerce Street*, conveniently across from the Northern Pacific headquarters.

With the delirious decade came the temptations of vice. Saloons, boardinghouses, and hotels crowded Whiskey Row on the east side of Pacific between 7th and 9th. Right next to City Hall, at *610 Pacific*, is a remnant of the row: the **Pacific Brewing and Malting Company**, which opened in 1897, was shut down by statewide prohibition in 1916 but opened again in 2014. At *815 Pacific*, the Theater Comique, a raucous saloon, was replaced in 1909 by the **Olympus Hotel**. The hotel was built by Leopold Schmidt, the same man who founded the Olympia Brewing Company in Tumwater and owned a hotel in Bellingham. The building now houses low-income apartments, but a "ghost sign" proclaims its history.

On the bluff between 7th and 9th Avenues, explore **Fireman's Park,** the city's first park, so named because it was situated near the fire department headquarters at Engine House No. 6. Fire departments were very important to cities whose core buildings were made of wood. During the summer of 1889, fires swept through Seattle, Spokane, Vancouver, and Ellensburg, prompting Tacoma's fire department to parade its new equipment to calm nervous residents.

The guy with a saw is a **bucker,** who cut felled trees into logs, thus *Clearing the Way,* as the statue is titled, for new cities like Tacoma. The **totem pole** in the park dates from 1903 and is said to be the tallest in the nation, carved by Alaskan Indians from a massive cedar tree growing in the forests of the St. Paul and Tacoma Lumber Company. Wealthy Tacoma businessmen commissioned the pole at a time when Seattle and Tacoma were competing as the "Gateway to Alaska" during the Yukon gold rush. In time, the pole rotted, but it was restored in 1976 and shored up in 2014, when it once again threatened to return to the earth.

In the early 1900s, Tacoma spread out from the cluster of buildings on the bluff as bridges over ravines and trolleys opened neighborhoods to the west and north. New Tacoma remained the business and entertainment center of the city.

Return to the old City Hall on 7th between Pacific and Commerce. Uphill and a block north on Commerce Street, the white stone building was the **Elks Temple,** erected in 1915. The steps leading uphill beside it are the **Spanish Steps,** built a year later to satisfy city fire code requirements for a second-story exit. The steps are patterned after the *Scalinata di Spagna* in Rome, a nod to the classical tradition. The temple building has been largely unoccupied since 1967.

Walk up the steps to Broadway. Broadway was an early residential street. The area to the immediate south had a small stretch of Chinese businesses before the Chinese were forced out of Tacoma in 1885.

Jog north to 6th Avenue and west two blocks to St. Helens Avenue. The Chamber of Commerce building, which was demolished in 1950, had on its roof a copper Goddess of Commerce statue. That statue was melted for scrap, but a new statue has arisen on this corner, funded by donations and sculpted by Marilyn Mahoney. The goddess sports crane earrings (the freight-loading kind, not the peace crane). The first container crane, "Big Red," started work at the Port of Tacoma in 1970.

Walk southeast on St. Helens across 7th Street to **Ledger Square**, *at Market Street and St. Helens.* The *Tacoma Daily Ledger* was an early newspaper; it was later folded into the *Tacoma News Tribune and Ledger.* A teletype would transmit news of major events on a display board passersby could see. Thousands gathered in October 1926 to read a description of the seventh game in the World Series between the New York Yankees and the St. Louis Cardinals, the local favorite. Despite the efforts of Babe Ruth, the Cardinals won. A large photograph recalls the scene in a remnant of the square.

Continue south on St. Helens to the Five Corners intersection (Broadway, St. Helens, and 9th Street). Note the small, triangular **Bostwick Building**, formerly a hotel built in 1889 by Dr. Henry Clay Bostwick, Tacoma's first practicing physician. At a meeting of a veterans' group here four years later, members stood and doffed their hats during the national anthem, starting a national tradition.

Five Corners was the heart of the theater district, host to speakers and entertainers including Sarah Bernhardt, Mark Twain, William Jennings Bryan, and Susan B. Anthony. Across the street from the Bostwick is the **Pantages Theater**, built in 1918, the second in a chain of seventy theaters operated or built by Alexander Pantages, a Greek immigrant who had financial assistance from his mistress, Kate Rockwell. Also known as Klondike Kate, she had built her wealth as an entertainer in the mining camps and brought some of that prosperity back to Puget Sound. The Pantages featured live vaudeville acts but converted to screening movies in the 1930s and is now part of the Broadway Center for the Performing Arts. *A half block west,* the **Rialto** opened the same year; it was and remains a movie house.

Return on 9th to Pacific Avenue, which was the artery of New Tacoma, used by the common folk, and a popular parade route. The Pacific Avenue Line trolley ran until the 1930s, when streetcars were replaced by buses. New Tacoma became old in the 1960s, when the Tacoma Mall lured shoppers away from the department stores on Pacific and Broadway. Automobiles and highways altered travel patterns and spurred the demolition of buildings to make room for parking lots and garages. Now the Tacoma Link light rail runs on Commerce Street, from the Theater District to the Tacoma Dome, a remnant of the 125 miles of streetcar lines Tacoma once boasted.

Before leaving New Tacoma, visit the **Tacoma Historical Society Museum** in the Provident Building at *919 Pacific. Then continue south on Pacific to take a walk along 11th,* where several buildings, including the **Rust Building** *at Pacific and 11th (950 Pacific),* were built in the Chicago style of architecture, emphasizing function more than form. Rust was William R. Rust, who built the Tacoma smelter and created the town of Ruston.

The massive stone building on the *southwest corner of 11th and A (1102 A Street)* is unmistakably a federal government building, meant to convey power. It was built in 1909 and has served as a customhouse, **U.S. Post Office**, and U.S. Courthouse. Within its walls, Teamsters Union president Dave Beck was convicted of tax evasion; the Seattle Seven were tried for conspiracy in organizing protests against the Vietnam War; Judge George Boldt interpreted 1850s treaties to mean that fish should be shared equally by Native American tribes and the state; and Jack Tanner, son of a Tacoma longshoreman, served as the first African American federal judge west of the Mississippi.

The cream-colored building on the *northeast corner of 11th and A (1073 A Street)* was the headquarters of the Weyerhaeuser Company. At first the company had an agent in the Northern Pacific headquarters, but it moved into this **Tacoma Building** in 1910 to administer its timberlands.

Continue east on 11th to the **Murray Morgan Bridge**, formerly the 11th Street Bridge, first built in 1894. From the time the railroad arrived on Commencement Bay, the city provided good jobs for the working class. Thousands walked down the hills from boardinghouses and homes each day, over this bridge, to get to work at the port and the lumber mills. The old bridge was replaced in 1913, then repaired and reopened in 2013. It was also renamed for Murray Morgan, journalist and historian of Tacoma and South Puget Sound. He had been a bridge tender and felt kinship with the workers crossing the bridge, declaring, "I'd like to walk with the lunch bucket brigade."

At times, the bridge has carried the weight of strife between labor and corporations. During the West Coast longshoremen's strike of 1934, Tacoma escaped violent conflict because employers did not hire strikebreakers, but the following year a strike of lumber mill workers was more destructive. On July 12, 1935, as many as 5,000 men and women gathered on this bridge to prevent those who had broken the strike from returning home after work. They stopped the 11th Street streetcar line and blocked lumber trucks. National Guardsmen, using tear gas and supported by a machine gun, confronted the demonstrators. One was killed. The strike ended a few weeks later with an increase in the hourly wage and a forty-hour work week, but no holiday pay or seniority system.

If you're feeling ambitious, cross the bridge, walk a mile or so on 11th Street, and climb the four-story **observation tower of the Port of Tacoma**. Built largely on the filled tideflats of the dredged mouth and channels of the Puyallup River, the port continues to drive Tacoma's economy, exporting wood and paper products, wheat, meat, industrial machinery, vegetables, fruit, nuts, and vehicle parts to Asia, Europe, and South America.

From New Tacoma, head southeast toward the industrial tideflats that kept railroad cars and ships full after the delirious decades of the late 1800s. *Travel Commerce Street on the "cars" (Link light rail) or walk south on Pacific Avenue, then east* to the esplanade that begins *at the foot of 15th Street.* The esplanade borders the Thea Foss Waterway for several blocks, passing new condo developments, marinas, and repurposed industrial buildings.

At the end of the esplanade at the eastern edge of Commencement Bay, follow the sidewalk over the D Street overpass of the tideflats—now a mishmash of warehouses, storage lots, engineered and natural waterways, docks, streets, and factories, essentially hostile to human exploration. The very first commercial enterprise on the tideflats was a sawmill set up near the river's mouth in 1852 by a Swedish immigrant, Nicholas Delin. He left when the Puyallup went to war to dispute the size and location of the reservation they had been given, including the very land Delin had claimed. Almost 150 years later, an agreement allocated most of the tideflats to the Port of Tacoma, with the Puyallup tribe retaining only land at the northeastern edge of the bay plus a casino and tribal headquarters in Fife. Puyallup habitation of the tideflats is recalled in artwork along the overpass.

Pause where the overpass meets D Street to look down at the railroad yards, a busy network of lines and sidelines for loading. Watch for great blue herons fishing silently on the waterway against the squealing and clunking of trains pulling oil tankers.

Walk south to E 25th Street and **Freighthouse Square**. For the first thirty years of Tacoma's railroad history, the Northern Pacific monopolized rail service to Tacoma and wharf space on the waterfront, but in 1909, the Milwaukee Railroad and others built this freight house, three blocks long. Painted green then and now, the structure was visible to the immigrants who arrived in the port, drawn to jobs in the western United States at the turn of the century. It is now a public market with stores and restaurants. Still a transportation hub, the square handles 1,735 Sounder train boardings and alightings each day. You may take the Link back downtown if you're tired of walking.

East of the square, surrounded by parking lots, the Tacoma Dome and American Car Museum host thousands of visitors, most arriving by car. Like the vote for a port district in 1918, the public vote to build the Tacoma Dome in 1980 was overwhelmingly in favor; the entertainment venue opened in 1983, the same year the old Pantages Theater reopened as a performing arts center.

Return to town along the esplanade/waterfront park and read on **interpretive plaques** the sobering story of plans for cleanup and restoration of the waterway that has become a Superfund site. *Just past the repurposed* **Albers Mill***, climb the steps or ramp to the* **Museum of Glass Plaza***. Look beyond the railroad tracks below to* **Union Station**. Its construction marked the end of Northern Pacific's unchallenged domination of Tacoma. For thirty years, city founders had urged the railroad to build something fancier than its first depot, a wooden shack on the tideflats. By the time the railroad decided to build, its headquarters had moved to Seattle, and other railroads had moved in. These railroads joined forces to construct the massive, copper-domed station in 1911. It served for some twenty-five years before automobiles replaced trains as the preferred mode of transport, and the station started a long, slow decline. The wonderfully restored and reclaimed building still looks like a train station—those expecting Amtrak will be graciously redirected by a security guard who frequently fields this question—but now it houses a federal courthouse and overlooks a freeway. (The more modest Amtrak station sits along tracks a mile east on Puyallup Avenue.)

Cross the **Bridge of Glass** *to Pacific Avenue.* In front of Union Station, in the new heart of Tacoma, greet the **statue of a traveler** arriving a century ago, looking for opportunity, adventure, and fortune. Along Pacific Avenue, the Tacoma Art Museum, Union Station, and the **Washington State History Museum** share a plaza. The arches of the history museum mirror the arches of Union Station, an image of railroad history central to the growth of the state. Where the old Prairie Line came down the hill amid rows of warehouses, the **University of Washington Tacoma** has created a campus, extending from roughly 17th to 21st and from Pacific to Market Streets. The Prairie Line itself has become a walking trail through campus.

Walk up the steps at the center of the campus to the trail. *To the right,* at the intersection of the Prairie Line trail with 17th, a sculpture symbolizing harmony memorializes the Japanese Language School as the cultural heart of Tacoma's Japanese American community. *To the left,* the transformer house of the Snoqualmie Falls Power Company now houses the university library. The backs of former warehouses, such as the **West Coast Grocery Company**, line Commerce Street.

After exploring the campus, return on 21st to Pacific and cross to small **Don Pugnetti Park**, surrounded by pavement and the site of the Occupy Tacoma encampment in 2011 and 2012. Pugnetti was a Tacoma journalist, but the park was originally named for John Bolander, the head spiker for the Northern Pacific who drove the last spike on the Prairie Line. At the back of the park is a misplaced and half-forgotten **rock**, marking a cold December day when, to the cheers of the hopeful, "the Northern Pacific rails met the Pacific Ocean sails," and Tacoma began.

Resources	Tacoma Historical Society Museum, 919 Pacific Avenue
	Tacoma Public Library, 1102 Tacoma Avenue S
	Tacoma Visitor Information Center, 1500 Broadway
	Washington State History Museum, 1911 Pacific Avenue
	Washington State History Research Center, 315 N Stadium Way

CHAPTER FIVE

Seattle

Gateway to Gold

Everything is "Klondike" and "Yukon" out here now
and the people are all crazy.

Eugene Semple, letter to his daughter, August 17, 1897

oday, Seattle is the Queen City of the Pacific Northwest—the largest, richest, and most dynamic city in the region. It was not always so. San Francisco was the first big city in the West, and it treated the Northwest as a hinterland. In the mid-1800s, Portland dominated the fertile Willamette Valley and the Columbia River. Vancouver, Olympia, Walla Walla, Spokane, and Tacoma all flourished before Seattle hit its stride, but what distinguished Seattle from its rivals was hubris, location, and a certain amount of luck. In 1897, a ship ironically named the *Portland* arrived with prospectors and gold dust from the Yukon, docked on the city waterfront—and disgorged prosperity.

Seattle had begun modestly in 1851 when the Denny party of ten adults and twelve children anchored off the tip of a surf-swept peninsula ringed by the camps and villages of the Duwamish people. The newcomers had traveled to Puget Sound from Illinois via Portland and, once the rain stopped, were wildly optimistic. In the tradition of ambitious entrepreneurs, they named their landing place New

.rk, soon amended to New York Alki, meaning New York "by and by" in the Chinook trade jargon. In that first wet winter, the women fed clam juice to their babies, and the men shipped evergreen trees to San Francisco and traded with a chief whose name they pronounced Seattle. But New York would not come easily to the wind-battered peninsula, now Seattle's most popular beach, pronounced "Alkee" by natives. In the spring of 1852, Arthur Denny, Carson Boren, and William Bell borrowed a canoe, paddled east in Elliott Bay beyond the wide opening of a river, dropped a line with a weight to test the water's depth, and found an excellent harbor.

"After the survey of the harbor, we next examined the land and timber around the Bay, and after three days careful investigation we located claims with a view of lumbering, and, ultimately, of laying off a town," Denny wrote later. They filed land claims to that deeper and more sheltered end of the bay, much of it on shifting soil at the base of a bluff. The Duwamish and Suquamish called it Zechalalitch, the "crossing-over place" between the Duwamish River and Lake Washington. Today, it is Pioneer Square.

The Dennys, the Borens, and the Bells—along with Henry Yesler and Doc Maynard—carved up the waterfront with their individual claims and platted a town. Like other Puget Sound ports attuned to the San Francisco market, the first industry was Yesler's sawmill, whose laborers cut down the huge trees ringing the shore and skidded them down a "road" to the water. City-building dreams were deferred but not totally deflated when the Northern Pacific Railway chose Tacoma as its Puget Sound terminus. Biding their time and building their own railroad to the coalfields east of town, Seattle's founders were gratified when the Great Northern Railway reached their town in 1893.

With the legislature handing out government plums across the territory, Arthur Denny offered ten acres of land, mostly his own, if Seattle could have the university. Classes began in a wooden building north of Pioneer Square in 1861. The university almost failed due to inadequate funding in its early years, but the first persistent graduate, a woman named Clara McCarty, received her bachelor's degree in science in 1876. She became a teacher and was later elected the first superintendent of schools in Pierce County.

For several decades, Seattle grew relatively slowly, hampered by broad tideflats at the mouth of the Duwamish River and hills rising smartly above Elliott Bay. The downtown built of wood was almost destroyed in the great fire of 1889, but the city rebuilt in brick and stone, raising sidewalks out of the tidal muck above the first layer of buildings, giving rise to a popular underground tour of Seattle. Although the financial panic of 1893 throttled speculation and hampered investment, in the late 1890s Seattle had a well-established center of commerce in Pioneer Square, standing largely on fill. The Yesler Building; the Maynard Building, with the city's first bank; and Schwabacher's mercantile bespoke stability. A Japanese freighter, the *Miike Maru,* arrived in Seattle in 1896, bringing a few passengers, many immigrants, soybean oil, silk, tea, ginger, and straw matting. It returned to Japan with lumber, coal, wheat, and metals, foreshadowing the trade on which the city would grow.

The pace accelerated on July 17, 1897, when the steamship *Portland* docked at Schwabacher's Wharf. Alerted by a special issue of the *Post-Intelligencer,* 5,000 citizens met the boat and prospectors cheered from her decks. There was a ton of gold dust in the hold—"enough gold to almost startle the world," according to the rival *Seattle Times.* The prospectors scurried downtown to stash their dust and nuggets and spread the good news in saloons.

Gold had been discovered along the Klondike River in the Yukon Territory of northern Canada. At a time when U.S. gold reserves were low, the discovery was the largest concentration of gold ever found. Seattle was the closest major American city to the Klondike. Although it was possible to trek all 2,000 miles to the goldfields over snowy mountain passes, the best route went first by water to Alaska (purchased by the United States from Russia after the Civil War) and then overland to the Yukon.

During the height of the Klondike gold rush, crowds gathered on a Seattle dock in 1898 to welcome argonauts returning from the Yukon. Courtesy Seattle Public Library.

"Seattle is all 'agog' with this gold fever and the streets are crowded with knots of men so worked up over the news that they can scarcely avoid being run over by the cars and carriages," wrote Eugene Semple, the former governor, to his daughter. The Chamber of Commerce hired a publicist, Erastus Brainerd, to tout the city as the Gateway to Gold.

Within two weeks of the *Portland*'s arrival, 650 men had headed north with outfits purchased in Seattle. Each day, 200 more arrived in the city seeking a piece of the action. Within six weeks, more than 8,000 gold seekers had sailed from Seattle. Of the 100,000 men and women who started for the Yukon from all points in the next couple of years, only 4,000 actually reached the territory and found gold; about 300 found enough to be considered rich, and only about 50 of those managed to keep their wealth. But merchants in Seattle had better odds. Restaurants, dry-goods stores, supply stores, saloons, and brothels were veritable gold mines. In less than a year, Seattle garnered $25 million in Klondike trade. Seattle's marketing rush made it more profitable than other ports on Puget Sound, and the city's population finally surpassed Tacoma's.

The Yukon gold rush abated fairly quickly with the discovery of gold at Nome, Alaska, and the distraction of the Spanish–American War in 1898, but Seattle continued to supply miners, and some of those who came back, like George Bartell and John Nordstrom, invested their money in businesses. They joined clubs like the Alaska Club and the Arctic Club, which celebrated the city's connection to Alaska.

Confident in their new wealth, city leaders undertook massive civic projects in the first two decades of the 1900s. Riding the national tide of Progressive ideals, they believed that both society and nature could be improved through legislation and engineering. The landscape architect John Charles Olmsted drew up plans for parks and boulevards. Using the authority granted by the reformist state legislature, voters created the Port of Seattle and wrested control of the waterfront from the railroads. Under the leadership of Hiram Chittenden of the U.S. Army Corps of Engineers, the port dredged and straightened the Duwamish River and filled the tideflats, creating more shoreland for industry. On the city's northern edge, the corps built a canal connecting Puget Sound with the fresh waters of Lake Union and Lake Washington.

Even before the gold rush, Seattle had hired a city engineer, Reginald H. Thomson. "Looking at local surroundings, I felt that Seattle was in a pit, that to get anywhere we would be compelled to climb out if we could," Thomson said. He launched an ambitious plan to level hills and create more land downtown. In the era before bulldozers, contractors used techniques developed during the gold rush to sluice hills into the bay along Jackson Street and Dearborn Street. The Denny Hill regrade allowed expansion of the city northward with more room for manufacturing, shipbuilding, and utilities, but regrades also dislodged many of the poorer residents. The filling of tideflats and railroad expansion forced Japanese and Chinese into today's International District.

In the midst of the Progressive Era, Seattle paused to celebrate its new status. Hoping to cement the connection not only to Alaska but to the markets of the Pacific as well, the city hosted an exposition and invited the world. Following the example of the Chicago World's Fair of 1893 and Portland's Lewis and Clark Centennial Exposition of 1905, Seattle staged the Alaska-Yukon-Pacific Exposition (AYPE) in 1909. It was one big coming-of-age party, drawing more than three million people. This time, Seattle was touted as the Gateway to Alaska and the Orient.

Progressive ideals lost steam during the cataclysm of World War I, creating doubts about the ability of humans to shape society for the good or to create wealth that benefited all. After the war, Seattle weathered a general strike in 1919, a huge Hooverville encampment of the unemployed and homeless during the Great Depression, and maritime strikes in the 1930s. The city boomed beyond its ability to provide housing and transportation during World War II, when thousands of workers came to Boeing's airplane factories and to the shipyards. That renewed prosperity continued during the Cold War and was celebrated again in 1962 with a world's fair that touted Seattle's technological future. After a downturn in the 1970s, when Boeing lost a potentially huge military contract, the city rebounded yet again with Microsoft in the 1980s and Amazon in the twenty-first century, renewing faith in the economic and social power of technology. The University of Washington became a major research university with a campus design that still captures Northwest beauty. The gateway became a destination.

The gold rush and the AYPE shaped Seattle's can-do spirit, its confidence, and its cockiness. A 1997 article in the *Economist* identified that period's impact: "It was through the gold rush that Seattle learned the marketing flair it now applies to selling computer software or persuading people to pay $2 for a cup of coffee."

This chapter's walk explores the waterfronts that made Seattle wealthy. It begins where optimistic settlers landed on Alki; takes a water taxi to downtown Seattle and Pier 57, where the gold landed; and explores Pioneer Square and the businesses that supplied the gold rush. The walk then follows crowds along the east shore of Lake Union to the site of the AYPE on the University of Washington campus, where Seattle introduced itself to the world in a fair.

Pioneer Walk: Alki

START: Alki Avenue and 63rd Avenue SW

DIRECTIONS: From I-5, take the West Seattle Bridge to the Harbor Avenue exit; drive northwest on Harbor Avenue as it becomes Alki Avenue. Or take the King County water taxi (passengers and bikes only) from Pier 50 in Seattle to Seacrest Park, and do the walk in reverse. The water taxi runs more frequently during the summer than during winter months. Check the schedule at www.kingcounty .gov/transportation/kcdot/WaterTaxi/WSeattle.aspx.

DISTANCE: 2.3 miles on sidewalk, multi-use path from Alki landing monument to Seacrest Park (with an optional 0.5-mile extension to Jack Block Park)

AMENITIES: Free parking along Alki and Harbor Avenues and side streets; restrooms at Alki Beach Bathhouse, Seacrest Park, and Jack Block Park

Seattle began on a windswept beach at the tip of a peninsula formed by Puget Sound, Elliott Bay, and the Duwamish River. The Denny-Boren-Bell party landed here on a schooner from San Francisco on a rainy November day in 1851. They were met by young David Denny, who had gone ahead to build a cabin but injured himself and hadn't finished the roof. Despite mishap and tears and rain, they had ambition and energy to form a city they hoped would rival New York. After the first dreary winter, when the people of Chief Si-ahl (Seattle) helped them survive, they moved their land claims to a deeper harbor on the east side of the bay.

Follow that wise move by walking the Alki Trail to Seacrest Park and taking a water taxi across the bay to downtown Seattle. Begin at the **landing monument**, *on the waterfront at 63rd Avenue.* The names of the founding fathers are listed on one side of the pylon, with the names of the mothers, children, and welcoming Duwamish added as an afterthought on the other sides. Three blocks away is the oldest house in Seattle, *at 3045 64th Avenue,* but this is not the unfinished cabin that greeted the settlers. According to historian Paul Dorpat, Doc Maynard probably had the house built in the 1860s as a refuge from city life.

At 61st and Alki is the **Statue of Liberty plaza**, featuring one of many replicas of the Ellis Island statue placed around the country by Boy Scouts in the 1950s. This one was fully restored sixty years later; the original is in the **Log House Museum**, *one block south at 61st and Stevens.* This "Birthplace of Seattle" museum, built as a carriage house in a rustic style favored by vacationing Seattle families, interprets the history of southwest Seattle. Although Alki did not thrive as a center of commerce, land developers built enough streetcar lines and housing to make West Seattle a separate city until it was annexed by Seattle in 1907.

After the founding families moved their land claims east, Alki became a vacation destination and playground for Seattle. The **Bathhouse** *at 60th and Alki Avenue* has served bathers and beachgoers for more than a century. The beach is now more popular for campfires (a heritage from Duwamish camps) and beach volleyball than it is for swimming. A half mile farther along, an **anchor** marks the site of Luna Park, an amusement park that flourished into the 1920s.

As you round Duwamish Head, the skyline of downtown Seattle

comes into view. The King County water taxi leaves from Seacrest Park, where ferries landed tourists, vacationers, and residents more than a century ago. Ferry Avenue still leads from the waterfront to homes and West Seattle's old streetcar junctions and business district at the top of the hill.

The multi-use trail continues for another half mile to **Jack Block Park**, a reclaimed Superfund site with an overview of Elliott Bay, the mouth of the Duwamish River, and the Port of Seattle. After the park, the trail leads all the way downtown along sidewalks and bike trails through the industrial heart of Seattle. It crosses the low bridge over the Duwamish River, then follows the waterfront and truck route along the port. Although hundreds of bike commuters use the trail daily, it is not an attractive walking trail. Instead of walking or driving downtown, you may take the King County Water Taxi from Seacrest Park to the Pioneer Square loop in downtown Seattle.

Duwamish River

Of all Seattle's early 1900s engineering projects, the straightening and dredging of the Duwamish River produced the most significant economic result. After its creation in 1911, the Port of Seattle dredged and straightened the northern five miles of the meandering river and filled tideflats to create a navigable waterway and flat industrial land. The only river that runs through Seattle became the Duwamish Waterway, the industrial heart of the city. The Duwamish River Trail begins at the mouth of the river where bridges connect West Seattle to the rest of Seattle, at the community of **Riverside**, *17th Avenue SW and Marginal Place SW.* The hiking/biking trail extends more than ten miles to Tukwila and the former confluence of the Green, White, and Black Rivers, which joined to form the Duwamish.

A small **plaza** lined with tiles identifies the mostly Croatian fishing families who settled Riverside in the early 1900s. A block north of the plaza, you may walk up the pedestrian/bike walkway on the **low bridge** to gain a view of the **Duwamish Waterway** as it flows into Elliott Bay. The bridge is a swing bridge that opens for marine traffic several times a day but is used mainly by trucks carrying containers from Harbor Island and cyclists commuting downtown.

A half mile south on the trail is **T-107 Park** (Herring's House), at *4570 West Marginal Way,* the only remaining natural bend of the river in its first five miles. This was the site of a Duwamish village. The **Duwamish Long-house and Cultural Center,** at *4705 West Marginal Way SW,* is across the street. The trail extends south along the waterway, through the community of South Park, past **North Wind's Weir**, past nineteenth-century river towns, and finally along the route of the Interurban through Fort Dent Park, 6800 Fort Dent Way. A Duwamish village stood at the confluence with the Green River here well into the early twentieth century.

Seattle Loop: Pioneer Square

START: Pier 57, 1301 Alaskan Way

DIRECTIONS: From Highway 99 or I-5, take Seneca Street and head west toward the water. Pier 57 is at the foot of University Street, one block north of Seneca. (The King County water taxi from West Seattle arrives at Pier 50 at the foot of Yesler Way, several blocks south of Pier 57.)

DISTANCE: 1.5 miles round trip

AMENITIES: Paid parking on streets or in lots; restrooms at Miner's Landing (at Pier 57), Washington State Ferries Terminal (at Pier 52), or Klondike Gold Rush National Historical Park

Begin where the *Portland* landed in July 1897 with its ton of gold, greeted by a crowd gathered at Schwabacher's Wharf. The Schwabacher brothers came from Bavaria and by the 1870s had established stores in

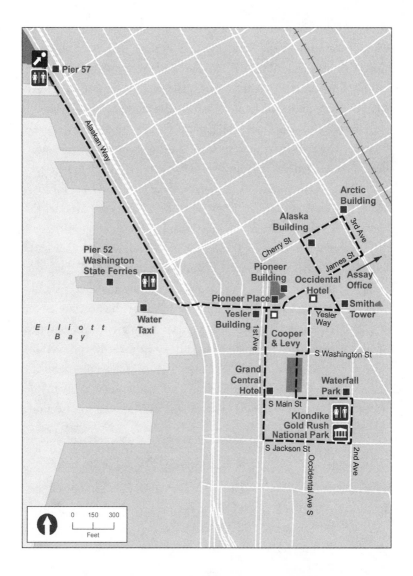

both Walla Walla and Seattle. Their wharf sat at the northern edge of the commercial district and escaped destruction during the great fire of 1889, which raged to the south. It is now Pier 57, called Miner's Landing, rife with souvenirs of Seattle's gold rush days.

Hustle south for six blocks along the waterfront, following miners as they rushed to deposit their gold in banks or ship it to San Francisco via railroad express. The Seattle waterfront has changed dramatically since that July day. Railroad Avenue, a planked roadway built on pilings, burned in the great fire but was replaced by the aptly named Alaskan Way, built on landfill and shadowed by a viaduct in the early 1950s. Colman Dock, built in 1882 and rebuilt after the great fire, received coal from mines east of Seattle and served a mosquito fleet of boats where cars now mass for the ferries. Henry Yesler's sawmill sat at the foot of Mill Street, the original skid road for logs. *Walk up the street renamed Yesler Way two blocks to* 1st Avenue, the heart of Seattle's commerce in the 1890s.

In front of you is an odd triangle called Pioneer Place. The early landowners, Arthur Denny, Carson Boren, and David Swinson "Doc" Maynard, disagreed about how surveying for streets should be done. Denny and Boren made their claims to the north of Yesler Way and Maynard to the south. (They had given Henry Yesler a strip of land between their claims.) Maynard used the cardinal directions (north/south, east/west) for his land. Boren and Denny laid out streets running parallel to the shoreline, which curves off to the northwest. The competing grids resulted in irrational intersections and triangles.

Look around this intersection of Yesler and 1st. In the early decades, logs skidded down a trace to the waterfront. Yesler's cookhouse was Seattle's first public space and restaurant. Yesler Pavilion hosted theatrical events. Yesler Hall sheltered mass meetings, including the mass meeting of the Puget Sound Anti-Chinese Congress in 1885. A mob hung three men accused of murder from Yesler's maple tree in 1882 after a preliminary trial in the hall. These early wood buildings did not survive the great fire of 1889, but Yesler rebuilt, commissioning three substantial stone buildings.

The first Yesler Building began in 1890 on the approximate site of his cookhouse, *on the northwest corner of this intersection, at 605 1st Avenue.* Bought by a New York insurance company, which renamed it the **Mutual Life Building**, it housed the First National Bank, one of eighteen banks in Seattle in which Yukon argonauts could deposit their gold. Another of those eighteen was the Scandinavian-American Bank in the second **Yesler Building**, *on the southwest corner at 95 Yesler Way.* Known historically as the Bank of Commerce Building, it housed a succession of banks that financed the rebuilding of Seattle after the fire.

The *Portland* was due to make a return trip to Alaska in two weeks. If you had bought a ticket—they were in short supply—you could head to **Schwabacher's store**, the "leading mercantile house of the Northwest," next door to the bank at *99 Yesler Way.* The store had been in business since 1869, managed by Bailey Gatzert, who married into the Schwabacher family and in 1875 became the city's first Jewish mayor. The store's building surrounds the Yesler Building and has a plaque and name engraved on the 1st Avenue side.

If Schwabacher's didn't have what you needed, Cooper & Levy Pioneer Outfitters probably did. Isaac Cooper and Louis Levy were brothers-in-law who formed their business in 1892. They had a store in the **Olympic Block** *on the southeast corner of 1st and Yesler.* During the gold rush, they stacked bags of flour, sugar, and beets on the sidewalk and employed twenty men night and day packing supplies. They sold their business ten years after the gold rush to a department store called the Bon Marché. The Olympic Block also housed the Northern Pacific Railway's ticket office. A corner of the building collapsed during a remodel in 1972, and the original was demolished.

Walk south on 1st Avenue, formerly known as Commerce Street. A **marker** *on the west side of 1st* describes the scramble to supply the 70,000 stampeders who left from Seattle. Cooper & Levy workers and goods are posed in a photograph in front of the **Lippy Building**, *on the east side of the street at 104 and 106 1st Avenue.* During the first year of the gold rush, Thomas Lippy, a former secretary of the Seattle YMCA, returned from the Klondike with $65,000. Taking three family members with him, he went again to the goldfields and came back with even more. Like many of the newly wealthy, he spent his money on a building, which was designed as a warehouse with a retail store facing 1st Avenue. The **stone column** on the north side of the facade is said to be a vestige of the Olympic Block.

If you rushed to Seattle after reading about the discoveries in the Yukon, you needed a place to stay. The Northern Hotel on the top floors of the **Terry Denny Building** at *111 1st Avenue* offered rooms for miners and loggers. The building had been commissioned by Seattle founders Charles Terry and Arthur Denny after the great fire.

If the Northern was full, you could try the State Hotel in the **Delmar Building**, on the *northeast corner of 1st and Washington*. The State offered rooms for 75 cents, as advertised in a **sign** that still hangs over the sidewalk. The building also housed a Chinese laundry and the city's first pharmacy. *On the northwest corner* is the **Maynard Building**, which housed another of those eighteen banks, this one managed by Dexter Horton.

Near the southwest corner of 1st and Washington is the **J. & M. Café**, which was a bar in gold rush days. Even before argonauts, a transient population of loggers, dock workers, and sailors would spend winters in the city. They frequented the saloons, brothels, and casinos in this Skid Row district of Seattle, bounded roughly by Yesler Way, Jackson Street, Railroad Avenue, and 5th Avenue. Robberies and assaults were common, and Seattle gained a reputation as a wicked city.

In the next block, pass the **Grand Central Hotel** *at 1st and Main*, in the **Squire-Latimer Building** which was converted to a hotel with the sudden influx of miners. The **Maud Building**, once owned by George Carmack, who is credited with the first discovery of Klondike gold, offered rooms *mid-block at 311 1st Avenue. On the southwest corner of 1st and Jackson (401 1st Avenue S)* was a later Schwabacher Hardware Company Store.

When the gold rush started its second season in March 1898, hopeful ship passengers again left Seattle daily, ideally with a good pair of shoes. *Head east on S Jackson Street. One block east, at Occidental, you will pass the* **Washington Shoe Manufacturing Company Building**. In business beginning in 1891, the company specialized in rain boots; the building is now used by a game company. *In two blocks* reach the **Klondike Gold Rush National Historical Park** in the **Cadillac Hotel** building, which also housed stampeders. Operated by the National Park Service, the museum interprets the gold rush in video and exhibits and hosts guided walking tours of the neighborhood in the summer.

Walk north on 2nd Avenue, then west on Main Street to **Waterfall Garden Park**. In 1907, when telephones were still uncommon, two nineteen-year-olds started a bicycle messenger service in the basement of a saloon here. Claude Ryan and Jim Casey, whose father had died in the gold rush when he was a boy, developed new wealth in what would become the United Parcel Service.

Walk north through **Occidental Park**. This location has many histories, beginning as a lagoon whose southern banks were part of a high-tide island and was, before the 1850s, the site of a Duwamish village. A narrow strip of land to the west was the Little Crossing-Over Place. The Sun and Raven totem pole, a shorter Killer Whale pole showing a man riding a whale's tail, and 1975 carvings of Tsonqua and Bear facing each other recall this Duwamish heritage. This space was also the birthplace of the Salvation Army, a free speech corner, a hotel, a parking lot, and finally a park created in 1971. The brick plaza features many interpretive plaques, an information booth, and maps showing different walking tours, including a Boom and Bust tour. A more recent addition is the Fallen Firefighters Memorial sculpture, inspired by the deaths of firemen fighting a warehouse fire in the nearby International District in 1995. Occidental Park is still home to itinerants who find common ground near the waterfront.

Exiting the park, continue north on Occidental Avenue past the **Interurban Building** *on the southeast corner of Occidental and Yesler Way.* This building housed the ticket office for the Interurban at its Seattle terminus. The line bustled with passengers between Bellingham and

Olympia, reaching a peak in 1919 with three million passengers, but the completion of State Highway 99 in 1917 signaled the decline of the Interurban and the rise of the automobile. Until a tunnel is completed, cars still rush overhead through Seattle on the viaduct, three blocks to the west.

Walk east on Yesler Way to 2nd Avenue. This intersection was a horse market during the gold rush. Dogs were also imported from Chicago, St. Paul, and other eastern cities and corralled 200 to 400 at a time at a dog yard on Beacon Hill to the south. A single dog could haul 200 pounds on a sled, and the Seattle-Yukon Dog Company did a booming business in fattening, training, selling, and transporting dogs to the Yukon.

At 2nd Avenue, walk north, passing the **Smith Tower**. Built in 1914, the tower ranked as the tallest skyscraper west of the Mississippi and a symbol of "Seattle's manifest destiny," in the words of historian Walt Crowley. Such skyscrapers featured elevators and a reinforced steel framework. The twenty tallest buildings in Washington are in Seattle, all built after 1962 except for the Smith Tower.

Walk east on James Street one block to 3rd Avenue. On the southwest corner is the **Morrison Hotel** at *501 3rd Avenue*. Members of the Arctic Club who had become wealthy in the gold rush met at the Morrison to hatch plans for the Alaska-Yukon-Pacific Exposition (AYPE). The stained-glass window above the door celebrates the Alaska connection.

One year into the gold rush, Seattle landed an **assay office** where successful prospectors stood in long lines to exchange their gold dust. The dust would be melted into bars in exchange for a government check, a check argonauts were likely to spend in town. To find the office at 609 9th Avenue between James and Cherry, continue walking six blocks uphill on James, under I-5, which was completed through Seattle in 1979. The assay office became the home of the German Club in the 1930s.

Foregoing that excursion, *walk one block north on 3rd to Cherry.* After the AYPE, Arctic Club members merged with the Alaska Club and commissioned the **Arctic Building** for their meeting place, *at 700 3rd Avenue, on the northeast corner of 3rd and Cherry.* Notice the many walruses decorating the facade, another connection to Alaska. The 54 walruses' tusks were removed as a precaution after an earthquake in 1949 but were later restored. *Return west to 2nd Avenue* and the **Alaska Building**, *at 612 2nd Avenue.* Built with fourteen stories in 1904, it was the Northwest's first steel-framed skyscraper. A gold nugget was embedded in its front door for many years.

Walk south on 2nd to James and then west along the side of a parking garage popularly known as the Sinking Ship. This was the site of the Occidental Hotel (later the Seattle Hotel), which dominated Pioneer Square in grand fashion from 1884 until it was torn down in the 1960s and replaced with this garage. That demolition spurred Seattle's preservation community to advocate for the Pioneer Square Historic District, created in 1970. At the point of the "ship," note the **Metropole Building** to the *south on Yesler,* which was a drug store in 1895. Next to it, the three-story **Merchant's Café** building, *at 109 and 109½ Yesler,* is Seattle's oldest continuously used restaurant but earned its fame as a Skid Row saloon and brothel. A lot of gold passed over the thirty-foot bar, which had been brought around the Horn in a sailing vessel in 1889.

On the northeast corner of 1st and James, at 606 1st Avenue, is the **Pioneer Building**, one of the three commissioned by Yesler and the first "tallest building in Seattle" until the construction of the Alaska Building. It was home to various mining firms, a speakeasy in the 1920s, an elegant cigar store in the 1930s, and an ice-cream parlor. An earthquake toppled its central square tower in 1949, simultaneously dropping it from the tall building rankings.

In the burst of activity that followed the gold rush, civic leaders named the triangle we return to as **Pioneer Place**. For a century and a half it has been a public square. Businessmen stole the original totem pole from a Tlingit Indian village, an indication of the region's fascination with Alaska. An arsonist burned the pole in 1938, and the city paid Tlingits to carve a replacement. The drinking fountain with the bust of Chief Seattle dates from 1905. The pergola was added the same year to shelter patrons of an underground lavatory and passengers waiting for the Yesler Way cable car to carry them up the hill.

The economic legacy of the gold rush extended beyond this tour of Pioneer Square. Seattle's downtown core moved north along 1st and 2nd Avenues as the city expanded toward Lake Union, two miles away. A walk in that direction would pass through the warehouse district on Western Avenue between University and Columbia; the Pike Place Market, which opened in 1907; stores like Bartell Drugs and Nordstrom, whose founders poured gold rush gains into their businesses; and the Cooper & Levy successor, the Bon Marché (now the Macy's store in Seattle), which designed a special china plate for the AYPE.

To sense the celebration of Seattle's new place in the world, head for the site of the AYPE, around the eastern shore of Lake Union, to the University of Washington campus. Early Seattle walkers could follow a plank sidewalk from downtown to a boat landing on Roy Street at the south end of Lake Union. By the 1880s, streetcar lines connected downtown to points north. By the 1890s, one of the most popular ways to get around was by bicycle, a new health fad, particularly liberating to women. In 1896, the Lake Union Path led from 8th and Pine to the lake, then another 2.5 miles up the east shore on sidewalks, streets, bridges, and a dedicated bike path. Nearly 200 cyclists paraded with lanterns on their bikes to celebrate the opening.

Most visitors to the fair arrived by streetcar or boat. Variations of those options remain. Hopping over downtown—by walking, biking, taking the bus or streetcar, or even driving—we'll start at the south end of Lake Union and walk.

Extended Walk: South Lake Union to the University of Washington

START: Museum of History and Industry (MOHAI) at Lake Union Park, 860 Terry Avenue N

DIRECTIONS: Take the streetcar from Westlake Mall to the South Lake Union stop. Or, from I-5, take the Mercer Street exit to Fairview Avenue; turn right onto Fairview, left onto Valley Street, and right onto Terry Avenue.

DISTANCE: 4.3 miles one-way to Red Square, on the University of Washington campus

AMENITIES: Paid parking in lots near Lake Union Park; restrooms in MOHAI or in University of Washington buildings

In the spring and summer of 1909, more than three million Seattle citizens and visitors boarded streetcars, trains, and boats, drove their cars, walked, or rode bicycles to reach the large new campus of the University of Washington, which had moved north from downtown in 1895 to the ridge between Lake Washington and Lake Union. The school had only a few buildings, but for two years Seattle civic leaders had been erecting a vast exhibition on its campus to showcase the city's importance as a gateway to the Orient and to Alaska. Patterned after the fabulously successful Chicago World's Fair of 1893, the Alaska-Yukon-Pacific Exhibition (the AYPE) featured exhibits from other cities, counties, states, Alaska, Hawaii, and the Philippines.

At the time of the AYPE, the shores of Lake Union hosted industry, streetcars, and homes. In the Chinook trade jargon, the lake was called *tenas chuck* ("little waters") in contrast to *hyas chuck* ("big waters") for the larger lake to the east. The Duwamish chief Cheshiahud had only recently left his home at the north end of the lake. Alki pioneer David

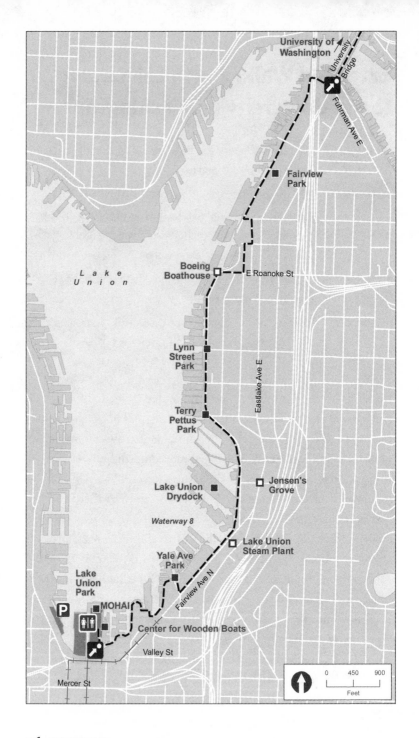

University of
Washington

University
Bridge

Fuhrman Ave E

■ Fairview
Park

*Lake
Union*

Boeing
Boathouse ▫   □ E Roanoke St

Lynn
Street
Park ■

Eastlake Ave E

Terry
Pettus
Park ■

Lake Union ■
Drydock

□ Jensen's
Grove

Waterway 8

Lake Union
Steam Plant □

Yale Ave
Park ■

Fairview Ave N

Lake
Union
Park

🅿

MOHAI ■

■

Center for Wooden Boats

Valley St

Mercer St

0   450   900
Feet

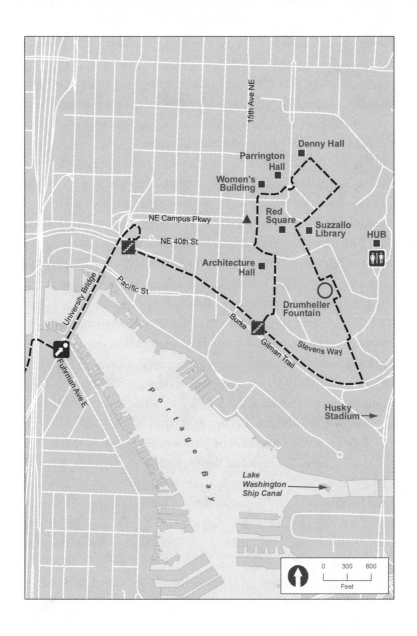

15th Ave NE

Denny Hall

Parrington Hall

Women's Building

NE Campus Pkwy

Red Square

Suzzallo Library

HUB

NE 40th St

Architecture Hall

University Bridge

Pacific St

Burke

Drumheller Fountain

Gilman Trail

Stevens Way

Fuhrman Ave E

P o r t a g e   B a y

Husky Stadium →

Lake Washington Ship Canal →

0   300   600
Feet

Denny had claimed land on the south side and built a mill. Thomas Mercer had also claimed nearby land. He gave a Fourth of July speech to neighbors in 1854 proposing a canal that would connect the salt water of Salmon Bay to the lakes. He proposed calling *hyas chuck* Lake Washington, honoring the nation's first president, and *tenas chuck* Lake Union because it would unite bodies of water.

By 1909, work on the canal had started and Denny's mill was flourishing. As in other areas of Seattle, the first economic enterprise on the lake had been cutting down the trees around it and sawing logs into lumber. For a few years in the 1860s, coal was carted on railcars and barges from the coalfields of Newcastle across Lake Washington and the ridge separating it from Lake Union and across that lake to railcars bound for the coal bunkers on Elliott Bay. Streetcars opened up new neighborhoods such as Fremont, Edgewater, Latona, and Brooklyn. The Seattle, Lakeshore and Eastern Railroad ran along the waterfront and the north side of Lake Union, connecting downtown Seattle with the university campus. The Eastlake streetcar ran along what is now Eastlake Avenue. We'll follow the Cheshiahud Lake Union Loop, which roughly parallels this route (see http://www .seattle.gov/parks/lakeunionloop/ for maps).

Begin at Seattle's **Museum of History and Industry (MOHAI)** or at the **Center for Wooden Boats (CWB)** on the south shore of Lake Union. The lake originally extended more than a block and a half south of here but the shoreline was filled in. Denny Hill separated the lake from downtown Seattle until the Denny regrade was completed in 1930. The Space Needle piercing the sky to the west dates from the 1962 world's fair.

You will not find any remnants of the village of the Lake Band of the Duwamish who first lived here (buried under fill), the Roy Street boat landing (likewise), or Denny's Western Mill (displaced by the armory and then by MOHAI). You will find all kinds of boats. The MOHAI building was once an armory for the U.S. Navy Reserve, which housed replicas of George Vancouver's ship, the *Discovery*, and the schooner *Exact*, on which the Denny party arrived. The Marine Heritage Park and the Center for Wooden Boats display Native American canoes and many other historically significant boats, including the *Arthur Foss*, a tugboat that went to Alaska during the Klondike gold rush. A history panel to the right of the walkway to the CWB describes the work of Blanchard Built Boats on Lake Union from 1904 to 1969.

Ford Motor Company

Visible across the street at Valley and Fairview is the reinforced concrete and red brick building that housed the Ford Motor Company's first assembly plant west of Detroit. Henry Ford chose Seattle as an assembly site when he visited the AYPE. The plant opened four years later but moved to south Seattle in 1932 and closed soon thereafter because of decreased demand for cars during the Great Depression. The original building is now used for public storage.

East of the CWB, find the blue wooden pennant for the **Cheshiahud Trail**. The Cheshiahud Lake Union Loop, named for the Duwamish chief, is a six-mile multi-use trail that circles the lake on boardwalks, paved trail, gravel and dirt trail, sidewalks, and low-traffic streets. The route is lightly marked by pennants on posts, generally heading northeast around the lake.

On the first part, *follow the Waterside Walkway* on docks for Waterways 4 and 5 along the southeastern shore. The waterways around the lake are numbered, beginning with Waterway 1 at roughly 10 o'clock if the lake were a clockface with the north end as noon. They continue counterclockwise through Waterway 23 at about 11 o'clock. This walk extends past Waterway 11 at 2 o'clock, then veers off to the university campus.

Walk among yachts and restaurants and shops along the boardwalk. The trail moves closer to the street after passing through **Yale Avenue**

Park, the first of several street-end parks. In the early twentieth century, the Olmsted Brothers recommended the creation of a thousand acres of parks in Seattle, which resulted in Volunteer Park, Woodland Park, Washington Park (now the Arboretum), Ravenna Park, and Leschi Park. A century later, street ends are some of the last remaining pockets for new parks. The Lake Union street ends are available because Seattle legislators asked the state for $1 million to finance the AYPE. The legislature funded the request by selling shorelands, submerged parcels that extended approximately one block from shore. Much of the shoreland was bought by property owners upland from the lake who had regarded the shoreline as theirs anyway. A century later, many of these property owners have cooperated with neighborhood volunteers to develop the street-end parks.

The trail continues on the sidewalk along Fairview Avenue, then turns back toward the lake. St. Mark's Cathedral is visible high on the hill above I-5. *On the Fairview Walkway,* a floating dock, *pass below* what were the smokestacks of the **Lake Union Steam Plant**. Seattle City Light was a publicly owned utility created in the early 1900s to provide electricity, a radical counterpart to privately owned utilities. When its dam on the Cedar River was no longer adequate to the growing needs of the city, the utility selected this site for its first powerhouse, using water power from the overflow at the Volunteer Park reservoir on the hillside above. The first plant is the small hydro house on the south; the much larger plant to the north was started in 1914. Near Waterway 8 are the remains of a **wooden pier** that was used to unload coal and then fuel oil for the larger plant. The plant closed in the mid-1980s and was restored by ZymoGenetics, which cleaned up oil pollution, remodeled the interior, and replaced the exterior smokestacks with replicas.

Seattle Seaplanes flights leave from a dock just south of **Lake Union Drydock**, at *1515 Fairview Avenue E*, probably the oldest continuously operating marine business in the city. The company built wooden Lake Union "Dreamboats" on the lakeshore from 1904 to 1969, flourishing especially during the 1920s Prohibition years, when it built yachts for both the rumrunners and the Coast Guard. One of the wooden buildings dates from 1919 and the two dry docks from the 1940s.

Seattle residents looking for a Sunday afternoon family outing took the Eastlake streetcar to Jensen's Grove, a German beer garden near the intersection of Eastlake and Garfield, a block east of the trail. The intersection now hosts a bank, parking lot, apartments, and the former home of the Bill and Melinda Gates Foundation, but no grove of trees.

The trail veers away from the shoreline at E Blaine Street, then returns at the foot of Newton Street, at **Terry Pettus Park**. North from here, houseboats line the lake, housing the Seattle lifestyle made famous by the 1993 movie *Sleepless in Seattle*. The first houseboats in the city were probably built among the fishing boats on Elliott Bay in the 1880s and 1890s. In a booming city where housing was scarce, laborers scavenged available material to fashion shacks on water, an attractive alternative to flophouses. Lake Union was the last waterfront in the city to host houseboats, but there were only a few in the early 1900s, inhabited mainly by sawmill workers. Now almost 500 houseboats ring the lake. Pettus was a labor journalist and houseboat activist who led efforts to make Lake Union more accessible to the public.

Two blocks farther north, at Waterway 10, is the **Lynn Street Park**, created in the 1970s by the Seattle Floating Homes Association and Eastlake Community Council. This park is known more colloquially as "Pete's Park," for Peter Omalanz, who provided beer to the workers and coordinated construction from his store across the street.

At the foot of Roanoke Street was the boathouse where the first **Boeing plane** was constructed. After piloting a seaplane on its first test flight over Lake Union, William Boeing declared, "Gentlemen, we are in the airplane business." The company soon moved to south Seattle and eventually expanded north to Everett and south to Renton, becoming a mainstay of the Puget Sound economy. The hangar was torn down in 1971, replaced by the Roanoke Reef houseboat community.

From here, the loop trail detours uphill from the waterfront on a series of streets—east on Roanoke, north on Yale Avenue, east on Edgar, north on Yale Terrace, west on Hamlin—and then returns to the lake. **Fairview Park** is the site of Cheshiahud's cabin and potato patch on land that David Denny had claimed and given to him. Cheshiahud and his wife, Madeline, were living here as late as 1900. After she died, he moved to the Suquamish Reservation and died there one year after the world's fair opened. In their landscape design for Seattle, the Olmsted Brothers recommended this terraced site for a park. It now hosts the Eastlake P-Patch.

At the northeastern curve of the lake, follow Fuhrman Avenue E, cross Eastlake, and then walk over the east side of the University Bridge. The bridge crosses the canal between Lake Union and Portage Bay, named for the portage the Duwamish people made across the ridge separating the two lakes. In 1887 a narrow chute was dug through the ridge to allow logs to be floated from Lake Washington to Lake Union, which was lower in elevation. A wider canal was completed in 1917, connecting the salt water of Salmon Bay through Lake Union and Portage Bay to Lake Washington. The University Bridge replaced the Latona Bridge, which had carried visitors to the fair.

Walk down the steps at the end of the University Bridge. At the foot of the steps is a most peculiar artwork, the *Wall of Death*, a reference to a motorcycle race and, obliquely, to bicycles speeding along the Burke Gilman Trail. *Turn back east and walk along the trail,* the former route of the Seattle, Lakeshore and Eastern Railway, which came around the north end of Lake Union. Watch out for bikes on the heavily used trail. You are approaching the University of Washington campus, moved here from downtown in the 1890s so that it could be "removed from the excitements and temptations incident to city life," according to the Board of Regents report. The city leased the southern half of the campus for the AYPE. The site was chosen because it had clear views of Mount Rainier, more than fifty miles away, and because it could be reached by rail line and streetcar,

Crowds thronged the Paystreak, an avenue of concessions and amusements at the Alaska-Yukon-Pacific Exposition. Courtesy University of Washington Libraries, Special Collections.

one line arriving at the main entrance to the fair at 15th Avenue and 40th Street.

The approach described here follows the crowds who arrived by boat on Lake Union and landed at the esplanade, a lively venue of parades, fireworks, canoe races, lifesaving drills, gondola rides, and the Aero plunge, on which riders slid down a chute and splashed into the lake. Once dry, you could make your way up the most popular part of the fair, the Paystreak, a row of attractions and amusements whose name harked back to the richest seam of gold in a placer claim. The heavily built south campus has overtaken the fair's esplanade and easy access to the waterfront.

Continuing past 15th Avenue, approach the pedestrian bridge that crosses Pacific Street, connecting the main campus to the Health Sciences Buildings at its south end. *Look down* some steps below the pedestrian bridge, near the greenhouses, to see stone **arches** under the railroad bed/bike trail. They once curved above fairgoers entering the Paystreak. The construction of a large Life Sciences Building may obscure this artifact of pedestrian life.

Walk back and climb the steps leading north past Kincaid Hall to Stevens Way, one of many campus streets named for the counties of Washington. *Follow Stevens as it curves north past Guthrie Hall* and arrive at **Architecture Hall**, one of only two buildings remaining from the AYPE. The graduating class of 1909 had high expectations of the fair, that it would "erect its gleaming palaces on our campus, which will make our campus a spot on which will mingle all the races of the earth and a place where will be displayed all the wonders of science, art, commerce and inventions." During the fair, the hall was the Fine Arts Building, one of those gleaming palaces. It was built with a steel frame and brick cladding rather than the wood frame and lath-and-plaster exterior of buildings intended to be temporary. Inside were hundreds of paintings, including an entire room displaying three volumes of Edward Curtis's Native American photos.

Across the street was the Women's Building, which offered both respite to female fairgoers and an assertion of women's accomplishments. Six hundred members of the National American Woman Suffrage Association held their annual conference at the fair, and some climbed Mount Rainier with a banner proclaiming "Votes for Women," actions that helped move Washington's male voters to approve women's suffrage in 1910. The building was later moved farther north on campus to make way for the Molecular Engineering and Sciences Building. Nine signs placed on campus during the centennial of the AYPE in 2009 identify significant sites.

Women's Clubs

Immigrants to Washington brought the urge to form civic and social groups with them. Middle-class men formed fraternal orders as havens from both work and home—the Masons, the Eagles, the Odd Fellows. The first men's lodge was founded in Olympia in 1855, followed by Odd Fellows lodges in Olympia, Walla Walla, and Vancouver in the 1860s and Seattle in 1870. Women formed clubs, ranging from maternal associations to temperance societies, Ladies Aid Societies, literary clubs, library associations, relief societies, and suffrage organizations. Some advocated labor legislation to benefit working women and end child labor. The clubs flourished in an age of Progressive reform. The Seattle Woman's Century Club was founded in 1891 out of the belief that "the coming century would be the woman's century." From local strength, clubs consolidated into federations. It was the Washington Federation of Women's Clubs that lobbied successfully for a women's building at the fair.

Continue on Stevens Way as it curves west and intersects George Washington Lane; then walk north. Cross the square in front of the Henry Art Gallery and pause at the **statue of George Washington**, funded by schoolchildren's donations and the local chapter of the Daughters of the American Revolution and unveiled on Flag Day, June 14, 1909, in the first month of the fair. It was moved to this spot from its original location at 40th Street, where it greeted visitors coming in the main entrance.

Follow George Washington Lane north until it curves east past the rescued **Women's Building**, renamed for 1907 alumnae Imogen Cunningham and home to the UW Women's Center. *Continue northeast* to **Parrington Hall**, one of the few university buildings present during the AYPE. Its large circular ends were thought to be ideal for science lectures and labs. *Across Memorial Way* is **Denny Hall**, which was the first building on the new campus, finished in time for the fall quarter in 1895 and later named for Arthur Denny, donor of most of the land for the original campus downtown.

After the fair, a century's worth of buildings grew on the campus. A 1915 campus plan added an axis pointing northeast to the axis John C. Olmsted had designed pointing southeast. *Walk southeast from Denny Hall on King Lane* to the center of the new axis, the Liberal Arts Quadrangle, known as the Quad. *Then walk southwest on Pierce Lane* to a large central plaza where the two axis points joined. The square's red bricks replaced grass when an underground parking garage was built in 1969. In that politically conscious era of frequent antiwar protests, students started calling it **Red Square**.

On the east side of the square stands **Suzzallo Library**, named for university president Henry Suzzallo, who tangled with Governor Roland Hartley in the 1920s over issues of funding and power. Meany Hall, on the west side of the plaza, occupies the open space that was just inside the 40th Street entrance. The U.S. Government Building sat on the central plaza.

A side excursion to the east, beyond Suzzallo and the Allen Library, leads to the **Husky Union Building (HUB)**, where a second-floor mural depicts the early history of the university. The HUB replaced the decaying Forestry Building, which had been built for the fair with huge vertical timbers.

At the south edge of Red Square, pause at the top of **Rainier Vista,** a view sweeping to Mount Rainier on a clear day. Olmsted wrote of his vision for this vista: "The best things from an artistic point of view are the Olympic Mountains, the Cascades, Mount Rainier and the two beautiful lakes. These are things that cannot be matched anywhere else in the country. If the landscaping at the exposition has made the most of the natural beauties at hand, then it may be considered a success." The vista of mountains and lakes spoke as much to the beauty of Seattle as to its prosperity.

Rainier Vista was the north–south axis of the fair. *Gradually descend* concrete steps over which water once fell—the Cascades. *Reach* **Drumheller Fountain**, first called Geyser Basin, then Frosh Pond, the name hinting at a quaint dunking custom long abandoned, leaving the pond to the geese and ducks. The basin was the center-piece of Olmsted's design. On the east side of the descending walk, the Sylvan Grove contains the original wooden columns from the 1861 building downtown. At the foot of the walk on Stevens Way, the Torii gate, depicted in an **interpretive plaque**, marked the southern entrance to the fair. In 1905 the campus was described as a "wooded wilderness." Few trees from that era remain.

Retrace your steps to Lake Union on the Burke Gilman Trail, and complete the Cheshiahud Loop around the lake, or return to downtown Seattle on buses that run on 15th Avenue, or take light rail, the resur-rection of the streetcar. A pedestrian bridge leads from Rainier Vista over Montlake Boulevard to the station at NE Pacific Street in front of Husky Stadium. The Husky mascot, adopted in 1922, recalls the promotional theme of the fair.

When the AYPE closed in October 1909, it left many buildings on campus, few of them meant to be permanent and not its chief legacy. "The real exposition is the City of Seattle," wrote John Barrett, director of the Bureau of American Republics, "that wonder city which has sprung up while we were asleep."

Resources	Center for Wooden Boats, 1010 Valley Street
	Klondike Gold Rush National Park, 319 2nd Avenue S
	Log House Museum, 3003 61st Avenue SW
	Museum of History and Industry, 860 Terry Avenue N
	Seattle Convention and Visitors Bureau, 1 Convention Place
	HistoryLink, www.historylink.org
	Seattle Public Library, 1000 4th Avenue

CHAPTER SIX

Everett

Milltown

We were really proud of those smokestacks and the jobs that came
with them.

David Dilgard, Everett historian

T he idea of a city called Everett arose relatively late in Washington history, a year after statehood in 1889. A creation of
eastern capitalists and midwestern timber barons, the city
they formed hit its peak as a mill town in the first decades of the
twentieth century.

Henry Hewitt Jr. was a timber cruiser who made a fortune in Wisconsin. When the forests of the upper Mississippi Valley were stripped
of their trees, he looked to the Pacific Northwest as the next lumber
bonanza. Hewitt had already invested in land and a timber company
in Tacoma, but he envisioned a new port city farther north on Puget
Sound. He found deep water and heavy forest on a promontory
formed by the Snohomish River on the east and Port Gardner Bay
on Possession Sound on the west.

Seeking financial backing, Hewitt had dinner at the New York
home of Charles L. Colby, a board member of the Northern Pacific
Railway Company and a representative of John D. Rockefeller.

Colby's fifteen-year-old son, named for the famous orator Edward Everett, was present at dinner and asked for more dessert.

"That's it!" Hewitt chuckled. "We should name our city Everett. This boy wants only the best, and so do we."

With the backing of Rockefeller, Hewitt formed the Everett Land Company in 1890, with himself as president. He began buying up land and platted a town. After a legal dispute with the state over the ownership of tidelands, Hewitt was able to reserve the waterfront for industries that would be outside the town limits and not subject to its taxes. He boasted that Everett would become "a city of smokestacks," with mills, shipyards, docks, railroads, smelters, and ironworks. His ambitious plans were bolstered by the discovery of gold, silver, iron, and lead in the Cascade Mountains to the east at Monte Cristo. Hewitt persuaded Rockefeller to invest additional millions there, too, and convinced investor Hiram Bond to bet his money on the Everett and Monte Cristo Railroad, which would transport the ore to a smelter. Soon smokestacks lined Port Gardner Bay and the Snohomish riverfront, almost encircling the peninsula.

The financial panic of 1893 caused a temporary setback; the smelter closed and three of the city's five banks went down. Rockefeller fired Hewitt, cut ties to his Everett investments, and dumped mining properties at Monte Cristo, but both Hewitt and the city recovered. Hewitt built a mansion in Tacoma and eventually became the richest man in the state.

Everett was saved by James J. Hill, the railroad titan who created the shortest haul between St. Paul, Minnesota, and Puget Sound by bringing the Great Northern Railway to the nascent city. Where Hewitt had promised a city of smokestacks, Hill promised a mill town, which became the darling of industrialists. He fed timber from the Northern Pacific land grants, which he had acquired through the railroad's bankruptcy, to the freight lines of the Great Northern. By 1910, eleven lumber mills, sixteen shingle mills, and seventeen combination mills, as well as ninety-five manufacturing plants, ringed Everett's waterfront. "Hear Everett Hum," crooned the city's promoters. Founding families named streets after themselves, then built mansions. Community activists built a hospital, high school, library, and theaters.

Everett would become infamous, however, for the conflict between workers and the titans of industry that resulted in the Everett Massacre of 1916, the most violent instance of class conflict in Washington's history. As Everett prospered, immigrant workers flooded to the mills from Germany, Scandinavia, Canada, and other U.S. states. The city's population more than tripled, from 8,000 in 1900 to 25,000 in 1910. Many of the workers joined unions. In 1886, the American Federation of Labor had united craft unions to demand higher wages, shorter working hours, and safer working conditions as the country industrialized. The Everett Trades Council had representatives from more than two dozen locals, most of them organized by skilled workers such as carpenters and electricians.

Union activism was supported by the broader Populist revolt of the late 1800s and early 1900s, which attracted farmers as well as workers. It was directed against industrialists like Everett's, who went deeply into debt to make capital investments and had to make their enterprises profitable. Washington elected eight Populists to the state legislature in 1893 and a Populist governor, John Rogers, in 1895, but reforms were limited.

Labor leaders focused on gaining an eight-hour workday. Eugene Debs, president of the American Railway Union, sought support for the nationwide strike against the Pullman Company. Debs spoke to a sympathetic audience of 600 at the Central Opera House in 1895. Later, Anna Agnes Malley came to edit a socialist newspaper, and two socialists were elected to the city council. Mother Jones made an appearance in 1914 urging the labor movement to stick together in pursuit of its goals. Everett labor leader Ernest Marsh marshaled support to put an initiative on the Washington ballot for an eight-hour workday, but it failed in the November 1914 elections.

After that defeat, labor leaders turned to direct action. For many

The Clough-Hartley mill, owned by David Clough and his son-in-law, Roland Hartley, was said to be the greatest producer of red cedar shingles in the world. It employed 165 men and could produce more than a million shingles during a ten-hour shift. This photograph shows it at full production in the year before the shingle weavers' strike. Courtesy Northwest History Room, Everett Public Library.

years unions in Everett had had working agreements, not contracts, with industries. That arrangement unraveled in 1916. Shingle weavers did the most dangerous work of all in the mills, their hands moving around whirring saw blades, cutting shingles at an inhuman pace. Such a pace was set at the Clough-Hartley mill in Everett, reported to be the greatest producer of red cedar shingles in the world. It employed 165 men and produced more than one million shingles a day during a single ten-hour shift, at a deadly cost to workers. In all mills combined, one in three shingle weavers was either injured or killed by the work; survivors could be recognized by their missing fingers.

During an economic depression from 1914 to 1916, shingle weavers around western Washington had taken a pay cut with the understanding that the original wages would return when profits rose. When that didn't happen and mechanization increased, the shingle weavers went on strike. They asked for a higher standard wage in mills all around Puget Sound. Many owners agreed to an increase, but those in Everett dug in their heels. They hired strikebreakers and armed enforcers to keep mills open, and the strike ground on for five months. The bitter confrontation spilled onto the streets named for capitalists.

The Industrial Workers of the World, known as the Wobblies, saw an opportunity to support their fellow workers. Responding to rapid industrialization, the IWW had organized in Chicago in 1905. Their platform proclaimed that the members of the working class had nothing in common with the owners of industry. The Wobblies advocated one big industrial union rather than the craft and skilled unions of the AFL. Using the tools of passive resistance, free speech, and songs, they organized field hands and timber workers who moved from job to job and carried blanket rolls on their backs. When news of the strike sifted down to the boarding halls of Seattle, Wobblies headed for Everett. On a waterfront dock unmarked today, they were met by armed deputies. A tragic clash of ideologies ensued, known as the Everett Massacre.

The events of 1916 left a scar on the city's history. Not until early summer 1917, when strikebreakers threatened their own strike, did holdout mills in Everett agree to pay union wages. As the United States entered World War I and the demand for timber soared, strikes closed down 90 percent of the lumber industry in western Washington over demands for an eight-hour workday and improvements in living and working conditions. The country needed the support of workers, and by February 1918, federal pressure helped soldiers working in logging camps and mills gain the eight-hour workday unions had long been asking for.

After the war, Everett prospered again. The downtown core experienced a building boom. In 1918, the municipally owned Port of Everett was established. In the 1920s an earthquake in Japan created a demand for lumber for rebuilding. Well into the 1930s, the bayside reverberated "with the whine of saws, the strident blasts of whistles, the hiss of steam, and the clank of wheels as engines shunt cars of freight on the sidings," according to the Washington State guidebook financed by the Work Projects Administration during the worldwide depression. Everett remained a union town, with prolonged periods of no work stoppages, but memories of the waterfront conflict persisted for decades and polarized the community.

Everett no longer boasts of smokestacks but of being an aviation production mecca. In 1940, native son Henry Jackson was elected to the U.S. House of Representatives and served in Congress for the next forty-three years, moving to the Senate in 1952. Often called "the senator from Boeing," Jackson was known as a Cold War, pro-defense, pro-labor, pro–environmental protection Democrat who brought federal investment to his hometown. Boeing is now the city's largest employer; a giant plant just south of town assembles 747s, 777s, and 787s. Naval Station Everett is second in jobs provided. As less industry lines the waterfront, Everett has spread out in a typical pattern—adding a mall and surrendering the oldest sections of town to I-5. But industrial and labor pride remain strong. "We were really proud of those smokestacks and the jobs that came with them," said David Dilgard, historian at the Everett Public Library.

This walk through Everett history begins at a bend of the Snohomish River, where logs cut from its shores were floated. It ends on Port Gardner Bay, overlooking the dock site where Wobblies and deputies clashed. In between, it passes the houses of mill workers and the mansions of industrialists, grand hotels and run-down boarding-houses, theaters and libraries, and the free speech corner where the Wobblies proclaimed the woes of a bindle stiff.

Pioneer Walk: Lowell

START: Rotary Park on the Lowell Riverfront Trail, 3505 Lowell Snohomish River Road

DIRECTIONS: From I-5, take exit 192 (Broadway/41st Street).
Go east on 41st to the first traffic light and turn south
on S Third Avenue for fourteen blocks to the intersection
with Lenora Street, the first four-way stop. Turn left to
go downhill and across the railroad tracks. Park at Rotary
Park on the left.

DISTANCE: 1 mile

AMENITIES: Parking at Rotary Park and Lowell Park, 4605 S 3rd Avenue;
restrooms at Lowell Park

Everett's logging wealth began at this **bend of the Snohomish River**.
For at least a thousand years, Snohomish people canoed up the river,
making their seasonal food rounds. The riverbanks, called Chi-*cha*-
dee-a, were a place for picking berries and gathering salmonberry
sprouts. The major village of Hibulb was farther north, at the point
of the peninsula. Resources abounded. "We never knew hard times,"
one Snohomish woman related in a local history.

In 1863, Eugene D. Smith, who had twice gone broke at mining,
set up the first logging operation on the river with his partner, Otis
Wilson. Because the water was deep and the undercurrent strong at
this bend, it held logs against the bank until they could be driven
downriver to a mill. Using oxen, Smith cleared the land on the banks
for a home and camp.

Walk north along the riverfront on the Lowell Riverfront Trail to
the pedestrian bridge over the railroad tracks. (The Lowell Riverfront
Trail continues in a northward direction from the park for a total of
1.75 miles.) This grade was first used in 1891 by the "Three S" railroad,
a forerunner of the Great Northern Railway, which arrived two years
later. The tracks passed directly over the first cottage Smith had built
near the present intersection of S 1st and Lenora; nothing remains
of the cottage, which was covered with vines by the 1890s. By then,
Smith had moved up the hill with much more ambitious plans. He

bought out his partner and established three separate logging camps, employing more than 150 men. Smith then developed a wharf, blacksmith shop, post office, sawmill, two hotels with a boardinghouse, homes, and a mill that became the town's main employer. He named the settlement Lowell after the industrial town of Lowell, Massachusetts.

Cross the bridge to the intersection of S 2nd Avenue and Main Street on the west side of the tracks. Two blocks to the south is Lenora Street, once the route of a **log flume** that carried logs from the ridgetop 200 feet down to the river. As reported in the *Port Gardner News,* crowds would gather along the flume to see "the immense sticks dash by 'on the wings of the lightning.'" One particularly brave and foolish newspaper reporter undertook to use the chute as a toboggan slide. He nailed a board for a foot brace across a large log and tacked on leather straps as handholds. Willing loggers pushed him on his way. As the log gained momentum, he blacked out twice and likened the ride to "falling from the top of the Eiffel tower." Hitting the river was like two planets colliding, but he survived to write about it.

On the northwest corner of S 2nd and Main is **Lowell Community Church**, built in 1891 with land and lumber donated by Smith. The church burned a few years before its hundredth birthday. Although the original siding was replaced and some features remodeled, the building retains many original characteristics and remains the oldest church in Everett. The house next door *at 5214 S 2nd* is the **Campbell House**, the first home of mill superintendent Frank R. Killien and Cora Jane Anderson Killien, built in 1910.

Lowell was well established by the late 1800s, when East Coast investors scented profitable investments to be made on Puget Sound. The Everett Land Company had its first offices in Smith's boardinghouse, and in 1891 he donated land along the river on the condition that the financiers use it for industrial development, thus staking Lowell's future. That's how the Puget Sound Pulp and Paper Com-

SUPER CALEDERS E.P.&P. MILL

Women and boys worked at the Everett Pulp and Paper Company in 1915. Lowell was a company town for seventy-five years, starting in 1895. Courtesy Northwest History Room, Everett Public Library.

pany, which became the Everett Pulp and Paper Company, started in Lowell and made it a mill town for the next eighty years. The **brick building** *at 5205 S 2nd* and the one-story building north of it are the last remaining company structures. The latter housed the office where workers clocked in and out. The mill and other industries lined the riverfront between the railroad tracks and the river.

For many years Smith's logging enterprises at Lowell were the strongest economic force on Port Gardner Peninsula. Once the pulp and paper mill arrived, daily life centered around the plant, the Sumner Iron Works, and other mills that lined the riverfront where the Lowell Riverfront Trail crosses wetlands. "You could just take your lunch pail and go down there and ask in the office if they needed any work, and they'd send you out to find so and so on the floor and see if he needed any help," commented one retired mill worker.

Smith and his wife, Margaret, and her brother Martin Getchell and his wife, Olive, platted thirty-three blocks of the town in 1873. *Walk the hillside* to see a variety of homes that date from the 1890s and early 1900s. *On the southeast corner of 3rd Avenue and Main* is the **A. E. Prudden home**; *4918 3rd* was the second Killien home. The **Le Clere home** *at 5101 3rd Avenue* is a typical worker's cottage in a Victorian style. Four more **mill worker cottages** are *at 5013, 5014, 5018, and 5102 3rd Avenue.* Visible across the river is the **Getchell farm**, dating from the 1880s.

If you continue walking north on 3rd past Lowell Park, you will pass **Acrowood Forest Products**, formerly Sumner Iron Works, in the 4100 block. Its large wooden buildings are visible through the trees to the east. The original ironworks, started in 1892, made marine, mining, and mill machinery and built ships. City police and private detectives protected strikebreakers at the plant in 1910 when striking ironworkers called for higher wages and an eight-hour workday, a primary goal of the labor movement. The present factory was built in 1913 to replace a brick factory destroyed by fire, and it is the oldest continuously manufacturing plant in Everett. The Craftsman-style former **home of George Sumner**, a son of the business's founders, is on the hillside above the factory at 4100 3rd Avenue.

Lowell remains the oldest part of Everett. The town lost its independence when it was annexed in 1962 and the paper mill closed in 1972. More distressing was the construction of I-5, completed to Everett from the south in 1967. The interstate ran over the site that had once been Lowell School and cut right through the town, taking down thirty houses. The Riverview Market and Café in the old clocking-in office displays photographs and newspaper articles about the Lowell that was.

By the 1890s, the bay side of the peninsula and the riverside north of Lowell had grabbed the attention of investors and speculators, and the Everett Land Company had moved on from its small office in Smith's boardinghouse. Follow those entrepreneurs west to the city of smokestacks and mills they built on Port Gardner Bay. *There is no friendly walking route from Lowell to downtown Everett. To drive, return to 41st, go west, and take Broadway north to Hewitt, following directions for the downtown loop.*

Everett Loop

START: Depot Park, south of 2900 Bond Street

DIRECTIONS: From I-5 north, take exit 192 and merge onto Broadway. Go north on Broadway. From I-5 south, take exit 194 (City Center/Everett Avenue), stay right to turn right onto Everett, and then turn left on Maple. From either direction, turn west onto Hewitt Avenue (29th Street). Hewitt Avenue veers left onto Federal Avenue, which very quickly becomes Bond Street. Depot Park is on the right, just beyond 2900 Bond Street, the offices of the Burlington Northern Santa Fe Railway.

DISTANCE: 5.5 miles round trip

AMENITIES: Parking along Bond Street and other streets; restrooms at Everett Public Library, 2702 Hoyt Avenue (off-route two blocks)

This tour of Everett, like tours of other Puget Sound and river cities, begins where land was most prized—on the waterfront. For Everett, that included the Snohomish River to the east and north and Port Gardner Bay on the west. The peninsula promised unlimited potential to investors: a location for the terminus of the transcontinental railroad, a deepwater port, and water power for factories and mills. Such resources fueled capitalist dreams.

Early speculators hoped that James J. Hill would locate the terminus of the Great Northern Railway on the bay. Hill was wined, dined, and cheered at the Bay View Hotel near here in 1892. "We could be persuaded

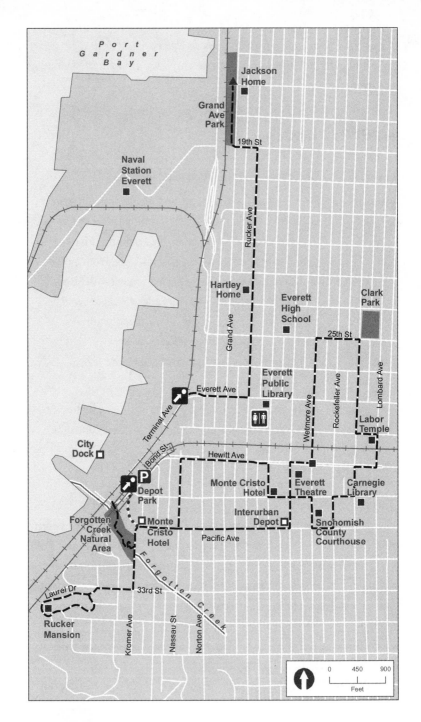

Port Gardner Bay

Jackson Home

Grand Ave Park

19th St

Naval Station Everett

Rucker Ave

Hartley Home

Everett High School

Clark Park

Grand Ave

25th St

Everett Ave

Everett Public Library

Rockefeller Ave

Lombard Ave

Wetmore Ave

Labor Temple

Terminal Ave

City Dock

Bond St

Hewitt Ave

Depot Park

Monte Cristo Hotel

Everett Theatre

Carnegie Library

Forgotten Creek Natural Area

Monte Cristo Hotel

Interurban Depot

Snohomish County Courthouse

Pacific Ave

Forgotten Creek

Laurel Dr

33rd St

Kromer Ave

Nassau St

Norton Ave

Rucker Mansion

0   450   900

Feet

not to haul our tonnage any farther than absolutely necessary to reach Puget Sound," he told the boosters. Everett, he went on, had "no reason to fear any city south of you." Just a year later the railroad came to Port Gardner Bay, but it also continued south to Seattle.

2900 Bond Street was the site of the first small railroad station, followed in 1910 by a much grander Mission-style building. Only a dim vestige of the original depot remains as the Northwest Division offices of the Burlington Northern Santa Fe. Amtrak service moved to the new Everett Station on the east side of town in 2002. **Depot Park**, with a garden and caboose-like kiosk just to the south, recalls a more bustling time.

To see what success and prosperity looked like for early investors, climb to the Rucker mansion overlooking Port Gardner Bay. *Find the trailhead at the southern end of Bond Street* for the **Forgotten Creek natural area**. The creek was once culverted and obscured by the industrial growth of Everett, including one of the city's first major industries, the Puget Sound Wire, Nail, and Steel Company. Contemporary Port Gardner neighbors have worked to restore the greenbelt. *Follow the trail uphill 0.25 miles to Kromer Avenue,* named for an early homesteader.

(As an alternative, walk up Bond to Kromer Avenue and follow Kromer uphill to Pacific Avenue. From this intersection, walk south on Kromer past the natural area to join the Rucker mansion loop or pick up the downtown loop at this intersection.)

At the top of the bluff, *walk south on Kromer to 33rd.* Take an optional walk three blocks east on 33rd to 3306 Norton, the former home of Tennessee and William Boner, built in 1906. Boner was the manager of one of the largest lumber mills in the world and the city's largest payroll—Weyerhaeuser Mill B—which opened on the tip of the peninsula in 1915. The lumber to supply the mill came from a deal made by Frederick Weyerhaeuser in 1900. He bought 900,000 acres of timberland from James J. Hill at the price of six dollars an acre, a deal that has prospered the timber company to this day.

Matthew Norton, after whom the street is named, helped raise millions for Weyerhaeuser's purchase.

From Kromer and 33rd, walk west two blocks to Laurel Drive, the street that angles to the left. *Veer left* at Rucker Hill Park *to make a clockwise loop of the hill.* Stay on Laurel to pass by the porte cochere of the **Rucker mansion** *at 412 Laurel Drive.* Here, the Ruckers, early land developers, could alight from horse and carriage under cover from Northwest mist.

Brothers Wyatt and Bethel Rucker and their widowed mother, Jane, moved west from Ohio in 1888, looking for investment opportunities, especially wherever the Great Northern planned to terminate on Puget Sound. They were the first to dream of a city on the bay and start buying up land, then were persuaded to join forces with the even more ambitious Everett Land Company. Succeeding grandly, the family built this mansion in 1905, the first on what is now Rucker Hill. Water was pumped by windmill from a newly completed reservoir, which facilitated development over the next thirty years. Descendants of the family donated the land for Rucker Hill Park in the 1950s.

To the west and north of the mansion, the sweeping expanse of Port Gardner Bay comes into view. British explorer George Vancouver named the bay in 1792 for Alan Gardner, who had been his commander. Vancouver claimed waters and land all along the coast for King George III of England, including Possession Sound, the arm of Puget Sound where the bay is located. He named Mount Baker, too, visible on the northern horizon. *Finish the loop and walk east on 33rd back to Kromer; go north,* crossing the ravine of Forgotten Creek.

At Kromer and Pacific, walk three blocks east to Nassau Street, and take Nassau downhill to Hewitt Avenue. On the way, pass three single-story workers' cottages on the east side of the street. In Everett's heyday, mill whistles blew at 6 A.M. for a wake-up call and again at 7 A.M. for the come-to-work call. Hundreds of workers streamed toward the waterfront from downtown boardinghouses and hillside cottages.

Hewitt Avenue was just a path through huge tree trunks in 1891, according to Eva Jones Davis, who arrived as a child. Her family was so seasick after their voyage from Olympia that they alighted on the bay side and walked two miles east "through the bushes" to their cabin. Davis grew up on the east side of town, known as the riverside. When Everett incorporated in 1893, its commercial center moved toward the bay side, with Hewitt Avenue as the connector, named after Henry Hewitt Jr., the "father of Everett." Everything happened on the 1.5-mile-long avenue—circus parades, Labor Day parades, presidential processions (Theodore Roosevelt in 1903), ship-launching celebrations—everything except free speech. (A city ordinance prohibited public speechmaking within fifty feet of Hewitt to protect the free flow of traffic.) In an oral history interview, Davis remembered that Snohomish Indian women would walk along Hewitt and that she would buy salmon from them.

At the corner of Hewitt and Nassau, note remnants from working lives that once centered on the waterfront. **Jones Stevedoring Company**, at *1017 Hewitt*, has handled cargo in North Pacific ports since 1858. A bench in front of **Local 32** of the International Longshoremen's and Warehousemen's Union, just *west of the corner,* proclaims "An injury to one is an injury to all."

The early Hewitt Avenue was home to brothels, taverns, and gambling joints. Taverns date from 1907 at **1001 Hewitt**. Formerly a saloon, **1105 Hewitt** is the oldest frame structure on the avenue, dating from 1899. There were forty taverns in town, and the brothels were also licensed to sell liquor, but most were on the riverside end of Hewitt, known as the "less righteous" end.

Walk east on Hewitt for six blocks. In later decades, the avenue became Everett's auto row. The last remnant was Dwayne Lane's Dodge *on the southwest corner of Hewitt and Rucker,* but the Spanish Mission Revival–style building now houses exercise facilities, an antidote to the car culture. *On the northeast corner at 1401 Hewitt* is the **Marion Building**, from 1893. Once a saloon, it became a hardware store after Prohibition.

Two blocks farther east, at Hoyt Avenue, walk south one block to Wall Street, an aspirational name. Hewitt insisted that downtown's north-south streets be named after investors—Charles Colby, his partner Colgate Hoyt, the Ruckers, John D. Rockefeller, Hiram Bond, and Thomas Fletcher Oakes. *At the northeast corner of Wall and Hoyt* is the **Monte Cristo Hotel**, named to capture the aura of wealth surrounding the mining town in the Cascades. The investors of the Everett Land Company met frequently and entertained eastern financiers at the old Monte Cristo, a wooden palace built in 1893 at Pacific and Kromer. The Sisters of Providence turned the hotel into a hospital in 1904; Providence Regional Medical Center now commands the original site. This newer hotel opened in 1925, using 500 bricks from the old, which was demolished.

Walk east on Wall two blocks to **Wetmore Avenue**, passing **Everett City Hall**, now a police station, on the southwest corner. The street was named after Charles W. Wetmore, a New York capitalist who built distinctive whaleback ships with decks rounded like the back of a whale. They carried ore on the Great Lakes, and Everett Land Company investors convinced Wetmore to open a West Coast operation. Soon the whaleback *Wetmore* came around Cape Horn bringing materials for the factories of Everett and iron to build more ships like itself at the Pacific Steel Barge Company on the Snohomish River. The *City of Everett* was launched in 1894, and celebrants paraded on Hewitt Avenue. Unfortunately, whalebacks ultimately proved unseaworthy, and the first ship was the only one built at Everett.

Walk south on Wetmore. With prosperity assured after the Great Northern Railway arrived in 1893, the community had the confidence to build civic institutions. Facing Wetmore between Wall and Pacific is the **Snohomish County Courthouse**, built when Everett supplanted Snohomish City as the county seat. Architect August Heide and his partner, Charles Hove, prospered with the city. The first courthouse designed by Heide burned in 1909, but a year later his new Mission-style courthouse opened, using three surviving arches.

On the southwest corner of Pacific and Wetmore, First Baptist Church was once the site of the Coliseum Skating Rink, which not only housed a skating rink but also hosted rallies and conventions. The renowned lawyer Clarence Darrow spoke there in 1910, arguing against a city prohibition law.

Prohibition

The same year as Darrow, evangelist Billy Sunday had brought his anti-saloon message to town as part of a nationwide campaign to curb the sale of alcohol. His preaching in a temporary tabernacle on the west side of Lombard, between California and Everett, drew crowds that totaled 220,000 people during a five-day crusade.

Sunday also indirectly succeeded in rallying the forces for women's suffrage. A speaker with his campaign claimed she had been harassed by the local suffrage club. Denied an official chance to respond, the club's president, Ella M. Russell, stepped up on a bench in front of the hall packed with 5,500 people and said that the claim was completely unfounded. Her speech garnered more newspaper headlines and possibly more converts than the rally that day.

Everett adopted prohibition in November 1910, under a local option provided by the legislature, but it lasted only two years before city coffers were drained by the missing income from taxes and licenses. Four years after the Everett vote and after women got the right to vote in Washington, the whole state voted to go dry. In another four years, in 1920, the whole country prohibited saloons. Always a bit ahead of the curve, Washington repealed statewide prohibition in 1932, a year before national repeal, and saloons flourished again.

Walk east on Pacific one block to **Rockefeller Avenue**, named after the financier who first bankrolled Everett. "He was an owner, either visibly or underneath, of virtually everything that got developed here," says historian David Dilgard. His money attracted everyone else's money, but he visited the city only once, in 1899, when he was preparing to purge his portfolio of local investments.

Go one block north on the walkway through the Snohomish County campus; then note the **First Presbyterian Church**, completed in 1910, *on the northwest corner of Wall and Rockefeller.* The church tolled its bells every hour on Election Day in 1912, during the vote to repeal the city's prohibition ordinance, which succeeded despite the bells.

Walk one block east on Wall to Oakes, where the **Carnegie Library** sits on the southeast corner. The Everett Woman's Book Club first met at the old Monte Cristo, with the goal of creating a free public library. The group started a public reading room in 1894, gathered books, and four years later paid a librarian to open a library in three rooms in the city hall. Industrialist Andrew Carnegie offered Everett money for a library building, as he was doing all across the country, and the Everett Improvement Company matched his offer with two lots. August Heide prepared a design. This building served as the city's library from 1905 to 1934.

Go north on Oakes one block to Hewitt, then east one block to Lombard. On the northwest corner is the **Mitchell Hotel**, which became the city's first-class hotel after the Sisters of Providence converted the original Monte Cristo Hotel into a hospital. *Rounding the corner, go north to the* **Labor Temple** *at 2810 Lombard.* The current temple was built in 1930, replacing the original office built in 1902. Just south of the temple is the east portal of the railroad tunnel that burrowed under downtown Everett in 1901. It travels underground for seven blocks and emerges near the waterfront.

The region's *Labor Journal* was published at the Labor Temple, beginning in 1909 and continuing through the 1970s. Editors strongly supported the efforts of women to improve their working conditions as cigar makers, cooks, waitresses, and telephone, shirtwaist, and laundry workers. John Campbell, business manager of the *Labor Journal* and a state legislator from Everett, lobbied for a law granting the eight-hour workday to women. The year after striking ironworkers in Lowell demanded an eight-hour workday from the Sumner Iron Works, Washington legislators granted the eight-hour day to women in 1911.

The campaign for an eight-hour workday for men continued for the next few years. In 1914, timber workers vowed to secure an eight-hour day, but timber mill owners shut down the mills for a week to dispute the men's right to organize. *Follow* the path of 5,000 workers who walked from the Labor Temple to the city's first park to protest the shutdown. *Walk north on Lombard to California Avenue, then west one block to Oakes and north one block to cross Everett Avenue. Continue two more blocks north,* passing **Normanna Hall** at *2725 Oakes,* home to the Sons of Norway and thousands of Norwegian immigrants to Everett. *Reach tennis courts on the west side of* **Clark Park,** between 24th and 25th, first called City Park. Clark was John Judson Clark, a Wisconsin merchant who had been persuaded by Hewitt to invest in Everett. Symbolizing the importance of the region's timber resources, the park once contained a giant Douglas fir stump that had been exhibited at the St. Louis Exposition in 1904. It was big enough to house the caretaker's toolshed for many years.

The march from the Labor Temple attracted a crowd that grew to 8,000 and threatened a general strike unless workers could join unions. That's when labor leader Ernest Marsh promised to achieve the eight-hour day through a statewide initiative. When it failed, more radical labor leaders gained strength. Two years later, 15,000 people gathered in the park during the shingle weavers' strike.

Go west on 25th, past the new gymnasium for **Everett High School,** whose structures span more than four city blocks. The massive Beaux Arts–style school at the corner of Colby and 25th dates from 1910 and proclaims the importance citizens gave education. For decades, Norwegian was taught in the high school because of the large Scandinavian population. The school's football teams united the city's social classes and immigrant groups. It was "the crown jewel of the community, not just its appearance but the role it's played in the community," said historian and educator Larry O'Donnell.

Return one block east to Wetmore and walk four blocks south to the northwest corner of **Hewitt and Wetmore**, once the most volatile intersection in Everett, now a parking lot. When no one would rent a large hall to the Industrial Workers of the World (the IWW, or Wobblies), they took to standing on soapboxes and speaking and singing, just like the Salvation Army and other religious and political groups. Thousands stood against buildings or looked out of windows to hear the street speakers.

These constant harangues made Everett industrialists and authorities nervous. In Spokane, Wobblies had filled the jails with speakers, a tactic that forced the city to respond to their protest against the corrupt practices of some labor agents. In Everett, the sheriff responded in the same way, his deputies swinging clubs, arresting Wobblies, and hauling them to the city jail. Since free speech was constitutionally guaranteed, the speakers were charged with peddling without a license (selling leaflets) or with vagrancy. Most of those

Wobblies at Beverly Park

The most serious conflict in the free speech fight in Everett occurred in October 1916 just outside of town in an area called Beverly Park. Forty-one Wobblies had come by ferry to Everett to speak at Hewitt and Wetmore, but Snohomish County sheriff Donald McRae was zealous in his opposition to striking shingle weavers and to the street speakers. On this evening, McRae and a group of "law and order" officials rounded up the Wobblies and forced them to run a gauntlet as they were beaten with whips and with devil's club, the native plant with ferocious thorns. The injured men hobbled twenty-five miles back to Seattle on the Interurban tracks, bloodied and enraged by an injustice they would not forget.

arrested were eventually released. Sometimes they were beaten and deported by Interurban back to Seattle. To avoid arrest and beating, speakers could also simply run down the street to the depot.

Detour one block east to the Commerce Building on the northeast corner of Rockefeller and Hewitt, built in 1910 and designed by Benjamin Turnbull, another of early Everett's most prolific architects. The local women's suffrage movement was a tenant here, part of the coalition of organizations that won the right for Washington women to vote in November 1910.

From Wetmore, walk one block west to Colby and then south two blocks to Pacific. On the way, pass the historic **Everett Theatre**, *at 2911 Colby*, which opened as an opera house in 1901. During the summer of strife in 1916, striking shingle weavers were picketing the Jamison mill. One night Neil Jamison paraded the strikebreakers through town to a party at the theater for a celebration of their "efficiency." When they emerged from the show, fistfights broke out between strikers and strikebreakers. Although a fire damaged the building in 1923, the facade and interior were rebuilt a year later.

The building *at the northwest corner of Colby and Pacific* housed the **Interurban depot**, which served travelers from Everett to Seattle for almost thirty years, from 1911 to 1939. The dispatcher's bay window, from which he could see trains coming and going, was on the second story of the north side of the building. The window is highlighted in blue paint, but there are no trains in sight (the main rail station to Seattle is now on the east side of town).

In November 1916, 294 free speech advocates had been arrested in Everett and the shingle weavers' strike was entering its fifth month. *To witness the conflict's climax and return to the start of the walk, follow Pacific west many blocks to Kromer and down Kromer to the waterfront.* Visualize the scene: On Sunday morning, November 5, thousands of Everett residents have gathered on the hill above the city docks, expecting a free speech rally by the Wobblies. Some 300 Wobblies, intent on protesting the beatings at Beverly Park, are making their way from Seattle by ferry. On the dock, about 200 armed men are waiting for them, deputized by Sheriff McRae with the support of local timber barons. The waiting men wear white handkerchiefs to distinguish themselves from the Wobblies, and some hide inside a warehouse.

Position yourself north of the BNSF offices on Bond Street. The City Dock was on Pier 2, at the end of Hewitt Avenue. It no longer exists; the site is closed off with fences and barbed wire just north of where the cement storage dome is now.

Watch as the *Verona* comes slowly into view. Its decks are crowded with men singing the Wobbly anthem, whose last verse ends, "We'll join our hands in union strong, to battle, win, or die!" Some cheers go up from the gathered crowd of residents, unionists, strikers, businesspeople, professionals, women, and children standing along the tracks of the Great Northern. A wharfinger secures the ferry's bowline to a piling, holding the crowded *Verona* close to the dock. Norman H. Clark, author of *Mill Town,* a social history of Everett, describes what happened next.

Sheriff McRae calls out, "Boys, who's your leader?" and receives the usual Wobbly response, "We're all leaders!"

He tells them they can't land. "The hell we can't," yells a Wobbly.

Then a shot rings out, followed quickly by a volley of shots from the dock and the vessel. Those on the *Verona* run to the other side of the ship, and several jump into the water to escape the firing or are dumped by the sloping ship. The pilot finally pulls the steamer away from the wharf with enough force to break the rope and retreat into the bay, but by then four Wobblies are dead, one is dying, and fifty are wounded. At least six more Wobblies have drowned or been shot while in the water and will never be found. Two deputies are dead, and twenty others are wounded, perhaps shot by their comrades in the mayhem.

The crowds above the dock were horrified. The strike, the Wobbly

The Verona *sits at the City Dock in a photo used as evidence in a civil suit filed by Oscar Carlson, who was a passenger on the steamer but not a member of the IWW. He was shot eleven times during the Everett Massacre but did not win his suit. Courtesy Northwest History Room, Everett Public Library.*

campaign, the reaction of the lumber trust, and the deputized force severed years of community trust that had developed in Everett. Seventy-four Wobblies were arrested, to be tried for the murder of one deputy. When the first Wobbly was found not guilty after six months of imprisonment and trial, all other charges were dropped. Not until early summer 1917, when strikebreakers threatened their own strike, did the holdout mills decide they could pay union wages to shingle weavers, and the long strike ended. The city plans to place an interpretive plaque at the site of the event remembered for decades as the Everett Massacre.

Extended Walk: Grand and Rucker Avenues

START: W Marine View Drive and Everett Avenue

DIRECTIONS: From Hewitt Avenue, go north on W Marine View Drive to Everett Avenue. Turn right one block and find parking on Grand Avenue south of Everett.

DISTANCE: 2 miles round trip

AMENITIES: Restrooms at Everett Public Library, 2702 Hoyt Avenue

The founding members of the Everett Land Company; its successor, the Everett Improvement Company; and the employers who resisted union wages continued to prosper. These industrialists had entrepreneurial skills and energies of a high order, according to Norman Clark, but they were also ruthless in the extraction of maximum profit. Many erected grand homes on Rucker and Grand Avenues with the profits from their enterprises. For a tour of this legacy and a view of Everett's transition from smokestacks and mills, walk the neighborhood high on the bluff above the port.

Begin on Everett Avenue east of Marine View Drive, site of the first homestead in 1862; nothing that looks like a homestead remains. On the waterfront below stood the Kimberly-Clark Corporation, the last in a seventy-year history of paper manufacturers and the last of the smokestacks. Its brick building was demolished in 2013. In its heyday as Scott Paper Company, the plant employed about 2,000 people and rivaled Weyerhaeuser as the city's largest employer. Pulp mills shifted the city away from nearly total dependence on lumber and shingle mills but gave Everett a second nickname, "the armpit of the nation," a reference to the rotten-egg smell typical of pulp mills. "It's the smell of money," the locals told newcomers.

Walk east on Everett Avenue to Rucker Avenue. On the block between

Rucker and Hoyt to the east is the Everett Public Library. **Mural maps** of the city from the 1930s have been restored on the walls inside the main entrance.

Walk north on Rucker three and a half blocks to 2320, the **Roland Hartley home**. Hartley's father-in-law, David Marston Clough, a former governor of Minnesota and one of the toughest and shrewdest of the timber barons, lived a few doors north on the corner, at *2302*. Together they owned the Clough-Hartley mill, which figured prominently in the 1916 strike. Decades later, the Hartley home had a sign for the Democratic gubernatorial candidate on the lawn. With the diminished importance of the founding capitalists and the growth of Boeing and its strong unions, Everett had become a Democratic town.

Governor Roland Hartley

Roland Hartley was the mayor of Everett, a Washington legislator during the shingle weavers' strike, and governor of Washington from 1925 to 1933. His political approach reflected his business approach: eliminate waste and extravagance. As a legislator, he voted against the eight-hour day for women. As governor, he hated taxes, government spending, and unions, and he often used his veto power. In 1926 he dismissed Henry Suzzallo as president of the University of Washington because Suzzallo would not agree to allow the state to centralize power over the university. A recall movement was initiated against Hartley, but the petition failed to gain enough signatures.

Continue north on Rucker, passing the **McChesney home** *at 2230 Rucker Avenue.* William T. McChesney was James J. Hill's man in Everett and a mover and shaker in the Everett Improvement Company. *On the northeast corner of 22nd and Rucker is* the **Clark home**, where Margaret Clark, the first graduate of Everett High School, grew up. *At 2107 Rucker* is the **home of August Heide,** the architect for many buildings in Everett.

At 19th, walk west to Grand Avenue and the beginning of a paved trail through Grand Avenue Park overlooking the bay. *At 18th* is a **rock** commemorating the landing of George Vancouver "near here" on June 4, 1792. The rock was erected by a chapter of the Daughters of the American Revolution during the era of club building and civic stability in the early 1900s.

This hike through the industrial and labor history of Everett *ends at 17th and Grand Avenue* before a **bust** of native son Henry M. Jackson. As a boy, Jackson delivered papers to the house at *1703 Grand Avenue*, designed by August F. Heide for William C. Butler. Butler and his wife, Eleanor, came to Everett in 1892, dispatched by John D. Rockefeller to oversee construction and operation of the concentrator in Monte Cristo and the smelter in Everett. Butler stayed and invested in banks. It has been said that Everett's economy "rested on Jim Hill's land and Butler's gold." He was an iron-willed opponent of the shingle weavers' union. Senator Jackson, his wife, Helen Hardin Jackson, and their two young children moved into the house in 1967.

Senator Henry M. Jackson

Senator Henry M. Jackson was known for his strong support of national defense and Boeing contracts, but he was also known as the father/grandfather of all environmental legislation in the country. An advocate for conservation and preservation of wilderness, Jackson pushed through a deal that created North Cascades National Park. He steered the Wilderness Act of 1964 and the Wild and Scenic Rivers Act of 1968 through his Energy and Natural Resources Committee and through Congress. He also authored the National Environmental Policy Act of 1969, which said it would be U.S. policy to "encourage productive and enjoyable harmony between man and his environment." Signed by President Richard Nixon, it instituted environmental impact statements for major federal projects.

Early residents viewed the waterfront as work, its line of smoke-stacks signifying the conversion of ancient Douglas firs and Western red cedars into marketable products. Smoke turned the air to a smudged-out gray, according to historian Bob Wodnik, and at night the tops of sawmill waste burners grew red hot; their cinders became shooting stars. That changed with the National Environmental Policy Act, which cleared the air in many cities by mandating cleaner facilities. The smell is gone, and the scenic view is now money.

Look down at **Naval Station Everett**, a U.S. Navy homeport and a dream of Senator Jackson's. The **gingerbread house** in the foreground was completed as a wood products showcase by Weyerhaeuser in 1923 and at one time housed the Everett Chamber of Commerce. The Port of Everett marina below has slips for more than 2,000 boats. Jetty Island, the long island in the background, is the result of an attempt begun in 1896 to create a freshwater harbor, which would thwart saltwater borers' damage to wooden-hull ships. The attempt soon went awry, but the island is a recreational treasure today.

As you walk back south on Grand, find the **Bayside Park and P-Patch** *between 22nd and 23rd Streets, one-half block west of Grand.* Look down at the former Kimberly-Clark property, now a vast gravel field. Gardeners have views of Possession Sound marred only by long, open-car trains carrying coal.

There is much more to visit in Everett—Forest Park, the American Legion Memorial Park, Hilbulb Lookout, the Mill Town Trail along the waterfront, and, of course, Boeing's huge hangar south of town, which draws visitors from around the world. Like most cities, Everett has sprawled far beyond its downtown, tearing down and fencing off some reminders of its past but restoring others as the city has transitioned from smokestacks to mills to port and aircraft.

Resources   Everett Public Library, 2702 Hoyt Avenue

CHAPTER SEVEN

Bellingham

Reluctant City

All was "boom," rush and excitement.

Ella Higginson

L ocated in the most remote corner of the continental United States, hunkered below a wilderness cascading down from the mountains, early Bellingham occupied "the rough edge of the world," as described by Annie Dillard in her historical novel *The Living*. But the early settlement had ambition. Four villages—Whatcom, Sehome, Bellingham, and Fairhaven—grew along the waterfront of Bellingham Bay and rode every boom and bust that swept the Pacific Northwest in the late 1800s and early 1900s. Whatcom surged on sawmills and a gold rush; Sehome boomed on a coal mine and railroad hopes. They merged in 1891 to become New Whatcom. The next village south on the bay, Bellingham, had a brief fling with coal but was swallowed up by Fairhaven to the south, which had visions of railroads and ended up with canneries. In sequence, they inhaled opportunity, exhaled optimism, and built long docks into the bay.

Ella Higginson, who later became the first poet laureate of Washington, arrived in the village of Sehome in 1888: "There were no sidewalks . . . , and women waded about in rubber boots," she wrote. "But ah! the joy of those first years! All was 'boom,' rush, and excitement. . . . Fortunes were made overnight on corner lots and every frog on Sehome Hill said, 'Struck it—struck it'!"

Three creeks flow into Bellingham Bay—Squalicum, Whatcom, and Padden. The first boom began between the first two creeks in the village of Whatcom, a place of noisy water. A chief of the Lummi people, Cha-wit-zit, gave good advice to two entrepreneurs looking for a sawmill site in 1852. He told them of a place where a creek falls down to a saltwater bay. The bay was sheltered by a peninsula on the north side, where the Nooksack River flows in, and by an island offshore, which buffers it from the Georgia Strait. The Lummi lived around the mouth of the river, on the shoreline north and south, and on the San Juan Islands in the strait. They had a seasonal fishing camp near the falls of the creek.

Henry Roeder and Russell Peabody were looking for a profit-making venture. California was a new state rich from the gold rush, but San Francisco had suffered a great fire and offered a bull market for lumber. The lower falls on Whatcom Creek would provide all the power they needed for a sawmill close to shipping, and the ancient forest on its banks would provide the lumber. Roeder platted streets and house lots and saved land for a park. Whatcom was soon named the seat of Whatcom County, but the village grew slowly, and the mill did not prosper. By the time it was up and running and the creek had enough water in the fall, the lumber market in San Francisco had dried up, and prices had plummeted. The mill found a sporadic market in Victoria, in the colony of British Columbia, where the next boom beckoned.

Gold was discovered along the Fraser River in 1858. Thousands of miners rushed to Whatcom and camped on the beach, waiting for a trail to be built overland that would shortcut the more perilous water voyage north. By the time the Whatcom Trail was roughly laid out, the British had imposed a new requirement—that miners stop in Victoria on Vancouver Island first, thus undercutting the overland route. Meanwhile, the gold rush had moved east to the Cariboo.

As in many Puget Sound cities, Bellingham's economy started with exporting lumber from big trees. This "World's Tallest Christmas Tree" moves down Railroad Avenue on two trucks in 1949. Two cranes and fourteen trucks lifted the 153-foot tree upright, and it was decorated with more than a thousand lights. Newscaster Edward R. Murrow described the illumination in a national radio broadcast. Photo by Jack Carver, Whatcom Museum no. 1995.14.70.

When the miners decamped, the whoosh went out of Whatcom. By the 1880s, mills could use steam power instead of water to transport heavy logs, and mills moved farther away from the bay. A triumvirate of entrepreneurs—Peter Larson, J. H. Bloedel, and J. J. Donovan— started a lumber company on the banks of Lake Whatcom, the headwaters of Whatcom Creek, several miles east of town. Of the three men, Donovan became the city builder, the man whose impact earned him a bronze statue—but not in Whatcom.

As the Whatcom boom faded, the next village south—Sehome— grew around a coal mine. Two men who had come to work with Roeder discovered a coal deposit in a hole under the upturned roots of a fallen cedar tree. The discovery was exhilarating, but Roeder couldn't afford to start a mine himself. He carted a load of coal to the shoreline by wheelbarrow and sent an emissary to San Francisco to find investors. Under the Donation Land Act of 1850, early settlers could make large land claims, which came with mineral rights they could sell for coal mining. A group of investors secured land claims, bought the mineral rights, and formed the Bellingham Bay Coal Company in 1853. Under the leadership of Pierre Barlow Cornwall, the coal company built the mine, a wharf, bunkers, and a tramway in Sehome and brought sailing ships to deliver the coal to markets along the Pacific Coast, especially San Francisco. For a time, the mine made money, but in the long term, the coal proved to be of poor quality, and the mines were plagued by fires.

When the Sehome mine closed in 1878, a village on the bay was deflated once again, but the land belonged to the coal company, which would not let it rest for long. Cornwall suggested that the owners hang on to their real estate, and he formed the Bellingham Bay Improvement Company. So-called improvement companies were springing up all over Washington cities, usually with the goal of improving profits by selling real estate and investing in utilities and facilities. Cornwall was convinced that, based on "natural advantages, . . . someday Bellingham Bay would become the site of a great city."

A great city would need railroads. Cornwall was disappointed when the Northern Pacific chose Tacoma as its terminus in 1873, so he looked north instead of east for a connection. In 1883, he announced that the Bellingham Bay and British Columbia Railroad (BB & BC) would extend from Sehome north to connect with the Canadian transcontinental railroad at the border. That great plan went slightly awry when the first Canadian Pacific train arrived in town amid a Great Water Fight. Read all about it on Railroad Avenue.

With coal and gold booms subsiding, and a regional railroad built, Sehome and Whatcom merged to form New Whatcom in 1891, with the hope of spurring more growth. The BB & BC built a passenger depot near the waterfront in 1892. One year later, in the midst of a nationwide financial panic, the merged towns built a city hall high on a bluff overlooking the bay. A large cargo mill, cutting lumber for export, moved to the foot of the town dock. These improvements would become the core of downtown Bellingham, but not until Fairhaven had its day.

Such a welcoming name—Fairhaven—given by the town's first landowner, Daniel Jefferson Harris. His modest vision was quickly superseded, however, by the improvement company folk who envisioned "the next Chicago," an industrial city on the bay. Nelson Bennett, the man who had engineered the Northern Pacific's tunnel through Stampede Pass to Tacoma, came north bringing the rumor of another transcontinental railroad, the Great Northern, which was shopping for a terminus on Puget Sound. With J. J. Donovan and others, he formed the Fairhaven Land Company and bought out Harris's claim. By 1889, fearless railroad workers had blasted rocks along the waterfront with huge powder explosions and built the Fairhaven and Southern Railroad to reach Skagit Valley coalfields. Hoping the Great Northern would notice this energy, investors speculated wildly in land and built more brick buildings.

Instead, the Great Northern chose Seattle and Everett for its terminus. For the third time, a town on Bellingham Bay had to reinvent itself. First, Fairhaven gobbled up the village of Bellingham just to its north, where a coal mine had failed. It then joined neighboring New Whatcom in 1903, compromising on the name of the bay, Bellingham, for the new city. (Sir William Bellingham was a controller in the British Navy; his was one of many names George Vancouver sprinkled all over Puget Sound.) For a while, Bellingham was the fourth-largest city in the state.

Bellingham was well situated to extract the next natural resource the Pacific Northwest had to offer—salmon, so abundant that settlers had pitchforked the rotting fish for fertilizer. By the late 1800s, industrialists had figured out how to can and ship salmon vast distances without it spoiling. Large fish wheels scooped fish out of rivers, purse seiners plied the waters of Puget Sound and Alaska, and fish traps caught thousands of fish in underwater pens. By 1900, salmon in the Columbia River had already been overfished, and investment moved to canneries on Puget Sound. For the next forty years, Bellingham was at the center of the cannery universe, with access to fish in both Puget Sound and Alaska fisheries.

By 1925, there were eight canneries in Whatcom County, including two on Bellingham Bay, which packed almost 500,000 cases one year. Pacific American Fisheries (PAF) had the largest Pacific salmon cannery in the world at Fairhaven. The company set huge traps and employed thousands of workers in canneries on the docks from the early 1900s into the 1940s, until the salmon were almost wiped out.

As the towns on Bellingham Bay exported natural resources, they attracted workers. Scandinavians came to log. Croatians came to fish using purse seiners. South Asians brought in from Canada served as contract laborers largely in the lumber companies. At its peak, PAF employed 4,500 local residents and contracted with a Portland labor contractor, Goon Dip, for more than 1,000 Chinese laborers. They had the most unpleasant job—slitting and gutting the salmon. The company president, E. B. Deming, valued their work. "It is realized now that Chinese are not cheap labour," he noted during a labor shortage in 1902; "they are skilled and don't have to work for little money."

The Chinese had become more valued after the passage of national Chinese exclusion laws in 1882 and 1892, yet they experienced expulsion efforts and were confined to the waterfront area of Fairhaven. Many were displaced by the invention of a machine that would do the work of slitting and gutting. The South Asians (locally called Hindoos) were forcibly expelled by white laborers in 1907. The Asiatic Exclusion League, which was active in Bellingham, provided political pressure for national immigration laws that ended all Asian immigration to the United States in the early twentieth century. Anti-foreigner sentiment, aimed not only at Asians but at blacks and Catholics as well, continued into the 1920s, even in times of prosperity; in 1926, 780 Ku Klux Klan members paraded on Cornwall Avenue.

The vast exploitation of fisheries could not last; conservation efforts began with hatcheries, including one built at Whatcom Falls Park in 1936. In the 1930s, the state banned fish traps on Puget Sound, and canning moved to Alaska. PAF continued providing cans for a couple of decades but closed in 1966 after Alaska banned fish traps, and tuna became the canned fish of choice. The waterfront quieted along Bellingham Bay.

By the 1950s, the extractive industries on which Bellingham had grown—logging, mining, fishing, and canning—were no longer the basis of the regional or city economy. Sawmills, shingle mills, coal mines, and canneries had closed, leaving downtowns in decline. One pulp and paper mill remained on the waterfront. In the 1960s, Bellingham thought that an interstate highway running right through the middle of the city might revive the downtown core, but instead, I-5 divided the city a mile and a half east of downtown. Retailers cooperated to build a parking garage but were unsuccessful in fighting a vast mall to the northeast of the city, right off I-5, attractive to shoppers from Canada.

Yet early citizens had the foresight to encourage Bellingham institutions that would sustain it through leaner years, the ventures that anchor a community. With the support of land and funding from J. J. Donovan, the timber-wealthy son of Irish immigrants, two Sisters of Providence opened a thirty-bed hospital in 1891 that grew into the biggest employer in Whatcom County. Ella Higginson was already a distinguished writer when she walked those muddy Sehome streets in her boots. After the coal mine closed and Sehome deflated, she proposed a teacher training school. She and her husband, Russell, a druggist and real estate investor, helped launch it on ten acres donated by the land and improvement companies on Sehome Hill.

At first, Whatcom Normal College offered only one year of higher education, which was all teachers needed. By 1933, three years were required, then four, leading to a bachelor's degree. After World War II, the Western Washington College of Education expanded its curriculum to serve veterans attending school on the GI Bill. By 1961 it was Western Washington State College, and by 1977, a university, with enrollment increasing from 3,000 students to more than 10,000.

The city has not always been comfortable with a university in its midst. In 1935, a Bellingham committee investigated President Charles Fisher for contaminating the student body with "dangerously radical and subversive ideas." The investigation found no basis for the charge, but Governor Clarence Martin removed him three years later. A fountain on campus now carries his name. Dr. Eunice Faber, the first black professor hired at Western, in 1959, was fired in 1962 when she married a white man. She was reinstated after contesting the removal before the state Human Rights Commission. More protests came in 1970, when students opposing the Vietnam War closed a portion of I-5.

That same year, Huxley College of Environmental Studies was created at Western, an emphasis that has spilled down the hill, swaying Bellingham toward a recreation- and environment-friendly city wary of industrial expansion. A two-mile trail below the bluff reclaims railroad right-of-way for pedestrians and cyclists. Students from Western's technology department created the proposal for Boulevard Park on the trail just south of what had been a coal dock. With environmentalists in training on the hill, the county plans to clean up thirteen contaminated sites around the bay. Native son and journalist Fred Moody claims Bellingham has become a refuge from ambition, a city of underachievers. "It is a reluctant jewel of a city," he writes, "trying to be both commercial mecca and retreat from civilization."

Despite this reluctance, Bellingham's prime location at the eastern end of the Strait of Juan de Fuca, with its access to the Pacific Ocean and to Canada and Alaska, continues to attract industry. The issues have shifted from resource extraction to transporting, refining, and exporting resources from other regions of the country through ports on Puget Sound. Heavy industries have located just north of Bellingham: an aluminum smelter in Ferndale; an oil refinery at Cherry Point, which receives oil brought by oceangoing tankers; a pipeline; and railcars. Fuel is shipped out by truck and the Olympic Pipeline.

These industries have environmental and social costs. In 1895 an explosion at the Blue Canyon Coal Mine on Lake Whatcom killed twenty-three miners. In 1999, gasoline in the Olympic Pipeline spilled and exploded along the very creek where the village of Whatcom had started. The Georgia-Pacific pulp mill contaminated Bellingham Bay with mercury before closing in 2001. A proposed deepwater marine terminal at Cherry Point, if built, would vastly increase exports of coal and the number of trains that hog the waterfront in Bellingham. This coal is coming not from the old mines under Sehome Hill but from Wyoming. The county will decide whether to permit expansion of a coal terminal at Cherry Point, once a Lummi harvest fishing site called Xwe' chi' eXen. The proposal has highlighted the century-old conflict between industrial expansion and the protection of natural resources.

This walk traces Bellingham's industrial and social history. It follows a military road, an old village trail, the waterfront of Bellingham Bay, trestles that carried railroads, and the landscaped paths of a university. The hike begins at the site of the first sawmill on Whatcom Creek, then follows the bay through downtown Bellingham to Fairhaven and cannery heaven. It climbs Sehome Hill to Western and a broad view of the mountains, forests, islands, and bay that counterbalance ambition in this reluctant jewel.

Bellingham Loop

START: Whatcom County Courthouse, 311 Grand Avenue at Lottie Street

DIRECTIONS: From I-5, take exit 254 toward State Street. Turn left onto Iowa Street, left onto N State Street, right onto E Champion Street, and right onto Grand Avenue.

DISTANCES: 7 miles round trip (may be done in parts)

AMENITIES: Metered parking on streets near the courthouse, city hall, and Bellingham Public Library; restrooms at Maritime Heritage Park; Whatcom Transit Authority Station; Boulevard Park; Taylor Dock; Marine Park; and the Amtrak terminal in Fairhaven

The Bellingham loop follows a century and a half of settlement, business, industry, and education through a stunning landscape with Mount Baker to the east and Bellingham Bay to the west. The walk begins in the oldest and most weathered part of town, the early village of Whatcom, and winds through the second village of Sehome. At the southern edge of old Sehome, the walk straightens out on a railroad grade along the waterfront to Fairhaven. An optional climb to Western Washington University lifts the walker above the bay and the fray. Both walks return to the first settlement on Whatcom Creek.

Begin your walk where the boom began in 1852, on a bluff above Bellingham Bay. A **totem carving** in front of the county courthouse, *on the southwest corner of Grand Avenue and Lottie Street,* depicts the arrival of Henry Roeder and Russell Peabody, the first of many men looking for an opportunity. The carving by Lummi artist Joseph Hillaire places the men in a canoe with Lummi leaders Ts-likw and Cha-wit-zit, who guided them to the **falls on Whatcom Creek**, a perfect site to power a sawmill.

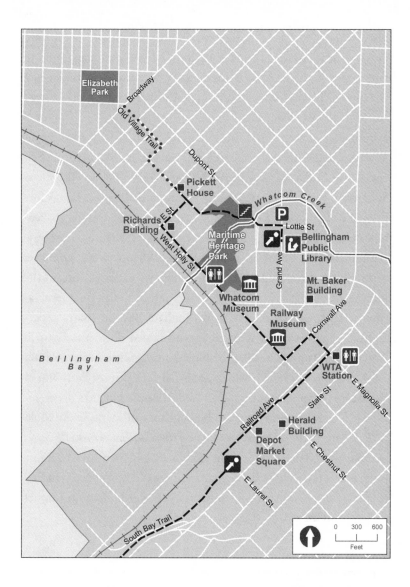

Walk west on Lottie Street to Prospect/Dupont Street, and cross **Pickett Bridge** *on Dupont.* The bridge was part of a military road built by U.S. Army captain George Pickett just a few years after Roeder and Peabody arrived. The road went as far south as the coal mine at Sehome.

On the north side of the bridge, take steps on the west down to the first landing to see the **falls**. The sawmill operated intermittently until 1873, when it burned. The Washington Colony, a utopian group of twenty-five families from Kansas, took over the mill, but it was abandoned by 1885 as large milling and lumber operations moved east to Lake Whatcom.

Continue down the trail in Maritime Heritage Park to the fish-holding pond at the Perry Center for Fisheries and Aquaculture Sciences, and find a map of the **old Village Trail**. The old village was Whatcom, the first of four strung out along Bellingham Bay before they joined forces as Bellingham. *Follow the trail* upslope to **Peabody Hill**, high ground above Whatcom Creek where a blockhouse was built by that same Captain Pickett. Blockhouses were a common protection settlers used for shelter at night in times of threat. The Lummi had signed treaties in 1855 and agreed to live on a reservation on the peninsula north of Bellingham Bay, but both settlers and natives feared northern tribes who raided down the coast in large warrior canoes. Besides the blockhouse, Pickett's soldiers built a fort three miles north, which soon fell into disuse. Early life in Whatcom was precarious, as portrayed in Annie Dillard's novel *The Living*. Dillard spent five years in Bellingham while writing the book.

Reach the **Pickett House***, set back on the southeast corner of F Street and Bancroft.* Built in 1856, at the time of early settlement, the house is the oldest building in Bellingham and the oldest wooden building in the state still on its own foundation. It was built from lumber milled from the Roeder-Peabody sawmill.

Pickett House

Captain George Pickett lived in this house with his Native American wife, Morning Mist. She died shortly after their son, James Tilton Pickett, was born in 1857. Pickett resigned his commission in the U.S. Army in 1861, left his son with a local family, and returned to his native Virginia to fight for the South in the Civil War. James grew up to be an artist and claimed the family home, but he never again saw his father and died at age thirty-two of typhoid and tuberculosis. The house was deeded to the Washington State Historical Society in 1936.

You may follow the old village trail two more blocks northwest along Bancroft through the neighborhood known as the Lettered Streets, then one block northeast on H Street (another one of those letters), and three blocks northwest on Clinton to reach **Elizabeth Park**, a park named after Roeder's wife, Elizabeth.

Continue the main walk into a more weathered Whatcom. *Walk down E Street toward the waterfront (there is no sidewalk)* to the **T. G. Richards and Company** building, the first and oldest brick building in Washington, *at 1308 E Street.* Thomas Richards, his brother Charles, and a third investor, all from San Francisco, built the warehouse and store in 1858, when several thousand miners camped on the beaches, waiting for the construction of a trail to the Fraser River gold rush. Built with brick shipped as ballast in ships from Philadelphia around Cape Horn through San Francisco, the building outlasted the gold rush, then became the county courthouse, jail, and center of social and political life. Described by historian Lelah Jackson Edson as a "tired, old building" more than a half century ago, it still sits near the original shoreline, surrounded by recycling activity.

Walk one block south on W Holly Street, the main business street of the village of Whatcom, *to D Street* and then an optional block west to the **Great Northern Railway passenger depot**, dating from 1927. The original tracks of the Fairhaven and Southern Railway were built on a high trestle over the waterfront. A long viaduct led from the trestle across the tideflats to the Whatcom Wharf. When the Great Northern took over the railway, it moved the tracks onshore and erected this brick passenger depot. It no longer functions as a station, but the Bellingham name is visible under the roofline.

Continue south on Holly to C Street. The shoreline here has been greatly altered by landfill. In 1883, the Washington Colony, the group that took over Roeder's sawmill, built a dock nearly a mile long to reach deep water and sailing ships in the bay. In the early 1900s, Whatcom Creek was dredged and widened to accommodate the larger ships that would come through the Panama Canal, anticipated in 1914. Dredged material was used to fill in the tideflats and create industrial land. Today, C Street extends along the south side of the Whatcom Waterway on the Colony wharf. Pulp and paper mills operated by Georgia Pacific were successors to the sawmills, claiming the waterfront for forty years until 2001, when they closed and left the large vacant hulks on the west side of Roeder Avenue.

On the east side of Holly Street, **Maritime Heritage Park** occupies landfill that replaced the beach; the homeless sit on benches where miners once camped. On fall days when the salmon are running, anglers line Whatcom Creek, casting for the fish that swim up the creek and attempt the falls but mostly flail against a metal gate, returning to the hatchery where they were born to be collected for artificial spawning. All aquatic life within three miles of the creek was killed during the Olympic Pipeline explosion in 1999, but restoration efforts have supported the return of salmon to the seasonal fishing camp at the mouth of the creek.

Olympic Pipeline Explosion

On June 10, 1999, gasoline leaked from a rupture in the underground Olympic Pipeline, which carries fuel from the refinery at Ferndale north of Bellingham to terminals in Seattle and Portland. The gasoline exploded upstream in Whatcom Falls Park and killed three youths fishing and playing along the creek. The leak spilled 277,200 gallons of gasoline into the creek and ignited a fireball that plunged 1.5 miles downstream, reaching I-5 but not downtown Bellingham. The tragedy led to the Washington Pipeline Safety Act of 2000, which allows the state to inspect intrastate pipelines. Banks of the creek that burned in the explosions have been restored. Pleasant trails in Whatcom Falls Park follow Whatcom Creek and the grade of a railroad that carried lumber and coal from industries on Lake Whatcom, including the Bloedel-Donovan lumber mill, to Bellingham.

Explore trails along both sides of Whatcom Creek, if you wish, then *continue on Holly to Champion Street.* At this intersection, on the west side of Holly, you will find the first of three cornerstones that mark the boundaries between the four original villages of Bellingham and describe the heyday of each. This boundary between Whatcom and Sehome was marked by an iron bolt driven into solid rock. It divided the land claims of Russell Peabody, the Whatcom founder, from Edmund Fitzhugh, a Sehome man. "Good-bye Iron Bolt," read the newspaper headline when the citizens voted to merge. Together the two towns built a **city hall**, which commands the bluff over the park as the city's major landmark. Steps in Maritime Heritage Park lead up to the museum, or you may visit it as the last stop on the longer loop.

Walk south on Holly into downtown Bellingham, which was the old town of Sehome, whose first boom came from a coal mine. Although coal mining failed, Sehome's hopes soared again between 1891 and 1893 at the prospect of a terminus for the transcontinental railroad (you've heard that one before). Entrepreneurs constructed buildings that promised wealth and stability. The **Oakland Block**, *in a triangle on the east side of Holly at 310–318,* housed the new city's offices until the city hall was completed in 1892. The Great Northern disappointed the town, but the merger of Sehome and Whatcom spurred new growth, evidenced by the **Flatiron Building**, built in 1907–8 *on the triangle formed by Bay, Prospect, and Champion Streets.* Note the mural of early 1900s Bellingham on the wall *at the triangular corner of Holly and Prospect.* All these triangles resulted from combining the different street grids.

Continue on Holly, crossing Commercial Street (the street signs are overhead and visible in only one direction on the one-way street) with a view of the **Mount Baker Building** and the tip of **Mount Baker** itself to the east. Unlike Seattle and Tacoma, where the full majesty of Mount Rainier is a backdrop to the city, Mount Baker is shielded by foothills and only partially visible from sea level on a clear day. *Continue one more block to Cornwall Avenue,* named for Pierre Barlow Cornwall, the primary coal mine investor. **Bellingham National Bank**, whose president was Victor A. Roeder, the son of Whatcom's founder, anchors *the southeast corner of Holly and Cornwall.*

Walk east on Cornwall one block to Magnolia Street. Most of the east side of this block was owned by Jacob "Jake" Beck, a brewer of Whatcom Beer. With wealth from a saloon and his Grand View Hotel, Beck built a splendid theater in 1902, but when Washington voters approved prohibition in 1910, saloons went out of business. Beck was able to save the theater but lost his hotel to the bank. His theater-turned-movie-house was razed in 1959, when this block became department store row.

Turn south one block on Magnolia to wide **Railroad Avenue**, the original right-of-way of the military road, usurped for the route of regional railroads. At different times, Railroad Avenue accommodated engines, tracks, switching yards, horse-drawn freight wagons, and trolleys. The contemporary avenue accommodates median trees and four rows of diagonal parking. This intersection remains a transportation center with a public lobby and restrooms in the **WTA Station** on the southeast corner. The **tracks** of a spur line leading toward the waterfront are still visible in the alley south of Railroad Avenue.

The Bellingham Bay and Eastern Railroad, constructed by J. J. Donovan, hauled coal through town from the Blue Canyon mine on Lake Whatcom to a coal and timber wharf on the bay. Donovan also had a hand in the Bellingham Bay and British Columbia (BB & BC)

Railroad, which eventually established a connection to Canada. A **kiosk** on the southwest corner of *Railroad and Magnolia* describes the Great Water Fight, which started as a celebration of the first Canadian Pacific train to arrive in town in 1891 and ended as a fiasco.

Walk west on Railroad Avenue. Although Bellingham never became another Chicago, as founders hoped, some business district buildings incorporated the "Chicago style" of architecture, known also as the Commercial style, which emphasized function over form. One is the **Bellingham Candy Company** building *at 1321–1327 Railroad.* Across the street is the **Spokane Block**, *at 1322–1324 Railroad,* which had rooms to let above and still has a feed store on the ground floor.

Between Chestnut and Maple on Railroad was the wholesale district of New Whatcom, once bristling with warehouses, machine shops, boardinghouses, and lunchrooms for warehouse workers. The station and office for the BB & BC and a hotel occupied what is now **Depot Market Square**. On the other side of the street, the **Washington Grocery Building**, at *1133 Railroad Avenue,* stored groceries waiting to be transported. With trains no longer loading wares, condos are changing the district's tone. The grocery company building provides low-income housing.

Continue another block through an apartment development to Laurel and an overlook of the southeast side of Bellingham Bay. There were seven sawmills and three shingle mills around the bay by 1890. The **Sehome coal mine** was located at the base of the bluff near here, in the present railroad yards. The first dock in Sehome was one block northwest, at the foot of Cornwall Avenue, then known as Dock Street. It extended to the waterfront. Coal was carried by railroad on a trestle out across the water so that it could be dumped directly into waiting ships.

This ends a one-way exploration of downtown Bellingham. To complete a longer loop and follow industrial history along the shore of Bellingham Bay, *veer southeast a half block to an alley where the railroad ran. On the south side of the street, find the posts with yellow stripes that mark* the start of the **South Bay Trail**, a two-mile walking and biking trail on railroad grade and boardwalks. The trail passes by the third old village—Bellingham—to reach the fourth—Fairhaven. **Numbered signs** on posts identify sites along the way—a story of railroads, lumber mills, coal export, canneries, and pollution.

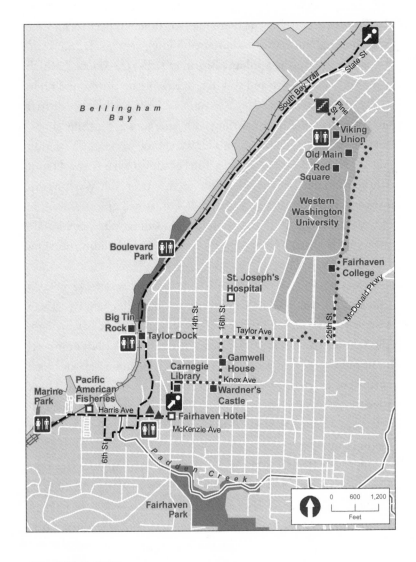

The trail begins on the grade of the old Northern Pacific tracks, on a long **trestle** that left the shore and stretched across the bay, avoiding the muddy tideflats. Most of the mill and dock sites are not visible through the trees except in winter. One huge endeavor was the Bellingham Bay Improvement Company Mill (#20 on the signs), which had a 1,200-foot-long wharf and access to railroad tracks for exporting logs by sea and land. It was sold in 1913 to Bloedel and Donovan, the men who started a lumber company on Lake Whatcom, and then to the Port of Bellingham in 1947. For more than forty years you could have heard one-ton Big Ole, the steam whistle at the mill. It blew for fifteen minutes nonstop, emptying the entire steam reservoir, to announce the end of World War I. The whistle is now on the Western Washington University campus and has been used for earthquake drills.

At about the 0.5-mile point, white plastic tarps are visible covering the site of the **Cornwall Landfill**, a dump at the end of Cornwall Avenue used for municipal waste from 1953 to 1965. The tarps cover sediment dredged from Squalicum Harbor, forming a buffer that slants away from the bay to prevent and contain contamination.

The **cornerstone marker** between Whatcom (now downtown Bellingham) and Fairhaven comes at the *1.2-mile point. At 1.4 miles, cross* the Burlington Northern Railroad tracks to reach **Boulevard Park**, which has replaced industrial land with lawns, benches, paved walkways over the waterfront, restrooms, and a playground. The coal dock for the Bellingham Bay Coal Company mine stuck out into the bay just north of the park. Pattle Point, named for the first white settler who found coal, is at the south end of the park. The boardwalk derives from a railroad trestle built out over the water on pilings because the Great Northern had monopolized the shoreline (#13). The shoreline tracks of the BNSF remain active, carrying loads of oil to a refinery at Cherry Point north of Bellingham and coal to Vancouver, BC, for export.

As you near Fairhaven, the story turns to canneries. By 1902,

During the salmon season, 700 women filled tins and labeled or packed cans of fish into cases at Pacific American Fisheries, the largest employer of women in Bellingham when this photo was taken in 1906. Photo by Asahel Curtis, Whatcom Museum no. 1973.24.159.

Fairhaven was the site of eight fish canning and packing companies. Pilings visible from the walkway mark the residue of two salmon warehouses and the Pacific Sheet Metal can factory. In 1899, the factory produced 27 million cans and still could not fill the demand from Puget Sound canneries. What looks like a rock between the shoreline and the walkway is actually the **Big Tin Rock** (#12), a pile of tin discarded in the process of making cans.

Fish Traps

Canneries drove pilings near a salmon migration route and enclosed the pilings with wire net. The trap gathered fish until they could be dipped out into the hold of a ship, which carried them to the canneries. One fish trap could hold an estimated thirty tons of fish.

Walk to shore at **Taylor Dock**, past benches, restrooms, and parking. *The South Bay Trail continues south on 10th Street for a block, resumes life as a gravel trail, and comes out at Mill Avenue. You will pass another* **cornerstone marker** for the boundary between the third village, old Bellingham, which was the site of the Pattle coal mine, and the fourth village, Fairhaven.

Walk one more block to **Harris Avenue**, the main street in Fairhaven, named after its first landowner, Daniel Jefferson Harris (referred to in more colloquial accounts as "Dirty" Dan Harris because of his unkempt appearance; he was, after all, the first settler). *Follow Harris west* past Padden Creek Lagoon. More than fifty paving-stone markers in Fairhaven designate historic sites, including several in the vegetation strip between the sidewalk and Harris. One marks "Sam Low's opium den." Respectable women did not venture this way, and Chinese cannery workers who lived in bunkhouses on the waterfront could not venture in the other direction.

Continue past the lagoon and the transportation hubs to reach the end of Harris. Walk south on the sidewalk to **Marine Park**. You are approaching the earliest alleged European history on Bellingham Bay. This spot of green and shoreline access has been variously known as Poe's Point, Deadman's Point, Commercial Point, Post Point, and now Marine Park. It is unclear exactly who died here—Spanish pirates attacked by a coalition of hostile tribes or local Indians attacked by raiders from the north. Both events exist in oral tradition and neither in recorded history. Clearly this is a point at which anyone arriving by sea might attempt to land. Harris sold the county four acres on the point for a graveyard, making it Graveyard Point for a few years before the graves were moved.

Return from the park past the Bellingham Cruise Terminal for the Alaska Ferry, a reminder of the city's ties to the north. The site of the multimodal transportation terminal for Amtrak and Greyhound was the headquarters of the most important industry in the city. By 1907, 65 percent of Bellingham's jobs were found in Fairhaven, and most were at Pacific American Fisheries. PAF grew to a company with thirty canneries under the leadership of E. B. Deming from Chicago. Take some time to sit on the bench in the terminal and look at a **mural** that depicts the huge cannery in action, including a picture of 25,000 fish on the floor. The steam whistle from the boiler room of the cannery could be heard three or four times a day. Until the fish gave out, this was Bellingham's most persistent boom.

With the decline of the canneries, the Port of Bellingham, formed in 1920, bought out PAF land, dry docks, and shipyards and began cleaning pollution from the waterfront. Some sites were redeveloped, including the terminals and Marine Park where the PAF shipyard had been, but many dilapidated buildings were demolished, leaving a relatively empty stretch of Harris. Where shipyards once flourished, the Fairhaven shipyard still has a floating dry dock for ship repair. Where Puget Sound Pulp and Timber processed logs, another business offers yacht service.

Walk east on Harris to 6th Street, and walk about a block south on

6th to a trail that goes both west and east. *Walk east toward Fairhaven* through early history: the site of Harris's cabin and land claim, an Indian campsite dating archaeologically from 1500 B.C., and a bunk-house that housed some of the thousand Chinese workers in the canneries. PAF depended for workers on a Chinese labor contractor named Goon Dip, whom Deming described variously as "shrewd, generous, fair, just, businesslike," and "the best known member of the Chinese race in the entire Northwest."

Fairhaven Park

Fairhaven Park, designed by the Olmsted brothers, was an auto camp-ground on Highway 99, the first north–south highway through the state. The park includes the trailhead for the Interurban Trail, a biking and walking trail that follows the old Fairhaven and Southern Railway grade six miles south to Larrabee State Park, land donated by a Fairhaven founder, C. X. Larrabee. Find the trailhead marked by brown posts with yellow stripes at Donovan and 12th Street.

At a junction in the trail, head east toward Fairhaven Park, but before the park, take the spur to **McKenzie Avenue**. McKenzie, extending to the waterfront, was the red-light district in a town with thirty saloons. That all changed in 1910, when a baseball player turned evangelist brought his national prohibition campaign to town. Wil-liam Ashley "Billy" Sunday preached to crowds that reached 25,000 a day at a temporary tabernacle in downtown Bellingham. His con-verts persuaded forty-six saloons in Bellingham to close. Nothing remains of the district except the trail and a set of concrete steps leading to a vacant lot.

One block east on McKenzie, take 9th Street back to Harris Avenue. Follow Harris east through Fairhaven's boom days, when forty real estate offices sold land. The **Bellingham Bay Hotel**, *mid-block* *between 9th and 10th at 909–911 Harris,* was a response to cannery employees' need for lodging. The **Morgan Block**, *on the southeast corner of 10th and Harris,* housed a hotel on the top floor and a saloon on the bottom. The **Terminal Building**, *at the northeast corner of Harris and 11th,* is the oldest surviving commercial building in Fairhaven, built in 1889. The bank in the **Nelson Block** *on the southeast corner of 11th and Harris* bankrolled the second boom in the early 1900s. The **Monahan Building**, *mid-block at 1209 11th Street,* opened as a saloon that catered to respectable people in 1891. The **Mason Block**, now Sycamore Square, *on the southeast corner of 12th and Harris,* housed five of those forty real estate offices as well as Russell Higginson's drug store.

The most opulent building of all was the Fairhaven Hotel, which towered above the others at 12th and Harris. Built in the tradition of grand railroad hotels, it hosted the likes of writer Mark Twain. The hotel became a luxurious in-town home for C. X. Larrabee, a founder of the Fairhaven Land Company, but did not survive past the 1950s. The site is now an abandoned gas station, a sore thumb left in boutique Fairhaven.

You will find **two bronzed men** claiming benches in Fairhaven: Daniel Harris and J. J. Donovan. First settler Harris hangs out, as might be expected, on the village green *on 10th Street between Mill and Harris.* Donovan, who had his hand in almost everything—coal mines, railroads, lumber mills, and a library, hospital, college, and church—is regarded as the most important man in Fairhaven history. *At 11th and Harris,* he is sitting on a bench writing a letter to his bride, Clara, which includes a sketch of the curve of Bellingham Bay showing the four towns.

Walk north on 12th to the **Carnegie Library** *at 1117 12th Street.* Libraries across the country were funded by money from steel magnate Andrew Carnegie. The Fairhaven Library provided an alternative to saloons as a place for men to spend their evenings. It still provides space for curious readers, a refuge from cold and dampness, and a rest for tired walkers. From here, you may return to Bellingham or explore South Hill and climb to Western Washington University.

Extended Walk: South Hill and Western Washington University

START: Fairhaven Library, 1117 12th Street

DIRECTIONS: See Bellingham Loop.

DISTANCE: 3 miles one-way, with elevation gain

AMENITIES: Restrooms at Viking Union at Western Washington University; street parking in Fairhaven

Beyond the industries on the bay and the brick buildings of downtown Fairhaven were the lower streets of South Hill, home to the many who came to work in fisheries and canneries. In the early 1900s, the modest homes on 10th, 11th, 12th, and 13th Streets were occupied by Croatian families who had come from the island of Vis in the Adriatic Sea. They were recruited by a large cannery near Astoria, Oregon, but settled up and down the West Coast. In Bellingham, men took purse seiners out to fish; women worked seasonally in the canneries and in large web houses, just south of the docks at the end of Taylor Avenue, where nets were made and maintained. When the fishing fleet was ready to leave for Alaska at the beginning of the summer, a priest from the Sacred Heart Church would bless the boats on the docks, asking for a bountiful and safe season.

South Hill is the south slope of Sehome Hill, where the Higginsons and J. J. Donovan proposed the state's third teachers' college in 1895. The Bellingham Bay Improvement Company and the Fairhaven Land Company offered ten acres for the school, near the Higginsons' home overlooking the bay. The hills, with coal mines underneath, have been a natural barrier separating Western Washington University on top from the city below, adding to the traditional separation between town and gown. Reaching the top of the hill is both a meta-phorical and physical climb to higher education.

One route to the university is to return to the South Bay Trail and walk 1.8 miles to the Pine Street staircase, which leads uphill on streets and steps to the university. You may also take a WTA bus from Fairhaven. The route described here climbs South Hill, reaching the south end of the WWU campus and walking north on wooded trails from there. This is not a casual stroll.

Starting at the Fairhaven Library, *walk north to Knox Avenue, then east to 14th Street. On the southeast corner, at 1100 14th,* is **Sacred Heart Catholic Church**, built in 1912. When the Church of the Assumption, the first Catholic church, moved north in the city, south siders asked for a parish of their own. Sacred Heart served a largely Slavic congregation.

Continue east, passing **Wardner's Castle** *at 1103 15th on the southeast corner of 15th and Knox.* Jim Wardner spent one year in Fairhaven and made $62,000 in sixty days selling lots. He built this house and then left for South Africa in 1891. In his autobiography, Wardner described his life as having a "feverish haste for gain." The twenty-three-room house was designed by Kirtland Cutter, an architect who earned fame building mansions in Spokane. The house was occupied for a long time by the Earles family; John Earles was a vice president of Puget Sound Sawmills & Timber Company on the Fairhaven wharf, the largest shingle mill in the world.

Walk uphill to 16th Street and one block north to Douglas Avenue. On the southeast corner at 1001 16th is the **Gamwell House**. The mansion built during the first boom in 1890–92 is a reminder of Fairhaven's aspirations. Roland Gamwell was a real estate agent from Boston with a preference for the Queen Anne style. He hired a Boston architect to design both his home and the Fairhaven Hotel, whose extravagance could not be maintained.

Continue north on 16th to Taylor Avenue, a longtime tobogganing hill, *and then walk east to 17th.* The house on the northeast corner was built in 1929 by the second generation of the family who owned the Bellingham Canning Company.

Two more blocks north, at 17th and Adams, was the original site of St. Joseph's, the first hospital in Whatcom County. As the most prominent Catholic in town, J. J. Donovan persuaded the Fairhaven Land Company to donate this block to two Sisters of Providence. They opened the hospital in 1891 with thirty beds and fresh vegetables served from the sisters' own garden. The site was traded for one on Forest when a new hospital was built in 1900–1901. PeaceHealth St. Joseph, which has moved farther north, is now the largest employer in Whatcom County.

Continue east on Taylor Avenue, going down steps when the street ends and continuing to 25th, sometimes on sidewalks and sometimes on trails. At 25th, turn north one block to McDonald Parkway. Cross McDonald Parkway and continue on 25th past the entrance to the Sehome Hill Arboretum. Find the trailhead for the Fairhaven Trail, which skirts the Arboretum and passes Fairhaven College on the way to the center of the campus. As the trail begins to climb, choose an exit trail, such as the one at Miller Hall, onto the campus of Western Washington University, a complex of residences, classroom buildings, library, performing arts center, student union, outdoor sculpture collection, and more. Compared to the two other Washington universities that started as normal schools, Eastern Washington University at Cheney and Central Washington University in Ellensburg, Western Washington University is the largest. From its modest beginnings, Western has expanded to cover 215 acres, with smaller college campuses within it.

Pick up a map at the **Viking Union** information counter or check kiosks along the walkways. Be sure to find **Old Main**, the first building, on the northern end of the campus up against the hillside; **Edens Hall**, an early dormitory; another dormitory, **Higginson Hall**, named for the Higginsons; **Red Square**, with its Fisher Fountain, named for the president who was fired for his liberal views; and the plaza next

When Martin Luther King Jr. was assassinated in April 1968, students at Western Washington University held a fifteen-minute silent vigil, the first public event on the new Red Square. Photo by Jack Carver, Whatcom Museum no. 1995.129822.

to Viking Union for its view of Bellingham Bay and all the walking you have done. *Come down from the heights on Pine Street to the South Bay trail.*

On the South Bay trail, *return to downtown Bellingham by retracing your route north. Exit the trail at State Street and loop back past* the **Herald Building** *at State and Chestnut.* The sign on top proclaims the prominence of the *Bellingham Herald* but is more visible from a distance. *Continue two blocks more on State to Magnolia; turn west three blocks to a triangle* formed by Magnolia, Commercial, and Champion streets, noting the railroad tracks in the alley between State and Railroad Avenue as you pass. The **Mount Baker Building**, a former theater, sits on Champion Street across from the triangle and mirrors with its tower a view of Mount Baker to the east.

Walk west one block on Champion to Prospect and then north one block to **Old City Hall**, *121 Prospect Street,* the Victorian landmark designed by local architect Alfred Lee. The hall sits on the bluff facing two directions. Since 1941, the hall has housed the Whatcom Museum of History and Art. *This walk ends two blocks north and one block east at the new city hall on Lottie Street, where you started the full loop.*

Resources Bellingham Public Library, 210 Central Avenue

Bellingham Railway Museum, 1320 Commercial Avenue

Fairhaven Library, 1117 12th Street

Visitor Information Center, 904 Potter Street

Whatcom Museum of History and Art, 121 Prospect Street

CHAPTER EIGHT

Yakima

Hub of the Valley

Ten acres of land will make you rich.

Anonymous boosters

Yakima history is Yakima Valley history, and the history of the valley is irrigation. "A history of irrigation in the Yakima Valley comes near being a history of everything," wrote historian W. D. Lyman in 1919.

The Yakima River emerges from the Cascade Mountains and flows southeast to join the Columbia River, threading the 200-mile length of the Yakima Valley in central Washington. The Naches River flows into the valley from the west. The city of Yakima sits at the confluence of the two rivers, between two sagebrush-swept ridges, Selah Ridge to the north and Ahtanum Ridge to the south. Prosperity depends on the snowpack in the mountains and the flow of the rivers.

Yakima is the shipping center for the valley's produce. With only a few tall buildings, wide-open streets, and near-empty hills stretching for miles around, Yakima hardly feels urban, yet it is the eighth-largest city in the state. It developed later than cities on Puget Sound or cities closer to the Columbia River. By the mid-1700s there were horses, providing wealth and mobility to the Yakama people. By the 1840s, the Yakama were also raising cattle traded from Fort Vancouver.

Following treaty negotiations and a brief war in 1855 and 1856, fourteen groups were consolidated into the Yakama Indian Nation (*Yakama* was the spelling on the treaty). They were given a 2,000-square-mile reservation southwest of the confluence of the Yakima and Naches, 13 percent of the land they had ceded.

Ranchers then swept into the valley. According to John Thorp, a settler who came in 1861, "A luxuriant carpet of nutritious bunch grass made the sagebrush hills a veritable paradise to cattle and horses." Thousands of cattle were driven to mining camps in Canada, and sheep followed. In this semiarid environment, the hillsides were soon overgrazed. With only eight inches of rainfall a year, farming was a challenge. "Ten acres of land will make you rich," boosters promised, but that wasn't quite true. By 1884, Yakima City was a town of merely 400 at the mouth of Ahtanum Creek.

As in many Washington cities, prosperity began with railroads, and, for Yakima, irrigation came shortly thereafter. The Northern Pacific Railway planned to pass through the valley on its way to Puget Sound. In a story recounted often in Washington history textbooks, the railroad said Yakima City was unsuitable either because the land was "swampy" or because owners wanted too high a price for their land. Instead, the railroad built a track and depot four miles north, where the land was unclaimed, and invited businesses to move there. More than a hundred did, very slowly. Structures were hoisted onto wagons or rolling logs and pulled by teams of horses or twenty mules. (A panorama at the Yakima Valley Museum portrays the move.) Hotel residents kept their rooms as the buildings rolled along, and business continued in the stores, with customers tying up their horses to the moving rail while making purchases. The new town was called North Yakima, but it changed its name to Yakima in 1918 to satisfy the post office; what had been Yakima City became Union Gap, and eventually the two melded into one.

In the years after the railroad arrived, Yakima grew slowly but steadily. Millions of sheep were shipped by train to Chicago and

Omaha. The first wine grapes were planted in the valley in 1869, the first hops in 1872, and the first commercial fruit orchard in 1887. While Olympia was given the state capital, Seattle the state university, and Walla Walla the state prison, Yakima received the state fair, which first opened in 1894. The fair provided a place for farmers to learn more profitable ways of farming.

The railroad opened the Yakima Valley to markets but needed products to ship. Its land grants in the valley were a hard sell despite ample sunshine and water power and rich soil nutrients from volcanic eruptions. Irrigation had not yet been widely successful. Individuals had tried digging ditches. Jesuit missionaries at Ahtanum Mission dug an irrigation ditch in 1852, and Yakama chief Kamiakin irrigated his garden nearby. Thomas and Benton Goodwin dug a ditch from the Yakima River in 1886 to water their five-acre wheat crop. But most individual farmers had neither the capital nor the labor to maintain large irrigation systems. So in 1889 the Northern Pacific formed the Yakima Canal and Land Company and the Washington Irrigation Company, which built the Sunnyside Canal southeast of Yakima, the largest irrigation canal in the Northwest at that time.

Even these larger private efforts were insufficient. Greedy landowners filed claims for water they did not need, and competing farmers sabotaged dams and threatened violence to forcibly take their share. The values of personal freedom and private property had to give way to government supervision in order to allocate water rights and build reservoirs for periods of low flow. It took the clout of the railroad and eastern investors and politicians to persuade the federal government to provide the type of large-scale irrigation that would be profitable. The most important event in the valley's development was the passage of the federal Reclamation Act of 1902, which provided aid for large-scale irrigation. President Theodore Roosevelt paraded down Yakima Avenue a year later to tout the legislation.

Under the Reclamation Act, the Yakima Project was authorized in 1905 to irrigate a 175-mile strip of land along the Yakima River. The project acquired the Sunnyside Canal, began construction of the Rim-rock Dam on the Tieton River west of Yakima, and constructed a string of canals and reservoirs along the Yakima River starting at the glacial lakes Keechelus, Kachess, and Cle Elum in the Central Cascades. Eventually there were nearly 2,100 miles of irrigation canals watering the most expensive farmlands in Washington and growing commercial crops marketed to distant cities and countries. By the 1920s Yakima Valley farmers were producing more than $40 million in crops annually in what they could legitimately call the "Fruit Bowl of the Nation."

Yakima makes no secret of its debt to large-scale, federally sponsored irrigation. Such collective action trickled down to city building. During the first decades of the twentieth century, a sense of stability prevailed as many local farmers invested their orchard profits. The heart of the downtown was Fruit Row, where fruit and vegetables were stored, dried, canned, or packed before shipping. A few skyscrapers rose on Yakima Avenue; a theater brought national entertainment; and the city built schools, libraries, fire stations, and churches. Irrigation canals ran down the sides of streets. After typhoid scares in the 1890s and 1900s, the city created one of the nation's first public health systems. By 1935, Yakima was ready to celebrate its golden jubilee with a pageant, a cast of 1,200, and a complete "Indian village" inhabited by 500 Yakama.

The wealth of the valley, however, depended not just on irrigation but on the labor of farmworkers. By the 1920s a migrant labor force of 20,000 workers was needed in season to harvest and process crops. As the Great Depression rolled across the country in the 1930s, local economies declined. Washington State stopped funding the state fair in 1930, but agriculture remained steadier in the Yakima Valley than elsewhere, thanks partly to the large irrigation projects. Yakima County was fifth out of all counties in the United States for total agricultural production in the mid-1930s. Thousands of migrants from the Dust Bowl areas of Oklahoma and Arkansas flocked to the valley, desperate for work at almost any wage. Unemployment in the county reached 28.5 percent the same year as the jubilee.

The tensions between farmers and the seasonal workers they depended on often spilled over into the streets of Yakima. After their success in the Spokane free speech fights of 1909, the Wobblies (the Industrial Workers of the World) spun off the Agricultural Workers Industrial Union (the AWIU) to organize farmworkers in the Yakima Valley, among other places. The union wanted to shorten the workday from ten hours to eight and to raise wages from 10 cents an hour for men and 8 cents for women to 35 cents for all. When Wobblies tried to hold street meetings on Front Street in Yakima in 1910, they were arrested, often on vagrancy charges. When they tried again in 1916 and 1917, they met stiff resistance from Yakima orchardists, police, and press.

During the 1930s, an estimated 35,000 workers flooded into the fields at the height of the harvest seasons. In the spring of 1933, the AWIU attempted to organize workers in the hop fields in Moxee, east of Yakima, and in August, workers went on strike at Congdon Orchards, a few miles from downtown. Pickets trying to persuade pickers to walk off the job were told by sheriff's deputies to get out of the orchards. Some moved to stand along the highway and others to a shaded triangle of land near the orchards, only to be harassed by a much larger group of farmers armed with clubs, pickaxes, and baseball bats. A short battle ensued during which one farmer was injured. The strikers were rounded up and marched several miles into town, where they were corralled in a stockade beside the Yakima County Courthouse. Charges against them were eventually dropped, but the stockade stood for the next ten years as a deterrent to labor organizing. In subsequent years, civic leaders resisted bringing manufacturing jobs to Yakima that might raise the wage scale.

The Wobblies were most successful at organizing white farmworkers. Historically, the valley has had a mixture of people: Yakama

Indians who worked in the hop fields; Hollanders, Dunkards, French, Germans, and Swedes who came early from the Midwest to make land claims; Japanese farmers, some leasing land on the Yakama reservation; Scandinavian laborers; and Filipino farmworkers. Many of those growing up in Yakima experienced both the stigma of poverty and the freedom of the countryside, as illustrated in the lives of two native sons.

William O. Douglas wrote of a hardscrabble life but also of a sense that everyone went to the same churches and schools as the elite. After his father died in 1904, when Douglas was six, his mother settled in Yakima with her three children. From his new home, Douglas could see both Mount Adams and Mount Rainier, a view that lured him into mountain hiking for the rest of his life. After teaching in the local high school, he went to law school. He was appointed to the Supreme Court by President Franklin Roosevelt in 1939, a position he kept for thirty-six years. The local newspaper disclaimed any responsibility for the justice's liberal views, and for years he kept its editorial headline in his wallet—"Don't Blame Yakima."

A generation after the Douglas family, the family of short-story writer and poet Raymond Carver emigrated to Yakima from Arkansas in 1934. Carver's father picked apples, worked as a laborer building the Grand Coulee Dam, and then landed a skilled job as a saw filer at the Boise Cascade mill. His mother worked as a retail clerk or waitress; other women in his extended family packed apples in the canneries. Carver remembered a childhood of fishing and hunting on the Yakima River and also of picking hops, which was "unimaginably hard work." His experiences growing up in a working-class family shaped his writing.

The 1940s brought wartime prosperity, with an influx of soldiers at the Yakima Firing Center, but wartime production drew thousands of workers away from the farms to factories and shipbuilding in Seattle, Vancouver, and Bremerton. More than a thousand Japanese Americans had to abandon their farms in the valley when they were interned during World War II. The subsequent need for farmworkers spurred the bracero program, an agreement between the United States and Mexico to import manual laborers to work in the fields during the war. Those workers could not bring families and were obligated to return to Mexico, but a pattern was established.

Generations of Mexicans returned to pick crops, and very slowly they organized for better working conditions and housing. Cesar Chavez, president of the United Farmworkers of America, led fruit boycotts in California, and in 1986 he led a march of more than 2,000 people in Yakima asking for farmworker rights. Not until 1995 would farmworkers sign their first union contract in Washington, with the Chateau Ste. Michelle Winery in the Yakima Valley. Farmworker families changed the ethnic dynamic of Yakima, where Hispanics now make up 37 percent of the population, compared to 7.5 percent in the state as a whole. That change is reflected in Yakima's two large high schools, Davis and Eisenhower. Each high school has close to 2,000 students, well more than half of whom identify as Hispanic or Latino. Students went on strike and walked out of the high schools in 2006, and approximately 15,000 people marched downtown that year, in support of immigrants' rights.

Today, the city's prosperity still depends on agriculture, with the enhancement of tourism, particularly wine tourism. Located at roughly the same latitude as the wine-growing areas of France, the Yakima Valley has nearly eighty wineries. Cyclists traveling the byroads smell both grapes and hops. Yakima County is the country's largest producer of apples, hops, and mint, with a high production of cherries, peaches, pears, nectarines, apricots, asparagus, hay, berries, and eggplant as well. Because people have to eat, Yakima chugs along, without the booms and busts other cities have experienced.

Yakima has a tradition of good public services, including four swimming pools, sidewalks, public transportation, an arboretum, a public library, fishing in rivers and creeks, and treated irrigation water for lawns and gardens. Its first high school, Davis (originally called

North Yakima) High School, was built to the state of the art in 1908; its auditorium, built in 1936, could accommodate 1,600 people. Eisenhower High School, founded in 1956, was replaced in 2013 at a cost of $104 million, making it one of the most expensive high schools in the state. Yakima voters had approved a twenty-year bond issue that also included renovations for Davis. Yakima has a community college that dates from 1928, predating the state's community college system. Although some historic homes remain, with a few exceptions, Yakima has not emphasized historic restoration.

This walk begins at the center of Yakima's commercial history— on Front Street and Fruit Row. It stops to browse the artifacts of Yakima Valley life at Millennium Plaza, then samples the downtown historic district, noting churches, courthouses, theaters, office buildings, statues, and sites of conflict. You may follow William O. Douglas on an extended hike toward the wilderness, stopping at the railroad bridge where he chatted with hoboes and then walking the Yakima Greenway along the rivers that made the city rich.

"Yakima has its own particular beauty," Raymond Carver wrote. "My heart lifts up when I see the Yakima Valley."

Yakima Loop

START: 100 N Front Street

DIRECTIONS: From I-82, take exit 33 from the south or 33B from the
                  north for Yakima Avenue, west toward the city center.
                  After several blocks, turn right one-half block on N Front
                  Street.

DISTANCE: 2 miles round trip

AMENITIES: Diagonal street parking or four-hour free parking lots
                  east of Millennium Plaza on N 3rd Street south of E Yakima
                  Avenue; public restrooms in government buildings

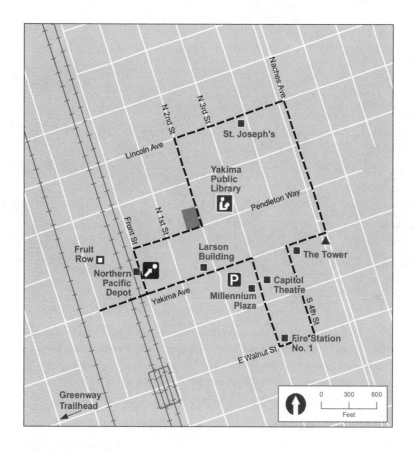

Begin on N Front Street between Yakima Avenue and Pendleton Way at the passenger and freight **depots** for the Northern Pacific Railway, the reason Yakima City moved here from four miles south. When the businesses and hotels moved, there were three streets: Yakima Avenue running east and west and 1st and Front Streets running north and south, fronting the railroad tracks. Hotels, restaurants, theaters, and stores lined Front Street. They were the center of social and economic life and remain the heart of Yakima's historic district. Restored brick and stone buildings with identifying plaques, old-style streetlamps, and a few street clocks recall the first hundred years of Yakima history.

The old depot, the third one built by the Northern Pacific, now

In May 1894, after the financial panic of 1893, hundreds of unemployed men gathered at the North Yakima station, planning to hop trains to Washington, DC, and demand jobs. Many members of "Coxey's Army," named for organizer Jacob Coxey, never reached the nation's capital, and the protest movement failed in its goal of obtaining federal work projects. Courtesy Yakima Valley Museum.

hosts a coffeehouse and fresh produce outlet. The first depot was simply a boxcar without wheels, the second a wooden depot built in 1886. The third and last depot was designed by Cass Gilbert in the Mission style in 1909–10. Coxey's Army passed through in 1894 on the way to Washington, DC, to demand jobs.

Across the street is the old **City Hall**, said to be the oldest commercial building still standing in Yakima, built in 1885. The fire department and police department shared the space. Cowboys passing through could stash their cash here, using a thumbprint for a signature. City government moved out in 1949, and the building is now a pub.

The **Opera House**, at *25 N Front Street*, was built by a developer, A. J. Switzer, in the 1880s. Yakima's first theater was on the second floor, lit by kerosene lamps and heated with two stoves. The antislavery play *Uncle Tom's Cabin* and *My Old Kentucky Home* were both performed here.

The **Lund Building**, or Greystone Building, on the northeast corner of Front and Yakima was finished in 1898, serving first as a saloon and then as a men's clothing store. It also was built by Switzer, of local basalt. All these buildings have different uses today, ranging from brewpubs and wineries to restaurants and florist shops.

In the downtown street grid, Yakima Avenue ("the Avenue") runs east and west, with the dividing point at Front Street. Numbered avenues run north and south on the west side of the railroad tracks; numbered streets run north and south on the east side of the tracks, both with the Avenue as the dividing point.

While the east side of Front Street was the center of civic action and commerce, the seasonally frenetic action took place across the tracks on Fruit Row. After the Northern Pacific arrived in the 1880s and the Union Pacific in the early 1900s, cold storage warehouses and packing facilities bordered the tracks for blocks. Fruit growers brought their fruit in bulk to be packed near the railroad.

From Front Street and Yakima Avenue, walk west across the tracks to a building *at 15 W Yakima* that stretches in two directions, north along the tracks and west along Yakima to N 1st Avenue. This opened as the **Fruit Exchange Building**, a sales agency for fruit growers, and then was, for decades, Pacific Fruit and Produce, a fruit-packing facility. More recently it houses Washington State Department of Agriculture offices. The **Union Pacific Freight Building**, *at 104 W Yakima Avenue*, sat on tracks that paralleled the Northern Pacific tracks, but the Union Pacific tracks have been pulled in this section. The **Union Pacific passenger depot**, *at 33 S 2nd Avenue,* has been remodeled and used by Yakima Schools administrative offices.

A 1941 guide to Washington State, compiled by writers employed by the Work Projects Administration, describes the scene along the tracks in the late 1930s when thousands of people packed cherries, peaches, pears, apples, and other small fruits: "With the beginning

Workers on a dock at the Perry Warehouse on Fruit Row pose during a break from loading boxes and baskets of apples. Courtesy Yakima Valley Museum.

of the cherry harvest, toward midsummer, Produce Row, always busy, becomes more hectic, and the narrow paved street is a shifting mass of trucks and shunting freight cars. Day and night the Row is a river of flowing traffic; gasoline fumes mingle with heavy odors of ripened fruit and the clank of hurried machinery." Everyone—transient fruit workers, "apple knockers" (packers), wives and daughters of nearby farmers, and townspeople—worked at terrific speed.

One hundred railcars pulled out of Yakima each day, loaded with fruit. It took 765 boxes of apples to fill a railcar. Before refrigerated cars became common after World War II, huge blocks of ice, weighing about 1,500 pounds each, were used to refrigerate the fruit. "A big thing was to come down around 5 P.M. and watch them ice the cars," recalls Del Bice, a Yakima Valley Museum curator of fruit box labels. Fruit Row lost much of its vitality as packing moved closer to the orchards. Contemporary orchardists use controlled-atmosphere storage for longer periods before fruit is transported by long-haul trucks and rail.

Retrace your steps along Yakima Avenue past Front Street to the **Larson Building** *at 121 E Yakima.* In the first two decades of the 1900s, Yakima's downtown expanded east along Yakima Avenue to Naches Avenue. Wooden buildings gave way to brick and stone, particularly local basalt. A. E. Larson was a lumberman who flourished during the 1920s. At the end of that decade, he wanted to leave a Yakima landmark, a building that would "stand as a sentinel of the Yakima Valley." Larson gambled that he could finance construction even as the Great Depression was taking hold; he spent three-quarters of a million dollars and finished in 1931. His Larson Building was the last of the state's skyscrapers to be built in that decade, made of reinforced concrete clad in fourteen shades of specially kilned tan brick, with the darkest on the bottom.

Continue another block east to N 3rd Street and turn south to **Millennium Plaza**, *between E Yakima Avenue and E Chestnut Avenue.* The plaza was completed in 2003 with a grant from the National Endowment for the Arts and the Mid-Atlantic Arts Foundation. Called *Water of Life*, the plaza was designed by artist Wen-ti Tsen to showcase all the important elements of Yakima Valley history. Walk among the objects mounted on basalt columns to find a saddle, a sewing machine, a miniature orchard, a berry basket, an irrigation valve handle, an "iron pot" (helmet) used by soldiers, and a short-handled hoe. The hoe, used in the sugar-beet industry, was outlawed in the 1970s because of its harmful effects on workers. Local artists and residents contributed thirty-nine totem objects displayed in window cases in two concrete walls. They relate many strands of history.

With the railroad no longer the heart of downtown, Yakima has been searching for its center. The plaza display will move if a proposed downtown plaza is constructed where the parking lot is now. The new plaza would include a small canal, signifying the importance of irrigation to the community, and a covered space for the farmers market, a microcosm of the valley's heart.

Across the street at 19 S 3rd Street, is a Yakima architectural icon, the **Capitol Theatre**, which hosted motion pictures, vaudevilles, and road shows beginning in the 1920s; it was touted as the largest and best theater in the West. Owner Frederick Mercy commissioned B. Marcus Priteca to design the building, as he had for several Pantages theaters; at one time Mercy owned six theaters in Yakima. The building came into public ownership in the 1970s and was restored after a devastating fire. It is now home to the Yakima Symphony Orchestra and host to lectures, musicals, and concerts.

Next to it is the **federal building and post office,** *at Chestnut and 3rd*, a center of federal power built in 1911. The U.S. Post Office is on the first floor, the federal court and U.S. Department of Justice are on the second, and the irrigation-important Bureau of Reclamation is on the third. The building was renamed the William O. Douglas Federal Building in 1978 in honor of the local lawyer who served on the Supreme Court longer than any other justice.

Continue southeast on S 3rd Street to 333 E Walnut Street and **Fire Station No. 1**. Like many cities in the late 1800s, main street businesses were built with wood and the fire department was often a volunteer bucket brigade. Yakima hired its first paid firefighters in 1905, and a year later, a downtown fire burned fourteen buildings, including the Northern Pacific depot. This brick building with tower and wide doors for vehicles housed the only completely automated fire department in 1912, which meant it used gas and some electric engines, not horsepower. The tower was used to hang and dry hoses.

Return to E Yakima on S 4th Street. West of the corner of Yakima and 4th, find the **Grand Hotel** *at 308–310*, built about 1911 with "200 modern rooms" renting for a dollar a night. It has been restored as apartments for senior citizens. The Grand was sandwiched by the two-story **Wilson Building** to the west, which still stands, and the Liberty Theater to the east, which does not.

Across the street, *at 321 Yakima Avenue,* is the Great Western Building, once the Masonic Temple, now the **JEM Building**, named after the company that restored it. The temple was built during the prosperity of the early 1900s. The luxurious Lodge Room on the top floor was inspired by King Solomon's Temple, only the second temple built on that model in the United States. (See photographs and column remnants in the Yakima Valley Museum.)

On the southeast corner of Yakima and S 4th Street is **The Tower**, a fourteen-story skyscraper that, unlike the Larson Building, was stranded mid-construction during the 1930s. It remained a skeletal framework until Frederick Mercy, the Capitol Theatre benefactor, took it over in 1946. The Tower opened as the Chinook Hotel in 1951.

Continuing east on Yakima, you are approaching the intersection with Naches Avenue, the edge of commercial development and the beginning of residential neighborhoods in the early 1900s. The **Weisenberger monument** in the median on the south side of the avenue commemorates a local company that fought in the Spanish-American War under John J. Weisenberger, who had no other connection to Yakima except for the men he commanded. Theodore Roosevelt made a speech at this intersection on May 25, 1903, as he swung through the West claiming credit for the passage of the 1902 Reclamation Act, which brought large-scale irrigation to the Yakima Valley.

St. Michael's Episcopal Church, the oldest church in the city, opened on Christmas Day 1889 on land donated by the Northern Pacific Railway *on the southeast corner of Naches and Yakima Avenues.*

Naches Avenue was the model neighborhood in early Yakima. Four irrigation canals, now covered up, ran along the street, one on each side and two down the middle. The canals watered the trees in the median. Homes lined both sides of the avenue, and squirrels were added for ambiance. *Note the* **irrigation covers** in the sidewalk. The city has provided irrigation water to residents since 1912.

Walk north on Naches Avenue, past the current YMCA to the old **YWCA** *at 15 N Naches,* which opened in 1935. The YWCA supported

28. CROWD FOLLOWING PARADE. 5-25-1

A crowd parades down a bunting-draped Yakima Avenue in 1903, following President Theodore Roosevelt, who toured the West to tout the Reclamation Act of 1902. Courtesy Yakima Valley Museum.

women and children in the valley; housed the temporarily homeless, the transient, and working women; and also served as an employment agency. Many women worked in the fruit-packing warehouses on Fruit Row.

In the next block, pass the original **First Church of Christ Scientist**, now a performing arts hall. On the east side of the next block are a few homes remaining from the original neighborhood.

At Lincoln Avenue, walk west to **St. Joseph's Catholic Church**, *at 212 N 4th Street.* The congregation dates from the earliest years of Yakima Valley history. Father Joseph Caruana was a Jesuit priest at Ahtanum mission among the Yakama Indians, southwest of the city.

For many years, Yakima had two water systems: one for drinking and one for irrigation. This ditch provided irrigation water to homes on Naches Avenue, which was a favorite subject of tourism postcards in the early 1900s. Courtesy Yakima Valley Museum.

The mission was burned by U.S. soldiers during the Yakama war in the 1850s, then rebuilt but closed in the 1870s and moved to nearby Yakima City. When everything else moved north to the railroad, the wooden church moved, too. This building dates from 1905.

On the northwest corner of Lincoln and 2nd is the home of the **Woman's Century Club**, originally built in 1890 as a family home. Woman's Century Clubs were organized in Seattle and Yakima as part of a movement of women's clubs that swept cities in the Pacific Northwest, including Olympia and Walla Walla. The clubs supported cultural and intellectual development for women as well as social services. The name came from the nineteenth century, which many

A temporary stockade on the grounds of the Yakima County Courthouse detained farmworkers arrested for picketing in 1933. This photograph is by Dorothea Lange, famous photographer of the Great Depression. Courtesy Library of Congress.

women active in the suffrage movement called the Woman's Century because of the advances made in women's rights.

As women advocated change through clubs, farmworkers during the 1930s took a more aggressive stance, seeking shorter working hours and better pay. *Proceed south on N 2nd Street,* past the Yakima County Court Administration building, to a small **park** *on the northwest corner of Pendleton Way.* Near here was the old Yakima County Courthouse, built of stone in 1909. Behind the courthouse a stockade was erected in twenty-four hours to contain striking farmworkers after the Battle of Congdon Orchards. The 1960 administration building arose on the lawn in front of the courthouse, which was then torn down in the 1980s.

Congdon Orchards

The Battle of Congdon Orchards, in which farmworkers struck for higher wages in 1933, took place in an apple orchard adjoining **Congdon Castle**. Chester Congdon was a resident of Duluth, Minnesota, who had built a family summer home called Westhome. It boasted more than eighty rooms, including eighteen bedrooms, and a swimming pool in the basement. The family also built the Yakima Valley Canal, known colloquially as the Congdon Ditch. A U-shaped inverted siphon, designed by a Congdon brother-in-law, drew snowmelt from Rimrock across Cowiche Canyon to the orchards, which covered more than 900 acres with 35,000 trees. Congdon Castle rests barely visible among the orchards, south of Nob Hill Boulevard, just east of the West Valley Wal-Mart. The **aqueduct** crosses Pecks Canyon Road off of N Powerhouse Road.

Return along Pendleton Way to the start of the loop at Front Street and Yakima Avenue. The early wealth from lumber and irrigation and the construction of churches, skyscrapers, and Egyptian temples were challenged in the 1930s by people concerned about great inequalities of wealth. Here, on the evening of August 24, 1933, a crowd of a thousand people gathered, most in sympathy with the striking farmworkers, some merely curious. National Guardsmen briefly mounted a machine gun, used tear gas, and displayed fixed bayonets to clear the crowd. Yakima would emerge from the Depression and take down the stockade in 1943, but the tension inherent in prosperous agriculture dependent on low-wage labor would continue into the twenty-first century.

For a sense of the rivers that brought sustainable agriculture and agricultural jobs to the valley and a sense of the wilderness that lured city residents, take an extended walk along the William O. Douglas Heritage Trail and the Yakima Greenway.

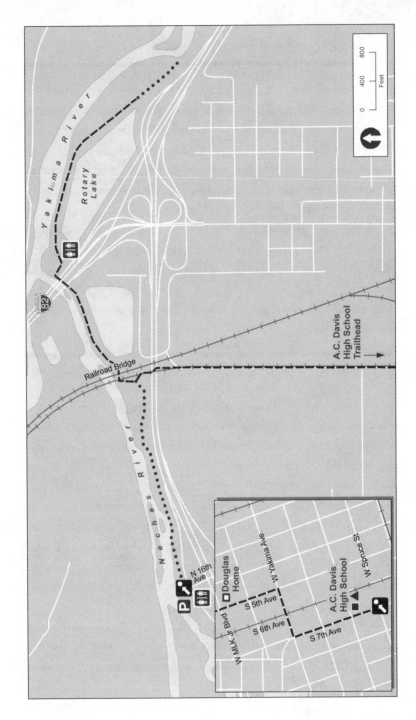

Extended Walk: William O. Douglas Heritage Trail/Yakima Greenway

START: A. C. Davis High School, 212 S 6th Avenue, or 16th
               Avenue Trailhead for Yakima Greenway

DIRECTIONS: See Yakima Loop.

DISTANCE: 2 miles from Davis High School to the railroad bridge
               over the Naches River; 0.7 miles from 16th Avenue
               trailhead on the Yakima Greenway to the railroad bridge;
               0.7 miles from the railroad bridge to Rotary Lake

AMENITIES: Parking at the 16th Avenue trailhead on the Yakima
               Greenway; restrooms at the 16th Avenue trailhead and
               Rotary Lake

William O. Douglas, a U.S. Supreme Court justice from 1939 to 1975, grew up in Yakima, where he found health and inspiration by hiking to the mountains. His route has been marked as the William O. Douglas Heritage Trail (www.williamodouglastrail.org). This walk follows the young Douglas as he headed out of town.

The heritage trail begins at his alma mater, A. C. Davis High School, where he worked as an English teacher and debate team coach before heading to law school. A **statue** of Douglas, with flowing judicial robes covering hiking garb, graces a courtyard in the school. Davis High School started in 1884 as North Yakima High School, and then was renamed for Angus Charles Davis, a principal in the early 1900s who subsequently became the Yakima schools' superintendent.

From Davis High School, go north on the west side of S 7th Avenue two blocks to W Yakima Avenue. Cross to the north side and go right two blocks (east) to S 5th Avenue. Turn left to go north on 5th for two blocks to W Martin Luther King Jr. Boulevard. Douglas grew up at **111 N 5th**

Avenue, a site designated with a banner on a concrete wall. His family was poor, as was his health, and, as he relates in his autobiography, *Go East, Young Man,* at the age of eleven, he began backpacking into the mountains.

From here, Douglas walked almost two miles to the Naches River. You may follow his route or shortcut it by starting at the 16th Avenue trailhead (see above). His route is not scenic in the traditional sense or studded with historic homes and sites. It follows 5th Avenue for eight blocks to I Street, then skirts one block west to 6th Avenue at I Street, and finally continues north on 6th, following the route of the Yakima Valley Trolley. It reaches the Yakima Greenway Trail at the historic **Naches River railroad bridge**.

Two bridges cross the Naches at this site near the confluence of the Naches and Yakima Rivers and an ancient village named Ti'mani. The upstream bridge carries the electrified Yakima Valley Trolley over the river to Selah on an early twentieth-century line. The downstream bridge carries the Northern Pacific mainline from Yakima through Selah Gap to Ellensburg. Hoboes gathered at the base of that bridge in the days when it was possible to hop a passing freight train to the next job.

Douglas crossed the bridge on his way to climb Selah Ridge, the ridge defining the valley on the north side. On days he was not hiking or picking crops or going to school, Douglas described sitting under the bridge and sharing coffee and stew with the "restless vagabonds while the wrath of their discontents against society bubbled out." The Douglas heritage trail extends seventy-five miles over Selah Gap and Cowlitz Pass to Mount Rainier.

At the bridges, the path joins the Yakima Greenway, which extends both ways along the Naches and Yakima Rivers for eighteen miles. *Explore as much of this trail as you like.* A little more than a half mile east, and beyond the smaller Berglund Lake, is the former Cascade Lumber Company millpond at Rotary Lake. Cascade started in 1903, milling logs floated down the Yakima River from logging in Easton and Cle Elum. During spring log drives, as many as a thousand logs arrived daily. Like many families in Yakima, the men in Raymond Carver's family all worked at the mill; "that was my entire frame of reference when I was a kid." The waters of the millpond commingled with drinking water in the 1890s and early 1900s, causing a typhoid scare that prompted the creation of a citywide public health system. The mill operated in later years as Boise Cascade until it closed in 2006.

Private efforts since then have reclaimed the riverfront for the walking, biking, and fishing that the citizens of Yakima have enjoyed for generations.

Yakima Valley Trolley

The Union Pacific competed with the Northern Pacific through Yakima. It operated the Yakima Valley Transportation Company as a feeder line, an electrified Interurban that also transported fruit from Selah, Ahtanum, and the Congdon Orchards into town. Freight operations were abandoned in 1985, but the trolley still runs during the summertime as a tourist adventure. It departs from the carbarn, shop, and powerhouse built in 1910 and 1911 at S 3rd Avenue and Pine Street. The trolley runs for five miles over the Naches River bridge and through Selah Gap to Selah on tracks constructed between 1907 and 1913. See www.yakimavalley trolleys.org for confirmation and current details.

Resources   Visitors Center, 10 N 8th Street

William O. Douglas Heritage Trail,
www.williamodouglastrail.org

Yakima Public Library, 102 N 3rd Street

Yakima Valley Museum, 2105 Tieton Drive

CHAPTER NINE

Spokane

City by the Falls

The downtown is to the city as the heart is to the body.
You can't let it die.

King Cole, President of Expo '74

T he defining feature of Spokane is the spectacular river and falls in its midst. The Olmsted Brothers saw it right away: "Nothing is so firmly impressed on the mind of the visitor to Spokane," the landscape architects wrote, "as . . . the great gorge into which the river falls near the center of the city. It is a tremendous feature of the landscape and one which is rarer in a large city than river, lake, bay or mountain."

It has been the defining feature for centuries. The Spokane River rushes west from the Coeur d'Alene Mountains to join the Columbia River. At the end of the last Ice Age, the great Missoula Floods carved channels in the river and left large basalt islands. Falls tumbled over those islands and made the river unnavigable, but it was rich in salmon that swarmed below a sixty-foot leap and could go no farther. The Middle Spokane Indian people came to the river to fish. The first settlers used the falls to power mills. The railroads surveyed routes that followed the river. Itinerant workers thronged its banks as they

FALLS OF THE SPOKANE.

In 1853, artist John Mix Stanley traveled with the exploration party for the transcontinental railroad and drew this representation of the falls in the Spokane River. It shows the large basalt island between channels of the river. Courtesy Eastern Washington University.

came and went to jobs in the mines, fields, and woods. Hoboes camped along it during the Great Depression.

Gradually the hum of machinery replaced the roar of the falls. During a century of use and abuse, some of the river's channels were filled in and its basalt islands blasted; dams, railroad trestles, tracks, and stations were built on its banks and remaining islands, and sewage and mine tailings were dumped into it. The river was obscured to the point where some residents hardly knew it existed. All of that changed in 1974, when Spokane restored the river and hosted the first world's fair with an environmental theme.

The Spokane people were the "children of reflected light," the light that rises from the spray of the falls. They were historically a prosperous people, with wealth and mobility from gathering wild plant food, farming, raising horses, and fishing at the foot of the falls. They traded with the Hudson's Bay Company post at Spokane House, several miles downstream. To strengthen the commercial relationship, Chief Illim-Spokanee sent his son, Slough-Keetcha, to the mission on the Red River in Manitoba to study English ways.

When Spokane Garry returned with a new name, new language, and new religion, he found nonnatives moving onto the Spokane land, first as missionaries and then as settlers. Garry worked to maintain a peaceful relationship with the incoming whites, but after failed treaty negotiations, the U.S. military subdued the Spokane at two battles west of the falls—the Battle of Spokane Plains and the Battle of Four Lakes—and slaughtered their horses. Soon thereafter, in 1861, a military road was built from Walla Walla through Spokane and across the Rocky Mountains to Montana, marking the American claim to the territory.

With the northern transcontinental railroad headed along the river on its way to the coast in 1881, President Rutherford B. Hayes created a reservation for the Spokane tribe, far from the falls. Garry was forced off his farm, but he refused to move to the reservation, sheltering instead in a teepee in a canyon west of the falls.

Early settlers wanted to be close to the falls, too. In letters home they spoke of the best water power west of Minneapolis. "Perhaps there is no better water power in the world," wrote one. They appreciated the beauty of the falls but wanted to use the water's power rather than just admire it. On the river's banks they built sawmills and flour mills to process logs and wheat. At first calling their town Spokan Falls, they incorporated with all of 350 residents the same year the Northern Pacific arrived.

Two years later, gold was discovered in the Coeur d'Alene Mountains, followed by the more important discoveries of silver and lead. For a time in the 1860s and '70s, Walla Walla had been the dominant agricultural and mining hub of the Inland Empire, a vast hinterland that stretched from the Cascades to the Rockies and from Canada to

Oregon. But the new mining discoveries and the routing of transcontinental railroads shifted the hub to Spokan Falls. The booming town quickly became the chief supplier of the mining districts, the exporter of mine products, and the beneficiary of personal wealth from citizens like August Paulsen, May and Levi Hutton, and "Dutch" Jake Goetz, who left behind statement buildings. The *e* was added to the town's name and the word *Falls* was dropped as the falls disappeared from public consciousness. Promoters called Spokane the "Imperial City," a reference to its prominence in the Inland Empire.

Like Everett, Bellingham, Seattle, and Tacoma, Spokane was touched by railroad fever, but location saved it much of the trouble of self-promotion. The northern transcontinental railroads wanted to reach Puget Sound, and they had to go through the Rocky Mountains. Going along the Spokane River Valley was the most direct route and the location near mining and agriculture provided products for the railroads to transport. Four transcontinental lines eventually went through Spokane: the Northern Pacific, the Great Northern, the Union Pacific, and the Milwaukee Road. In addition to those lines, a Spokane entrepreneur, Daniel C. Corbin, built rails to the mining towns of Idaho and to the Cariboo region just north of the Canadian border. This network of railroads reaching out through the hinterland and stretching from the Midwest to the coast made Spokane a chokepoint of rail travel. Promoters called it the "Railroad City."

Economic growth started with railroads and silver but soon fed on itself. Town boosting and land speculation was a sport in Washington Territory. The railroads were eager to sell land and develop regional markets for products they transported, and they pumped Spokane and its hinterland. "What's the matter with making money?" asked a real estate ad offering lots for sale. Thousands of immigrants moved west, land became valuable, and business boomed—at least in some towns. By the end of the 1880s, Spokane's population had soared to 19,000, securing it the county seat, with a grand courthouse to follow.

A 1920s photograph of the upper falls in the Spokane River shows the first power station on what was later named Canada Island. The Centennial Grain Mill is visible on the north bank of the river. Courtesy Northwest Museum of Arts & Culture/Eastern Washington State Historical Society, Spokane, Washington, L87-1.18000-20, Charles Libby Collection.

A single electric generator powered the Spokane Flour Mill in 1885, followed by electric streetlights a year later, making Spokane one of the first electrified cities in the West. Local investors formed Washington Water Power, a private utility that converted water power to economic and political power. With energy from a power station at the falls, the company ran electric streetcars to neighborhoods that would, in turn, use more electricity. By 1920, Washington Water Power had constructed three dams to provide electrical power. "Blasting powder ruined their charm," one pioneer said of the falls, "and they were turned from a thing of beauty to a thing of power." Promoters called Spokane the "Power City."

Spokane's growth hit a temporary snag in August 1889, when fire destroyed wooden buildings on three-quarters of the blocks downtown. Rather than devastating the city, however, the fire fueled ambitious growth. To residents, it was "the beginning of a new Spokane."

The call went out nationwide for carpenters, architects, stonemasons, and real estate investors to rebuild the city, taller than it had been before. Five hundred buildings were constructed of local basalt and brick in the next four years, many rising six and seven stories high. Spokane became a real city.

No sooner had Spokane rebuilt from the fire than a financial panic hit the nation in 1893. The bottom fell out of financing for big projects funded by eastern or European capital, and boomtowns in the Pacific Northwest felt the impact most severely. Seven of Spokane's ten banks failed. The panic not only ruined some Spokane developers but also hurt workers in the surrounding mines, fields, and lumber camps. Spokane swarmed with itinerant workers who came to find the next job or to spend the winter in single-room occupancy hotels. These thousands of bindle stiffs made Spokane a magnet for labor and Populist action.

In the fall and winter following the panic, workers could find work at starvation wages or no work at all. More than 2.5 million were unemployed across the country, with immigrants still arriving from Europe. A businessman in Ohio, Jacob Coxey, decided he would lead an army of the unemployed to Washington, DC, to "force the government to do something," such as creating jobs by building public roads. Spokane was a major launching point for Coxey's Army, which reached the lawn of the U.S. Capitol but failed to persuade the government to act. Not until the Klondike gold rush of 1898 would the U.S. economy recover.

Despite this setback, the labor movement was growing. The Knights of Labor had formed a Spokane chapter in 1886, bringing together unskilled workers. Workers who had skills and could live and work in one place—the home guards—formed trade unions. The Knights and trade unions combined in 1888 to create the Spokane Trades Council, which published a weekly newspaper, the *Labor World,* the oldest labor newspaper in the state. With the discoveries of silver and lead in Idaho, mining had changed from the luck of an individual prospector with a mule to a corporate enterprise, funded by distant capital. The freedom to be one's own boss gave way to wage work in often unsafe, unstable, and unhealthy conditions. The Western Federation of Miners organized miners in Coeur d'Alene, and the conflicts between mine owners and workers rippled into Spokane.

Advocacy for the rights of workers sparked in 1909 with the Spokane free speech fight, a national struggle organized by the Industrial Workers of the World, or IWW. Workers coming from one job and searching for the next often had to "buy a job" by paying a fee to an employment agency. Bindle stiffs would carry their blanket roll to the job they had paid for, only to find it didn't exist or lasted only a week; then another fee could be charged to the next temporary worker. The IWW, or Wobblies, began protesting these practices by standing on soapboxes and making speeches on the streets of Spokane, despite a city ordinance hastily passed to forbid political, but not religious, speech. After hundreds were arrested and jails filled, the city modified the ordinance and regulated the agents, but an association of Spokane with militant action had been formed, no promotion needed.

Militant action gave way to reform through the political process in the early 1900s. Progressives asserted the power of government to curb corporate monopolies. One issue especially important to Inland Empire farmers was the railroads' ability to set exorbitant freight rates. Because interior rates were higher than coastal rates, a Midwest merchant could ship goods to Seattle and then back to Spokane more cheaply than shipping straight to Spokane. The Washington legislature approved a railroad regulatory commission to monitor freight rates in 1905. A few years later, the Interstate Commerce Commission, with new powers granted by the Hepburn Act of 1906, ruled on a complaint in Spokane's favor, forcing the railroads to lower and equalize rates.

As the prosperity and growth of the early 1900s met the cataclysm of World War I, many of the causes that had roiled Spokane were suppressed by wartime patriotism. The Wobblies' loyalties were divided by the war and by the Russian Revolution of 1917. They were met with raids and arrests when they called for strikes in the fields and woods.

During the conservative 1920s, Spokane made its peace with sudden wealth and corporate control of the economy and settled into a slower growth mode. A few Spokane Indians continued to camp in areas west of the city as early skyscrapers rose downtown. Miners, lumberjacks, fruit pickers, railroad workers, and farmhands still gathered on streets close to the river to share news, rumors, and the promise of jobs, but the more conservative labor movement predominated over the bindle stiffs.

There was a renewed suspicion of the foreign-born—German, Irish, Italian, Norwegian, Greek, Chinese, and Japanese. The Ku Klux Klan brought its anti-immigrant, anti-Catholic, anti-Jewish, and anti-black message to the city, but the movement did not receive wide support. Chinese, Japanese, Greek, and Italian immigrants claimed a few streets and alleys downtown for their stores as the city became more socially segregated.

During the rest of the twentieth century, mining subsided as a source of economic growth, but agriculture and manufacturing remained strong. The Great Depression and World War II brought disruptions and expansion, including Fairchild Air Force Base a few miles west of the city.

By the 1950s, the vitality of downtown Spokane, built so confidently with brick and stone, was fading. Property values dropped, businesses left, retail and shoppers moved to the malls and residents to the suburbs. A major shopping center, NorthTown, was built in 1954 and lured Sears, Roebuck away from downtown. The railroad lines that crisscrossed the city had nearly obscured the Spokane River with their tracks, depots, viaducts, and yards built on its banks and islands, but with railroad travel decreasing, the property had little commercial value. The river and falls were still supplying power but also serving as a literal sewer and dumping ground. An industrial laundry dumped suds and dirt, which joined the city's sewage and mine tailings. During some summer weeks, the river and its falls were almost dry and invisible.

Something had to change. Spokane faced a challenge to its continued viability as a city with a center. The Inland Empire had been a promised land for immigration, growth, and the exploitation of natural resources to the extent that, in 1890, Spokane had hosted the Northwestern Industrial Exposition, which celebrated conquering nature. That approach had lost its luster.

As early as 1908, a report from the influential landscape architects the Olmsted Brothers had identified the river and falls as what set Spokane apart, and they urged the city to make the river its heart: "Any city should prize and preserve its great landscape features, inasmuch as they give it individuality." With financing from banks, Washington Water Power, and the Cowles family, who owned the major newspapers, city leaders commissioned a report to study downtown's health. The 1961 report channeled the Olmsted Brothers: if you want to do something for the city, reclaim the river.

Nationally, environmentalism had found expression in the Wilderness Act of 1964, the National Environmental Policy Act of 1969, the Endangered Species Act of 1973, and celebration of the first Earth Day in 1970. Spokane leaders decided that a world's fair with an environmental theme would "sell."

With a population of about 180,000, Spokane would be the smallest city ever to undertake such an ambitious venture. In a powerful spurt of self-interest and civic activism, downtown property owners and city government organized into a group called Spokane Unlimited to redevelop the central business district. They hired a planner named King Cole and mobilized residents to support the fair with the river and its islands as centerpiece. Instead of conquering nature, Expo '74 would be "Celebrating Tomorrow's Fresh New Environment" or, more informally, exhibiting "Progress without Pollution." They pulled up railroad tracks, restored much of the river's flow, cleaned up pollution, and invited the world to celebrate the difference.

Crowds celebrate the opening of Expo '74 with 50,000 balloons. Courtesy Northwest Museum of Arts and Culture/Eastern Washington State Historical Society, L2002-33-23.

President Richard Nixon formally opened the fair in May 1974, amid a few protests over the continuation of the Vietnam War under his leadership. Governor Dan Evans and Spokane's congressman, Tom Foley, who had secured funding for the U.S. Pavilion, attended the celebration. Opening day of the fair was "the greatest day in Spokane's history," declared Dorothy R. Powers, a longtime columnist for the *Spokesman-Review*. More than 5 million people visited that spring, summer, and early fall.

This walk begins at the great falls on the Spokane River, where the Spokane people fished and the city drew its first power. It explores both the wealthy and bindle-stiff blocks of downtown, walks through Wobbly Town to the train depot, then passes the edifices of the newly wealthy, the social establishments of the city, and the remnants of the footloose. Finally, the walk returns to the river, the source of the city's renaissance a hundred years after its founding.

Spokane Loop

START: Riverfront Park, 507 N Howard Street

DIRECTIONS: From I-90, take exit 281 to Division Street and go
                 north, following brown signs for Spokane Falls Views.
                 Go west (left) on W Spokane Falls Boulevard. Look for
                 street parking or go north (right) on Post Street, which
                 is one-way, to a small parking lot in Riverfront Park.

DISTANCE: 4 miles

AMENITIES: Paid parking on streets or in lots; restrooms at Riverfront
                 Park

Begin at the **lower falls of the Spokane River** in Huntington Park. *From Riverfront Park, cross Post Street at a crosswalk marked with hoops and find the sidewalks in Huntington Park that lead to the foot* of the most dramatic falls in the river. Despite the unnatural gondolas that hover over the maelstrom, this site conveys much of the awe-inspiring natural force of the river whose roar grows louder the closer you come, at least on a day in June when water is high. The river divides into three channels that fall thirty feet, then unite for this sixty-foot plunge, controlled by a dam.

At the bottom of the trail, a sculptural salmon chief holds up the first salmon, in tribute to the spirit of the fish that sustained the Spokane people for thousands of years. Despite their prodigious strength, salmon could not ascend the lower falls, and fish runs ended here. For several months in the summer, tribes could catch 700 to 800 fish a day, enough to last through the winter when smoked and dried.

Walk back toward Post Street. Frederick Post was the first to harness

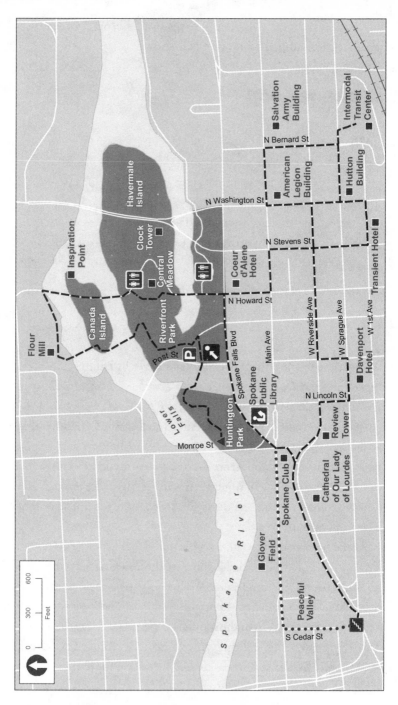

the river's water. His flour mill and house at the nearby site of City Hall gave this street its name. Post sold water rights along the three channels of the river to mine owners who formed a private utility. *Pass* the red brick **Post Street substation**, built in 1910 by the Washington Water Power company, whose name appears in large lettering at the top. Now named Avista, the company has harnessed hydroelectric power for Spokane for more than 120 years, longer than any other hydroelectric site operating in Washington.

Cross Post to Riverfront Park, where the town began, *and ramble the western part of the park, following kiosk maps.* This part of the park has been heavily used since Expo '74 and has been undergoing alterations according to a master plan developed in 2014, so some features, especially the meadows, may change.

The landscape itself has been greatly altered over a period of 150 years. Some of the original channels have been filled in and some new ones blasted into the rock. There are now three channels, one island (Canada), and a large peninsula that had been an island (Havermale) in the middle of the river. *As you head toward the suspension bridge to Canada Island, pass* the **Thomas R. Adkison theme stream**, a symbolic recreation of the old channel that made the peninsula you are standing on an island. From the suspension bridge, notice foundations of the city's first power plant on the western tip of Canada Island, which is named for that country's popular exhibit at Expo '74.

Continue across the suspension bridge over the north channel of the river to the **Flour Mill**, one of three early mills that ground grain into flour and shipped it as far away as London, England. The mill was transformed in 1973 into stores and restaurants but also displays historic artifacts such as large water wheels.

Return across the river on the bridge that extends south from Howard Street and find **Inspiration Point** *at the eastern tip of Canada Island.* Above the middle falls, medallions identify early religious workers in the inland Northwest. Catholic fathers worked northeast of Lake

Coeur d'Alene, and Protestant missionaries first settled at Tshimakain, twenty-five miles northwest of Spokane.

The bridge returns to what was **Havermale Island**, where five families took refuge during Indian wars in the 1870s. Once there, they were protected by water that flowed swiftly on both sides. The sawmill companies filled in the southern channel with earth in order to trap logs coming down the river. By 1924, the former island was overrun by railroad tracks.

Arrive at the Rotary Fountain in Riverfront Park at Howard and Spokane Falls Boulevard, first called Front Street. In 1873, James Glover sat on a "great rock" near the river and was overwhelmed by its beauty. He filed a land claim on its southern banks, bought out an existing sawmill, and stocked a store. He platted the town and named the streets: Sprague for a railroad superintendent, Howard for an army general who fought Indians, Stevens for the new territorial governor. This was Four Corners—the heart of Spokan Falls—a hotel on the northeast corner, a stable on the northwest, Glover's store on the southwest, and his home on the southeast.

With his town platted and lots ready for sale, Glover waited for the railroad to arrive. He knew that surveyors for the Northern Pacific had scouted a route along the river, and he was relieved to find they were not building across his land but a half mile to the south. Once the railroad arrived, the town filled in between the river and tracks. The first city hall was across the street on the *southwest corner of Howard and Spokane Falls Boulevard,* where a **plaque** now describes the city's founding. Wooden buildings started spreading south along Howard. Most would not survive the great fire of 1889. *Leave the park* to walk eighty years of early city history and return in the 1970s.

On the southeast corner of Howard and Spokane Falls Boulevard is the **Coeur d'Alene Hotel**, a solid remnant of the decades when railroads and mining wealth propelled Spokane's economy. German immigrants Dutch Jake Goetz and Harry Baer were saloonkeepers in a northern Idaho mining town, occasionally grubstaking a persistent miner. They struck it rich when they staked Noah Kellogg just one more time in 1885. Kellogg found what would become the Bunker Hill and Sullivan Mine. Newly rich from their investment, Goetz and Baer moved to Spokane with $200,000 and opened a hotel, which burned in the 1889 fire; a second hotel, which they lost in the financial panic of 1893; and finally this much grander hotel, an entertainment venue replete with multiple bars and restaurants. Remembering his humble beginnings, Goetz offered blankets on the floor in the basement to anyone who needed a place to sleep. Spokane was a wide-open town in the last decades of the 1800s, with soup kitchens, houses of prostitution, ninety saloons, and a shortage of beds. As laborers, carpenters, and architects poured in after the fire, men slept in chairs, on the floors of hotels and saloons, or crowded together in rooms.

Walk south on Howard to its intersection with W Main Avenue. This block of Howard is the **Bennett Block**. The most prominent building on a city block gave its name to the block, and the word *block* could also refer just to the building. Such business blocks usually spanned several lots with brick buildings two or more stories high. The buildings typically had retail on the ground floor and offices, apartments, or meeting halls on the upper floors. The **Bennett Building**, *on the northeast corner of Main and Howard*, was one of the first completed after the great fire of 1889; it housed a brewing company with a hotel on the upper floor and a saloon on the first.

Turn east on Main to N Stevens Street. On the southeast corner was the Bodie Block, also completed right after the fire, and now known as the **1889 Building**. Attached to the building and *halfway down Stevens, north of the alley,* is the **Levy Building**, whose name is visible at the top. Originally owned by Glover, the parcel's succession of owners illustrates speculative land frenzy. It sold fourteen times in twelve years, the last time to Samuel and Anna Maria Levy of Philadelphia, who never moved to Spokane. The first businesses in the building were those of a cobbler, a saddler, and a dressmaker, plus a carriage-trimming shop. Above the businesses was a twelve-room hotel, which for many years housed working-class men: a laborer, miner, lumberjack, hotel manager, saloonkeeper, railroad brakeman, cook, carpenter, and meat cutter. The Bodie Block also housed a single-room occupancy hotel. Modern brick has been added to the facades of both buildings.

On the south half of the block is the **Old National Bank Building**, the first skyscraper built in Spokane a decade after the fire. It was designed by Daniel Burnham, the architect of the Chicago World's Fair. Daniel C. Corbin, who built regional railroads to the mines, had a suite on the tenth floor.

Riverside Avenue evolved as the central business district in the 1890s. It paralleled the river and could extend east and west as the city grew. The **Fernwell Building**, *on the southwest corner of Stevens and Riverside,* was built in 1890 and was first known as the Hyde Building. Three Hyde brothers and a sister came to Spokane from Wisconsin. Samuel arrived as the newly appointed federal judge. Rollin and Eugene were experienced real estate developers, and Rollin commissioned this building. Eugene became chief of police and a state senator. Martha was one of Spokane's first two female schoolteachers, teaching the upper grades to students ranging from twelve to twenty-two years old.

Although buildings like the Levy and the Coeur d'Alene Hotel gave shelter to itinerants, Spokane could not accommodate the many unemployed who passed through looking for jobs or came to the city to live during the winter, especially the winter after the financial panic of 1893. That's when businessman Jacob Coxey called for a march to Washington, DC. An army of the unemployed responded from cities throughout the West, including Yakima, Seattle, and Spokane. We'll follow the job seekers as they headed for the Northern Pacific depot "under the flare of gasoline torches."

Cross to the south side of Riverside, and walk south on Stevens, crossing

W Sprague Avenue. The unemployed gathered nightly on Sprague in April 1894, determined to go on to the nation's capital "to see Grover" (Cleveland, the president). *At W 1st Avenue, walk east, passing* the **Transient Hotel** (Minnesota Building) at *421–423 W 1st Avenue.* As the name implies, the Transient was one of seventy hotels built in Spokane in the early 1900s to house workers on the second floor and businesses on the first. This block retains many of the original buildings.

Continue east on 1st for one block, then turn north on S Washington for one block to Sprague and continue east, passing the site of the Socialist Hall at *309 W Sprague Avenue,* which Spokane police raided during the IWW's free speech campaign in 1909, driving 200 members into the street, where they continued to make speeches. The buildings of the working class tend to be demolished more often than the stately brick of the wealthier class, and this site is now a parking lot. *Continue marching to Bernard Street* and the basalt-lined approach to the **Northern Pacific depot**, now called the Intermodal Transit Center.

Even though they had money from a generous donor, the railroad would not sell local Coxeyites tickets for the ride to Washington, DC, so they began slipping out on every train that came through town, a few at a time. "Every time a train goes through / It takes out a dozen or two," they sang. Only about 500 reached the nation's capital. Coxey was arrested for trespassing on the Capitol lawn before he could speak, and soldiers in his "army" drifted back to cities like Spokane, still looking for work.

Climb the stairs on the west side of the transit center for an elevated view of Spokane spreading to the river on the north and I-90 a few blocks farther south. (The tracks are open here, and buses leave on the roadway, so *pay attention*.) Notice the **ghost sign** for the National Biscuit Company, Home of SnowFlake Saltines, on a brick building to the southwest of the depot (*304 W Pacific Avenue*), one of many industries and warehouses that cozied up to the railroad tracks. The east part of the building was constructed for the **Washington Cracker Company** in 1891. It became part of a Pacific Coast Cracker

Trust and then was taken over in the 1930s by the National Biscuit Company, the largest biscuit company in the world—Nabisco. The combination of abundant wheat fields and demand for cookies, biscuits, and crackers drove production at the company and made it an important employer for Spokane in the early 1900s.

Turner Hall

With the national failure of Coxey's army, the efforts of workers to organize and secure jobs and better working conditions on the local level continued. Labor groups often had trouble finding a hall to rent for speakers. For a side trip of several blocks, walk east on Sprague and south on Division Street to 3rd Avenue. At 53 W 3rd is **Turner (Turnverein) Hall**, also known as German Hall and home to the German American Society, which was willing to host controversial speakers when other venues in town would not. The hall's caretaker was warned by the police not to rent to the IWW, for example, but members of the society backed him up when he defied the authorities. Theodore Roosevelt was slated to address the African American people of Spokane at Turner Hall in 1911, but his speech was moved to the Masonic Temple. Turner Hall is the only known building remaining where the more radical labor groups found a venue.

From the depot, walk north on Bernard Street two blocks to W Main Avenue. This part of town provided lodging, offices, and stores for itinerant workers and immigrants, as well as saloons and houses of prostitution. The blocks and alleys north and west of here were known variously as Chinatown, Japanese Alley, and Trent Alley. In the early 1900s, a thousand Japanese immigrants who had worked in the mines and on the railroads were living in these blocks. The Japanese American community increased during World War II because Spokane was outside the coastal exclusion zone and those who lived or moved here did not face internment. Despite that temporary growth, most of the neighborhood around Trent Alley was demolished in the 1970s and paved over during Expo '74. The alley name was changed to Spokane Falls Boulevard. The former alley now provides parking for the convention center and performing arts center.

One and a half blocks east, at 25 W Main, is the **Saranac**, which was a single-occupancy hotel for more than ninety years. The bottom floors housed various businesses between 1909 and the 1950s, including City Hand Laundry and North Coast Supply, run by Japanese immigrants who sold imported Asian foods.

Just east of the intersection, at 245 W Main Avenue, is the **Salvation Army Building**, where the army once handed out "soup, soap, and salvation" and operated the Red Shield Hotel beginning in 1891. The Salvation Army used street speech, songs, and bands to attract the down-and-out to its message, and a Spokane ordinance forbidding speech on the streets exempted religious proselytizing. During the Depression, the Salvation Army fed thousands. It has now moved to a larger location in Spokane that serves homeless families.

Walk west on W Main Avenue through the 300 block, which was known as **Wobbly Town**. In 1909, the Industrial Workers of the World started their free speech campaign close to the corrupt job agencies they were protesting. "We do not ask for the privilege of holding meetings on Riverside," the Wobblies told the local press. "We are sure we cannot get recruits to our ranks from the Silver Grill nor Davenport's. We want to work down here among the employment offices, where there are wage-earners."

The busiest corner was two blocks away at Stevens and Front (now W Spokane Falls Boulevard), not far from Wobbly Hall at 324 W Main (now a parking lot). A Wobbly would step up on a soapbox and begin, "Fellow workers," and the police would arrest him for disorderly conduct. Another would step right up and begin, "Fellow workers," until Spokane had more Wobblies in jail—300 to 400—than it could accommodate. After thirty days of choosing between working on the rock piles (breaking rocks into gravel) or eating only bread and water, the Wobblies were released, and city leaders revoked the street speech ordinance and began to regulate employment agencies.

Tensions increased again in 1917 when Wobblies tried to organize workers in the wheat fields and called for a general strike during World War I, arousing the ire of farmers who blamed Spokane's civic tolerance for this "curse in our midst." To prevent the strike, a National Guard company stationed at Fort George Wright raided Wobbly Hall and arrested leaders. After the war, the IWW faced increasing harassment by civic authorities. The Spokane police raided the pool halls of Wobbly Town, interrogating and searching more than a thousand itinerant laborers in a single day. Within a few weeks, the IWW was banned in Spokane, but the state supreme court overturned that ban in 1921.

As you reach Washington, you are leaving the bindle-stiff streets and approaching the million-dollar corners of the early twentieth century, corners marked by banks, office buildings, and retail stores reached by streetcar. Emblematic of this period is the **American Legion Building**, a half block south at *108 N Washington*. It was first commissioned for the Spokane Club by F. Lewis Clark, a bon vivant and yachtsman who became wealthy from mining. Clark was the owner of the Spokane Flour Mill and a vice president of Washington Water Power. After the Spokane Club moved to new quarters on the west side of town in 1912, the Chamber of Commerce occupied this building until 1932, when it next housed the offices of both mining companies and labor unions. The American Legion bought it in 1948. The corner ceded its million-dollar label when land value and traffic moved west along Riverside.

Continue south on Washington to the **Hutton Building** *at 9 Washington Street,* best viewed from the west side of the street. When Al and May Arkwright Hutton struck it rich in a silver mine and moved to Spokane, they invested their wealth in this building. They moved into a nine-room penthouse apartment on the top floor at a time when living downtown was fashionable; their business offices were housed below. Three stories were added to the original four in 1910. The

Huttons hosted national visitors such as suffragist Susan B. Anthony and labor leader Samuel Gompers, who shared their causes. Senator William Borah of Idaho, whom May had persuaded to run for election in 1907, had his office in the building for all of his thirty-five years in the Senate.

The Huttons

The lives of May Arkwright Hutton and Levi "Al" Hutton followed the national and local progression from Populism through labor unions through Progressive reform. Both had come from hardscrabble backgrounds. May was an orphan who left Ohio to work as a cook and then started her own boardinghouse in the Coeur d'Alene mining district. There she met Al, a railroad engineer whose train was co-opted by striking miners carrying dynamite to sabotage the Bunker Hill and Sullivan Mine in 1899. Al and a thousand of the strikers were rounded up and confined in a "bull pen" until May's crusading spirit freed him and others. She wrote a novel that captured the miners' cause and letters of protest to Spokane's leading newspaper, the *Spokesman-Review*, which was supporting the owners and operators of the mine.

Like many other risk-taking westerners, the hard-working Huttons also invested in a hole in the ground, the Hercules mine. After several years of pickax action, one of the co-owners they had grubstaked found pay dirt, a rich vein of silver. Suddenly rich, the Huttons moved to Spokane in 1907 and spread their wealth among buildings and charitable and Progressive causes. May had briefly enjoyed the right to vote in Idaho, and she became a leader in the fight for women's suffrage in Washington. She persuaded the city jail to provide a matron for female prisoners and took a home for unwed mothers under her wing. She served as president of the Spokane Non-Partisan League and was the first female delegate to the Democratic National Convention.

Return north to Riverside and walk west to 421 W Riverside Avenue, another product of wealth from the Hercules mine. August Paulsen was a dairyman who had bought a share in the mine and done a lot of the digging. He built the **Paulsen Building** a year after the Huttons built theirs; it was the first real skyscraper and tallest building in Spokane at the time, eleven floors supported by steel girders.

Continue four blocks west on Riverside to Post Street and south one block to Sprague. You are again in million-dollar territory from previous centuries. The valuable real estate *on the northwest corner at 1 N Post Street* belonged to the **Whitten Block**, built for Leyford B. and Georgia Ballou Whitten in 1890. Leyford came to Spokane as a carpenter but soon found more opportunity in mining and real estate investments. Georgia was a physician, one of Spokane's first female doctors. One of the largest department stores in the state, the Crescent, later occupied a desirable spot in the Whitten Block. Today the block houses the luxury Hotel Lusso. *On the southeast corner* is the **Peyton Building**, built in 1898, using the remaining exterior walls of another building that had burned down on the site.

Another enterprising businessman who flourished after the 1889 fire was Louis Davenport, who set up a waffle iron on the street. While living in the Whitten Building, he moved his business indoors, then built a fancy restaurant across the street *on the southwest corner.* It evolved into the **Davenport Hotel**, which opened in 1914 and now occupies an entire block and more *at 10 S Post Street.* In the tradition of grand hotels that came with the railroads, the Davenport was regarded as the finest hotel in the West and the most renowned in the state. Designed by Kirtland Cutter, an architect who became famous in Spokane, it was modeled after places in fifteenth-century Florence.

Such wealth coexisted somewhat uneasily with the working class of the city. Elizabeth Gurley Flynn, a fiery young speaker for the IWW, lobbed jibes at the Davenport at a public meeting: "If the police and city government refuse the Constitutional right of free speech, the workingman should refuse to work, and if the working man refused to work, there would not be a single fat capitalist eating turtle soup in Davenport's tonight," she proclaimed.

Just east of the Davenport, in the W 700 block on the south side of Sprague, the Spokane Labor Council met every Monday night in Eiler's Hall. Their members represented many of the more conservative home-guard unions. For example, skilled workers such as barbers and firefighters were working 144 hours a week when they formed a union in 1918 and joined the council. The building has not survived.

Walk west on Sprague to N Lincoln Street, noting the **Bing Crosby Theater** on *the southwest corner* of this intersection. The theater opened in 1915 as the Clemmer Theater during the first wave of "movie palaces" in the building owned by August Paulsen, the dairy farmer who struck it rich. Howard Clemmer was a showman who gave free admission to boys with red hair because he said life is harder for redheads. The theater was recently renamed to honor the crooner who grew up in Spokane and sang at the Clemmer early in his career.

Turn north one block to Riverside, passing the **Empire State Building** *on the southwest corner of Riverside and Lincoln.* The building was designed by John Dow in 1900 as the city's first fireproof building. It was financed by Charles Sweeney, an Anglo-Irishman from New York who briefly served as the deputy U.S. marshal during the labor violence in the Coeur d'Alene mines. When Sweeney's own mining claims were upheld, he became a millionaire and formed a holding company, the Empire State–Idaho Company. He and F. Lewis Clark bankrolled several important Spokane buildings.

Walk west on Riverside to Monroe and the **Review Tower**, home of the *Spokesman-Review,* owned by the Cowles family, which has been influential in shaping the region's history. This daily descended in 1893 from the third newspaper started in Spokane. It has been publishing for more than 120 years.

Cross Monroe and then cross W Riverside Avenue to stand in front of the **Spokane Club**, the first social club in the city. At *1002 W*

Riverside Avenue, it is another building designed by Kirtland Cutter. The club marks the western end of downtown and the beginning of a boulevard planned by the Olmsted Brothers, whose designs imprinted almost every Washington city of the early 1900s. John C. Olmsted's report to the Board of Park Commissioners recommended this curving parkway with linden trees in the median.

Next door is the **Spokane Civic Building**, *at 1020 W Riverside*, once occupied by the Chamber of Commerce. Then comes the **Masonic Temple**, *at 1108 W Riverside*, built in 1925; its many members marched along Riverside Avenue to the opening. The Masons are the largest fraternal organization in the world. Fourth in the row, *at 1116 W Riverside*, is the former **Elks Temple**. The clubs and fraternal organizations of the city were almost exclusively white and male through the 1960s. For several decades, the Spokane Club was the city's most important employer of blacks, as waiters.

West of Madison, on the south side of the avenue, is the **Cathedral of Our Lady of Lourdes**, built in 1903 to serve the Diocese of Spokane, which had begun in a carpenter's shack in 1881. The diocese has served a long-established Catholic working-class community, including southern European, Irish, and now Spanish-speaking immigrants. The power elite in Spokane has largely been Protestant, but the cathedral is the city's largest church building.

Peaceful Valley

The parkway becomes pedestrian unfriendly at Cedar Street, but you may want to take a side trip down the stairs toward the river just before the Maple Street bridge. The metal steps descend to the continuation of Cedar Street and the neighborhood known as **Peaceful Valley**, once an encampment site of the Spokane tribe, then a Finnish neighborhood of modest Victorian houses, and now a contemporary encampment of Volkswagen vans. Peaceful Valley Finns managed a pool hall and soft-drink establishment called the "Working Men's Place" in Wobbly Town.

Glover Field, east of where Cedar meets the river, was the site of the community's early Fourth of July celebrations and later provided a field for athletic competitions before high schools had their own fields. About a mile west of here, where Hangman (Latah) Creek flows into the river, is People's Park, first an Indian winter camp, once a free hippie-style camp for 5,000 visitors to the world's fair, and now a nudist beach in a section of High Bridge Park.

Return on Riverside Avenue, or up W Main Avenue from Peaceful Valley, to the **Spokane Public Library** *at Lincoln and Main.* The library was constructed on a hillside augmented by debris from the 1889 fire. Across the street from the north side of the library, the current **City Hall**, *at Spokane Falls Boulevard and Post Street,* occupies the former Montgomery Ward building on a choice spot above the lower falls of the river. Montgomery Ward was the innovator of retail trade in its day, first using a catalog order model to serve a rural population and in 1929 opening this store, which faced the city's retail core to the south and the railroad tracks to the north, quite convenient for shipping goods. Sears, Roebuck built a store the same year just one block away. Sears moved to a shopping center in the 1950s and Montgomery Ward moved to the east end of town in the 1970s and is no longer in business in Spokane.

The downtown blocks you have walked were the retail, business, and civic centers of the city. Institutions such as the newspaper, the Masons, the Spokane Club, the Chamber of Commerce, City Hall, the library, and the churches that spread out mainly south of downtown solidified the character of the city—home-owning, middle-class, somewhat conservative, predominantly white and Protestant, with a small African American population, a small Japanese population, Italians in Hillyard, and Finns in Peaceful Valley. Starting in the 1920s, Spokane comfortably dominated the Inland Empire, but that was not the end of the story.

Return to **Riverfront Park**, the site of Spokane's world's fair. When Spokane launched Expo '74, ten countries agreed to participate and build pavilions. Most of the fair buildings were modular, to be removed after the fair, but there are legacies throughout the hundred-acre park as well as later additions.

Pass the sculpture of the Bloomsday runners, a marker of the city's efforts to encourage recreation events in the heart of downtown. The Bloomsday Run started in 1977, inspired by Olympic runner Don Kardong. It attracts thousands every May, starting and ending in the park. The bike and pedestrian Centennial Trail, a legacy of the 1989 Washington State Centennial, winds through the park and generally follows the curves of the river for more than thirty-seven miles, west to Nine Mile Falls and east to the Idaho border.

Walk east past the popular **Looff Carousel**, designed by Charles Looff. It was originally installed in Natatorium Park in 1909 and moved here after the fair. The carousel is hand carved with horses, a giraffe, a tiger, and two Chinese dragon chairs. *East of Stevens Street*, between Spokane Falls Boulevard and what was the south channel of the river, is the **Radio Flyer Wagon**, created for the state's centennial. Beyond it is the fair's former Washington State pavilion, now part of the Spokane Convention Center and Opera House. Hoboes, twentieth-century counterparts to the earlier bindle stiffs, were dislodged from camps near here for construction of the fair.

Explore the park at your leisure. You may cross the south channel of the river on Washington Street to the east end of Havermale Island. The railroad tracks, trestles, and yards that had covered Havermale Island since the early 1900s were a major obstacle to reclaiming the river and hosting a world's fair. By the 1960s, rail commerce had declined, and railroad companies agreed to donate their valuable property as a contribution to the fair and the revitalization of downtown. Trestles were torn down and tracks were removed, but Spokane citizens were reluctant to let all the rail memories go. They lobbied to retain the **Great Northern Depot clock tower**, built in 1901. The tower still towers and still tells the time.

Arrive at the **central meadow**, west of the tower on Havermale Island. On this meadow Spokane Indians gather in August to pow-wow. By 1898, Indians had to obtain a pass, signed by a federal agent, to come into Spokane. Three areas significant to their former life are now golf courses: The Creek at Qualchan, Hangman Valley Golf Course, and Indian Canyon Golf Course, in the area where Spokane Garry last lived. The powwows reclaim a temporary right to camp by the river.

And what of the river itself? Redband rainbow trout are the indicator species of the river's health. On the opening day of the fair, 1,974 trout were released to demonstrate that the reclaimed river was healthy. The Spokane tribal hatchery releases 750,000 trout annually downriver, yet trout numbers have been declining in recent years. For many years after the fair, the river almost dried up every summer from heavy use of its water. As part of the relicensing of Avista's dams in 2009, under pressure from environmentalists, the power company agreed to allow year-round and all-day water flows. A new sewage treatment plant was built after the fair to address that pollution.

Expo '74 revived downtown Spokane as King Cole had urged, but the river at its heart faces continuing challenges from dams, condominium development, and mine tailings. Despite the powerful force of nature that made Spokane a city, the river in its midst runs a perilous course.

Resources   Spokane Historical, http://www.spokanehistorical.org/

Spokane Public Library, 906 W Main Avenue

Spokane Visitor Information Center, 808 W Main Avenue

Northwest Museum of Arts and Culture, 2316 W 1st Avenue

CHAPTER TEN

Bellevue

Edge City

We didn't have any pedestrians we could identify any place.
We had lots of cars.

Fred Herman, Bellevue city planner

Bellevue did not follow an ordinary course to cityhood. Homesteads nestled sparsely in the lowlands between Lake Washington and Lake Sammamish. No deepwater port lured a transcontinental railroad and pumped up local land speculation. No river provided power for mills. No heavy industry grew on its waterfront. Instead, Bellevue was a playground for Seattle, a destination for picnics and excursions, a source of strawberries and blueberries, and, after World War II, a bedroom. It did not incorporate until 1953, so how did this suburb become the fifth-largest city in the state?

Communities on the east side of Lake Washington, east of Seattle, began with the simultaneous discovery of coal and the passage of the Homestead Act of 1862. The coal mining was concentrated in the Issaquah Alps, ancient mountains southeast of what is now Bellevue. The Homestead Act promised 160 acres to any adult who would live on the land and make improvements. One of the first land claims in what would become Bellevue was made by William Meydenbauer, a Seattle baker who built a summer home on a bay. The first real homesteaders were Aaron and Ann Mercer, who settled for a few years along a slough that was once an arm of Lake Washington. Clark Merrill Sturtevant stayed longer. In 1873 he made a Civil War veteran's claim on 160 acres between NE 8th Street and SE 8th Street, from 112th to 116th Avenues, immensely valuable land today. When the post office needed a name for the settlement, homesteaders chose Bellevue to reflect the beautiful view of lakes and mountains to both east and west.

By 1900 there were more than 400 people clustered near the waterfront on Meydenbauer Bay, in neighborhoods like Killarney, Medina, the Points, and Clyde Hill. Ten years later the population had tripled. Promotional brochures touted a type of clean living on the east side of Lake Washington: "plenty of pure air and an abundance of the purest water (but no saloons)."

The construction of the ship canal from Puget Sound to Lake Washington in 1916 had two effects on Bellevue. To balance the relative heights of the bodies of water, Lake Washington was lowered by almost nine feet, which drew water from Mercer Slough and made it unnavigable, especially for the logging company at its northern end. On the plus side, Meydenbauer Bay suddenly had a saltwater connection. The American Pacific Whaling Company started storing its whaling ships there during the winter.

During the 1920s and 1930s Bellevue was a farming community, producing lettuce, apples, poultry, milk, grapes, rabbits, mink, and especially strawberries, most of which were grown by Japanese immigrants. Most Issei, the first-generation Japanese Americans, were not eligible for citizenship under U.S. immigration law and could not own land under the Washington Alien Land Law of 1921, so they leased land for periods of about five years. They would clear the stumps from logged-over land, create small farms, and then move on to another plot when their leases ended. In this manner, much of the logged land was made arable. "All you needed to grow strawberries was one horse, one plow, and lots of kids," one Issei commented.

The community celebrated with the first strawberry festival in 1925, and in ten years three times as many visitors (15,000) were coming to the festival as there were people living in Bellevue. Then came 1941, when the Japanese Navy attacked Pearl Harbor, bringing the United States into World War II. Sixty Japanese American families from Bellevue were transferred to internment camps inland; only eleven would return after the war. Most of the returnees had owned land through their children, who were born in the United States and were citizens; a few had bought land before the restrictive laws of 1921.

With internment and the wartime shortage of workers, harvesting and planting on small farms halted, never to be resumed. Instead, the cleared land proved ideal for housing developments. Bellevue's largest growth came after World War II. Veterans finished college on the GI Bill and started families. They bought homes with Veterans Administration loans at low interest rates in neighborhoods like Surrey Downs, Enatai, and Eastgate. In 1955, more than 4,000 homes were built in Lake Hills—"Bellevue's Levittown"—with its own small shopping center but no hills. These houses in the Northwest's largest planned community were not luxury homes, but they were modern and offered a new start after the privations of the 1930s and '40s. Vuecrest, built on a 160-acre farm just northwest of Main Street, promised "gracious living." Developments like Newport Hills, Somerset, and Robinswood promised easy access to the four-lane state highway that would become I-90.

"Imagine yourself in a country setting, just 15 minutes from work!" real estate brochures invited. Ranch and split-level homes were designed with off-street parking, acknowledging that each household would have at least one car. Many were built in the Northwest Modern style of architecture with wooden materials abundant in the region and sited to take advantage of a natural setting. Developments like Lake Hills, Newport Hills, and Somerset provided their own swimming pools and tennis courts. Many parents worked at an expanding Boeing, which hired British engineers who came home from work and coached their children's soccer teams.

Suburbs were not new. Ballard was a 700-acre housing development in 1883, connected to Seattle by the Seattle, Lake Shore and Eastern Railroad, a twenty-minute ride. West Seattle and Columbia City developed on the outskirts, too, until they were annexed to Seattle in 1907. Nor were developers new. James Ditty, a resident of Beaux Arts Village within Bellevue, began buying up land north of Main Street in 1928, envisioning 200,000 people living on the Eastside amid skyscrapers and hotels.

Such growth didn't happen until highways and bridges crossed Lake Washington. Everything depended on commuting easily by car. The term *Overlake*, used often on the Eastside, meant across (or over) Lake Washington from Seattle. When the first bridge to Seattle opened in 1940, Ditty's vision made sense. He sold off parcels of land, including ten acres to Miller Freeman and his son, Kemper, who built the second shopping mall on Puget Sound after Northgate. A square with a large parking lot surrounded by stores opened in 1946 just north of Bellevue's old main street, its goal to keep shoppers on the Eastside.

With a retail center in place, Bellevue incorporated in 1953 in order to improve roads, sewers, and fire and police protection and to gain control of planning and zoning. That same decade the city built a hospital and library. The city core was only five square miles, but over the next twenty years many outlying neighborhoods voted to annex to Bellevue so as to obtain better services. The supermarket chain Safeway located a distribution center to the northeast of downtown in 1958, the city's first major business. When Seattle finished its transition from private to public power, Puget Sound Energy, a private company, moved to Bellevue in 1956. Bellevue came of age as an edge city—a work, retail, and entertainment center that emerged outside an urban downtown (Seattle) in a place that had been mixed rural and residential.

Growth continued into the 1960s. A Dairy Queen and McDonald's opened, and the city's first skyscraper rose seven stories. In 1963, a second bridge opened across Lake Washington, the Albert D.

Rosellini Memorial Evergreen Point Floating Bridge, known collo-quially as the (Highway) 520 Bridge. Bellevue nestled snugly between the two bridges to Seattle. That same year construction began on I-405, which replaced the two-lane Highway 2A and cut through Bellevue neighborhoods and downtown, allowing access for Boeing workers to plants in both Everett and Renton. US Highway 10, across Lake Washington, became the last link of I-90 from Boston to Seattle. PACCAR International located its headquarters in the city in the early 1970s; Nintendo and Microsoft started up soon thereafter. By 1970, Bellevue's population had increased tenfold since incorporation, from approximately 6,000 to 61,000.

Bellevue became a city during the golden age of urban planning. Its council–city manager type of government gave staff a lot of influ-ence. "It was the nearest thing to a clean sheet of paper that I think any planner ever encountered," said Fred Herman, Bellevue's first and longest-serving city planner. There was no abandoned down-town or declining housing stock. "That was a beautiful thing to see because there was almost nothing here that you had to renew or tear down. Urban renewal was for some other place, not here."

Unlike cities built for horses and carriages or Interurbans, Bellevue was built for the automobile. "We didn't have any pedestrians we could identify anyplace," Herman said. "We had lots of cars," and so the city designed megablocks—roads placed far apart but with large capacity—six-lane arterials—which still make for easier driving than walking.

While building a commercial center, annexing sprawling neigh-borhoods, and touting a convenient commute, the city quickly built schools and preserved land for parks. When baby boomers crowded the schools between 1952 and 1972, Bellevue School District built twenty-five new elementary schools, six middle schools, and three high schools. The parks department used a "pearls on a string" approach, with public lands connected by proximity and trails to create a "city in a park." The city was one of the first in the nation to implement a storm- and surface-water utility, using streams instead of sewers to channel runoff and reduce flooding. Property owners were taxed more in proportion to the amount of paved land they owned.

When downtown businesses threatened to encroach on surrounding neighborhoods, Bellevue developed a wedding-cake approach to growth with step-down densities: retail and office buildings would be highest and most concentrated in the center, with lower building heights on the perimeter. When Bellevue Square wanted to expand, it built up rather than out. The square still symbolizes Bellevue's upscale aspirations and orientation to the automobile; its enclosed mall is accessed through multiple parking garages.

As glass office towers and apartment buildings rose downtown, Bellevue dropped out of the Suburban Cities Association in 1996, indicating its more urban than suburban identity. By the end of the century, it had more jobs than residents. The phrase "reverse commute" described the phenomenon of just as many people driving from Seattle to the Eastside to work as drive from the Eastside to Seattle. In 2003, the city celebrated its fiftieth anniversary, halfway to a centennial. What had been a largely white, middle-class enclave attracted diverse families; by 2010, more than 30 percent of the city's population was born outside the United States, with the largest groups from East and South Central Asia.

The evolution of Bellevue from bedroom community to edge city foreshadowed the path of similar suburbs, such as Kent, Federal Way, and Spokane Valley, which have also climbed into the ranks of the state's most populous cities. One challenge remains—that a city have a walkable downtown.

This chapter begins with a short heritage loop in the homesteading, logging, and farming history of Mercer Slough. It offers an extended walk through a midcentury suburban neighborhood. The downtown loop finds Old Main Street and the one building that dates from the 1890s, then skirts Meydenbauer Bay and ends at Bellevue Square and the downtown park, rimmed by glass towers that scream city.

Pioneer Walk: Mercer Slough Heritage Trail

START:	Winters House Visitor Center, 2102 Bellevue Way SE
DIRECTIONS:	Access the visitor center from the south on Bellevue Way. From I-90, take the Bellevue Way exit. From the north, turn around at the South Bellevue Park and Ride and return north to the visitor center. (Light-rail construction along Bellevue Way may make access difficult.)
DISTANCE:	1 mile round trip
AMENITIES:	Parking at Winters House; restrooms at Winters House and the Mercer Slough Blueberry Farm

To sample the first thirty years of Bellevue history, begin on the **Mercer Slough**, which was an arm of Lake Washington. Six interpretive signs recount natural and human history along the Heritage Trail, a walking loop on boardwalks and dirt paths.

Begin at the eclectic Spanish-style **Winters House**, which was built on the northwest corner of the Mercer Slough Blueberry Farm in 1929. The Winters family grew iris and daffodil bulbs and azaleas for their wholesale floral business on the slough. *Leave from the north side of the house and follow the walk clockwise* to a collapsing and almost-drowned **boiler room** for their greenhouses, the first stop on the trail.

The name *Mercer* comes from Ann and Aaron Mercer, who homesteaded on the west side of the slough beginning in 1869. Aaron was the younger brother of Seattle settlers Asa and Thomas Mercer, after whom Mercer Island was named. Ann and Aaron soon moved to south Seattle to be closer to schools for their eight children.

The slough was next used as a log storage pond by the Hewitt-Lea Lumber Company. Co-owners John and Henry Hewitt were the sons

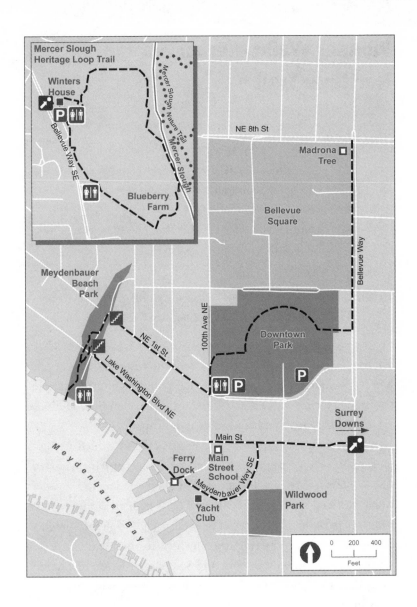

Mercer Slough
Heritage Loop Trail

Winters
House

Bellevue Way SE

Mercer Slough Nature Trail

Mercer Slough

Blueberry
Farm

NE 8th St

Madrona
Tree

Bellevue
Square

Bellevue Way

Meydenbauer
Beach
Park

NE 1st St

100th Ave NE

Downtown
Park

Lake Washington Blvd NE

Surrey
Downs

Main St

Meydenbauer Bay

Ferry
Dock

Main
Street
School

Meydenbauer Way SE

Yacht
Club

Wildwood
Park

0   200   400
Feet

of the Wisconsin lumberman Henry Hewitt, who invested in mills in Tacoma and Everett. Charles Lea was married to their sister Clara. The company supplied building materials for homes, a fitting precursor to Bellevue. In 1916, when the ship canal was built to connect Lake Washington with Puget Sound, the lake was lowered; the slough receded and became unnavigable to steamships. Only kayaks and canoes float it today.

Millworkers for the lumber company lived on Wilburton Hill to the east of the slough, but the construction of Highway 2-A in the 1940s (now I-405) eliminated any traces of the logging community except for a very high railroad trestle that crosses SE 8th Street at the northeastern corner of the slough. Completed in 1904, the trestle carried a Northern Pacific belt line that ran north and south along the east side of Lake Washington. It is no longer active.

At the bridge over the slough, go right toward the South Bellevue Park and Ride and the **Mercer Slough Blueberry Farm**, one of several enterprises that took advantage of the peat bog created by the lowering of the lake. Several trails branch off from the Heritage Trail here, crossing the slough and leading to the Mercer Slough Environmental Education Center. The last stop on the loop recounts the acquisition and restoration of the Mercer Slough Nature Park, and the trail returns to the Winters House.

Surrey Downs

For a sense of how a suburb became a city, walk from the Winters House through the neighborhoods of Bel Crest and Surrey Downs. Walk north along Bellevue Way, crossing 112th Avenue, then veering right on 108th as it moves uphill from the gas station that has been on this corner since the 1950s. It's sixteen blocks to Main Street, a round trip from the Winters House of three miles. The walk reaches the crest of what was known as Raine hill or Bellevue Park. From the crest, I-405 is visible to the east, as is a 1970s housing development on Somerset hill to the southeast. Just past the crest, pass entrances to the athletic fields and back of **Bellevue High School**, opened in 1949 as students outgrew Union High School downtown. The 2003 *Newsweek* ranking of the top hundred high schools in the nation included all five Bellevue high schools, placing three in the top twenty.

Just before SE 3rd Street, cross the street at a crossing and take a trail down stairs. At the bottom of the steps, make a short jog left and continue on an asphalt path to 109th; continue east along SE 3rd to 110th Avenue and the neighborhood of **Surrey Downs**, with homes typical of the 1950s. Many are ranch or split-level houses with carports or garages located beneath the living space. Thirty-five homes in Surrey Downs have elements that are still true to their original form of more than fifty years ago; fifteen were built in the Northwest Modern style. This cluster of mid-century designs makes the neighborhood a potential historic district in the National Register of Historic Places, a feature residents hope will protect it from the encroachments of light rail.

Almost every new neighborhood in Bellevue had an elementary school to go with it. Surrey Downs Elementary School opened in 1962 and closed in 1981, as homeowners aged and student populations moved farther away from downtown.

More change is coming. In just a few years, Sound Transit light rail will run north from I-90 along Bellevue Way. Avoiding the Bel Crest hill, it will veer northeast on 112th through low land along the east side of Surrey Downs. A form of transportation foreign to the car-dominant culture of Bellevue, light rail faced many political obstacles until Eastside voters approved it in 1996 and the Bellevue City Council approved the final route in 2013. Completion of the line with stations downtown is planned for 2023.

Take 110th Avenue north to Main Street. From here, you may walk west two blocks and loop back along 108th Avenue to the Winters House, or continue west on Bellevue's megablocks to begin the downtown loop at Main and Bellevue Way.

Bellevue Loop

START: Main Street and Bellevue Way SE (104th Avenue)

DIRECTIONS: From I-90, take the Bellevue Way exit and drive north to
                  Main Street. From I-405, take the SE 8th Street exit and
                  drive west to Bellevue Way, then north to Main Street. To
                  find parking at Downtown Bellevue Park, continue north
                  on Bellevue Way and turn west (left) on NE 2nd Street.

DISTANCE: 3 miles round trip

AMENITIES: Parking on streets and south and west parking lots of
                  Downtown Bellevue Park; restrooms at Downtown
                  Bellevue Park and Meydenbauer Beach Park.

Early commercial history began at Bellevue Way and **Old Main Street**. A few buildings from the early 1900s remain, and the street retains a smaller scale than the rest of downtown, but higher density is encroaching. The west corners of this intersection illustrate that change. A barber shop that operated for eighty years at *10251 Main Street* was torn down in 2013. A building across the street, *10246 Main,* built in 1920, remains (address numbering decreases as you walk west). Another remaining building on the same block on the south side, *10203 Main,* was first a bank and then a popular soda fountain, Lakeside Drugs.

The Philbrook House, believed to have been built as a farmhouse in the 1890s for Civil War veteran Alphonse Philbrook, was the oldest structure on the street *at 10135 Main Street* until it was demolished in 2015, erasing what little remained of a truly old Bellevue. An interpretive plaque on the new office building will commemorate the house. A decrepit building at 105 102nd Avenue SE, just south of Main, housed Bellevue Realty, founded in 1925 by Charles Bovee, who became Bellevue's first mayor.

Students pose on the steps of the Main Street School, built in the 1890s. The building was used as a school until 1942, then became a VFW (Veterans of Foreign Wars) Hall, and, in 1953, Bellevue's first city hall. It was condemned in 1965, when Bellevue schools had expanded greatly. Image courtesy of the Eastside Heritage Center.

Continue west on Main Street, passing the site of George Hanson's garage on the north side of Main near 102nd. *On the north side at 101st* was the McKee Building, built in 1924, which housed a variety of businesses in six retail units, including a candy shop, variety store, post office, drug store, and gas station. The original building was replaced in the 1990s by an apartment complex that retained small shop space on the street floor.

Main and 100th Avenue was the central intersection of old Bellevue and the site of the first schoolhouse in 1892. A kiosk on the southeast corner illustrates the Main Street School, which served

Cars from Seattle drive off the ferry at the Bellevue dock on Meydenbauer Bay, circa 1915. Early Bellevue was a vacation and recreation destination. Image courtesy of the Eastside Heritage Center.

grades 1–8 until 1912, then added four more grades until a new elementary school opened in 1923. The Main Street School continued as the city's first high school until 1942. It became the city hall when Bellevue was incorporated in 1953. The gas station replaced the condemned building in 1965.

Return east to 101st Avenue, and walk south past the northwestern end of **Wildwood Park**, a historic destination for Seattle residents who came over on the ferry for picnics, music, and boxing matches. *Walk west on Meydenbauer Way SE,* past the **Meydenbauer Bay Yacht Club**, which was originally part of the park, used for dancing, rollerskating, and other indoor recreation. It has been a yacht club since 1946. The ferry docked at the foot of 100th Avenue.

Continue along the City of Bellevue piers on Meydenbauer Bay to 99th Avenue SE. The bay was the winter home for seven boats in the American Pacific Whaling Company fleet. Freshwater helped kill barnacles and shipworms off their hulls. President William Schupp had moved the company's corporate headquarters to Bellevue in 1919 because he lived there. The company hunted whales along the coast of British Columbia and Alaska until 1941.

Walk north on 99th to Lake Washington Boulevard NE and *walk west* to a bridge that crosses a ravine. *Walk down steps* to **Meydenbauer Beach Park**, which was constructed in 1935 by the Works Progress Administration, a federal program to stimulate public works during the Great Depression. The park was forgotten in the 1940s but rediscovered in 1954 as one of the first park properties in Bellevue's string of pearls.

After visiting the beach, *walk uphill through the park and up stairs just past the turnaround circle* to NE 1st Street. *Follow 1st east* to the **Downtown Park** between 100th and Bellevue Way (104th). This is not a town square set aside in original land claims but a park developed from land sold by the Bellevue School District in the 1980s. As retail overtook housing in the downtown area, schools moved out. A city proposition to create the park failed by just a few votes in 1984, prompting private and corporate money to step in.

From the fountain at the north entrance to the park, a **concrete outline** of Overlake Elementary School is visible in the grass. The park includes memorials in the form of a flagpole and plaque and three **elm trees** (for three Bellevue citizens who were killed or reported missing in action in World War I). **Cherry trees** in the northeast corner recall Japanese American contributions to the city's history. The wide, flat land that characterizes downtown Bellevue was ideal for strawberry farming from the 1920s into the 1940s.

The park borders the south side of **Bellevue Square**, the icon of Bellevue's growth. Miller Freeman bought the land on which the square was built from James Ditty, the 1920s developer with an urban vision. Freeman's son Kemper visited several of the new shopping malls springing up around the country after World War II. The result was an assemblage of twenty low-rise buildings where shoppers could park as close to the front doors as possible. Frederick and Nelson

A much loved madrona tree stood on Bellevue Way in front of the first version of Bellevue Square until the tree died in 1961. Image courtesy of the Eastside Heritage Center.

opened its first department store in a shopping center at the square, as did J. C. Penney, in 1955, its first shopping-center store in Washington. In the 1980s, the mall was built up and enclosed.

Leave the park on the east side on a walkway at NE 3rd and walk north on the west side of Bellevue Way. After Bellevue's renowned strawberry festival ended in 1942, when Japanese American families were interned, an arts and crafts fair gradually replaced it. The first took place in 1947, one year after the shopping center had opened, on Bellevue Way between NE 6th and NE 8th Streets, in front of the Crabapple Restaurant and under a much-beloved madrona tree. It was at the fair that Kemper Freeman first met Dudley Carter, who was using an ax to carve a large cedar trunk. Freeman commissioned Carter to create Bellevue's first public artwork, called *Forest Deity*. (The twelve-foot carving now stands in a small planting area outside the massive north wall of the square's main parking garage on NE 8th Street.)

End the walk in comfort in the lobby of the Lodge *on Bellevue Way, just south of NE 8th Street*. Above the fireplace is a carving done by Anna Hanson, granddaughter of Dudley Carter. When the madrona tree in front of the Crabapple died in 1961, Freeman planted an Atlantic cedar to replace it. When that tree had to be moved because of the square's expansion, Hanson carted it to British Columbia and carved it in her grandfather's style, returning the carving to Bellevue with the name *Full Circle*.

Farms

For several decades, Bellevue was a community of small farms. Much of the farmland was leased to Japanese immigrants who practiced truck farming, growing a variety of crops harvested at different times from the same small plot. Crops were trucked to the Pike Place Market in Seattle or collected at a cooperative warehouse at 11660 NE 8th Street, near the railroad tracks. Besides strawberries, local farms also produced lettuce, apples, grapes, blueberries, cabbage, milk, rabbits, poultry, and mink. Most of that farmland turned to housing after the war, but some acres were too boggy for backyards. Some of those became city parks.

The **Mercer Slough Blueberry Farm**, known historically as the Overlake Blueberry Farm, still produces blueberries at 2380 Bellevue Way SE, in the Mercer Slough Nature Park on the heritage loop, as does **Larsen Lake Blueberry Farm** at 700 148th Avenue SE in the Lake Hills neighborhood. The farm is named for Ove and Mary Larsen, Danes who homesteaded in 1890. They harvested wild blue huckleberries and cranberries, then sold the land to others who became vegetable and blueberry farmers. In 1966, 152 acres of farmland were released to the city. The land now includes two miles of trails in the Lake Hills Greenbelt and a restored **cabin**, which was built about 1890 near Phantom Lake.

The hill to the east of downtown Bellevue had trees 200 feet tall that were logged early in the twentieth century. Calhoun and Harriet Shorts farmed the land and donated it and their home for a park in 1984. It became the Bellevue Botanical Garden at 12001 Main Street.

Finally, **Kelsey Creek Park**, at 410 130th Place SE, has introduced farm animals to generations of Bellevue children. The park was originally the Twin Valley Dairy Farm and retains barns built in the 1920s and '40s on a hill between two valleys. In the days before teaching could support a family, Bellevue's second schoolteacher, Henry E. Kelsey, owned the land surrounding the creek. The park has 1.5 miles of trails and a **log cabin** that dates from 1888.

Resources: Bellevue Public Library, 1111 110th Avenue NE

Eastside Heritage Center, 2102 Bellevue Way SE

Tourist Information Center, 11100 NE 6th Street

Sources

Sources used in this book range from books written in the nineteenth century to twenty-first-century blogs. This list provides bibliographic information for sources mentioned by name and sources for quotes.

Benbow, Mike. "Last of the Big Smokestacks." *Herald Business Journal,* September 2, 2011.

Berry, Don. *The Lowell Story: A Community History.* Lowell, WA: Lowell Civic Association, 1985.

Carver, Raymond. *Carver Country: The World of Raymond Carver.* With photographs by Bob Adelman and an introduction by Tess Gallagher. New York: Arcade Publishing, 1994.

Clark, Norman H. *Mill Town: A Social History of Everett, Washington, from Its Earliest Beginnings on the Shores of Puget Sound to the Tragic and Infamous Event Known as the Everett Massacre.* Seattle: University of Washington Press, 1970.

Curtis, Wayne. *The Last Great Walk: The True Story of a 1909 Walk from New York to San Francisco, and Why It Matters Today.* New York: Rodale, 2014.

Daniels, Roger. "Provision Camp." *Columbia, the Magazine of Northwest History.* Tacoma: Washington State Historical Society, Fall 2002.

Dillard, Annie. *The Living.* New York: HarperCollins, 1992.

Douglas, William O. *Go East, Young Man: The Early Years.* New York: Random House, 1974.

Edson, Lelah Jackson. *The Fourth Corner: Highlights from the Early Northwest.* Bellingham, WA: Whatcom Museum of History and Art: 1968. First published 1951.

Herman, John Frederick, Steve Cohn, and Betty J. Sellers. *Oral History of Fred Herman, Bellevue's First Planning Director: History Taken on October 16, 18, 1990.* Bellevue: City of Bellevue Planning Department, 1990.

Jacobs, Jane. *The Death and Life of Great American Cities.* New York: Random House, 1961.

Kleeman, Karl, and William Rink. *Rail Trail Walking Guide: Fairhaven to Bellingham.* Bellingham: Bellingham Railway Museum, 2013.

Lyman, W. D. *History of the Yakima Valley Washington, Comprising Yakima, Kittitas, and Benton Counties.* Vol. 1. Chicago: S. J. Clarke, 1904.

———. *Lyman's History of Old Walla Walla County, Embracing Walla Walla, Columbia, Garfield and Asotin Counties.* Vol. 1. Chicago: S. J. Clarke, 1918.

Moody, Fred. "Bellingham, My Hometown." *Pacific Magazine,* the *Seattle Times,* October 5, 1986.

Morgan, Murray. *The Mill on the Boot: The Story of the St. Paul and Tacoma Lumber Company.* Seattle: University of Washington Press, 1982.

———. *Puget's Sound: A Narrative of Early Tacoma and the Southern Sound.* Seattle: University of Washington Press, 2003. First published 1979.

Myers, Ronald A. "Labor Pains." *The Inlander,* September 9, 1998.

Newbill, James. "Farmers and Wobblies in the Yakima Valley, 1933." *Pacific Northwest Quarterly* 68 (1977): 84.

Newell, Gordon R. *So Fair a Dwelling Place: A History of Olympia and Thurston County, Washington.* Olympia: Olympia News Publishing Company, 1950.

Plan of Seattle. Report of the Municipal Plans Commission, submitting Report of Virgil G. Bogue, engineer. 1911. Seattle: Lowman & Hanford Co. 1911. Seattle Municipal Archives record series 9359-01.

"Report, Olmsted Brothers, to A. L. White, Board of Park Commissioners, Spokane." In *Board of Park Commissioners, Spokane—Annual Report, 1891–1913.* Spokane: Board of Park Commissioners, 1914.

Solnit, Rebecca. *Wanderlust: A History of Walking.* New York: Penguin, 2000.

Stevenson, Shanna. *Olympiana: Historical Vignettes of Olympia's People and Places.* Olympia: Washington State Capitol Museum, 1982.

Stilgoe, John R. *Outside Lies Magic. Regaining History and Awareness in Everyday Places.* New York: Walker and Company, 1998.

Wade, Richard C. *The Urban Frontier: The Rise of Western Cities, 1790–1830.* Urbana: University of Illinois Press, 1966. First published 1959 by Harvard University Press.

Wilkeson, Samuel. *Wilkeson's Notes on Puget Sound.* n.p.: 1869.

Wilson, Douglas C., and Theresa E. Langford, eds. *Exploring Fort Vancouver.* Seattle: University of Washington Press, 2011.

Woodridge, Sally B., and Roger Montgomery. *A Guide to Architecture in Washington State: An Environmental Perspective.* Seattle: University of Washington Press, 1980.

Work Projects Administration. *The New Washington: A Guide to the Evergreen State.* Compiled by workers of the Writers' Program of the Work Projects Administration in the State of Washington. Rev. ed. With added material by Howard McKinley Corning. Washington State Historical Society. Portland: Binfords & Mort, 1950.

Youngs, J. William T. *The Fair and the Falls: Spokane Expo '74: Transforming an American Environment.* Eastern Washington University Press, 1996.

Acknowledgments

The writing of this book depended on the work of local historians, librarians, archivists, and city planners. They have been researching and writing, guiding research, answering tourist questions, planning city trails and leading walks for years. I am indebted to the writings and comments of many—first, to veteran guidebook writer Joan Burton, who encouraged and accompanied me in researching and writing the early chapters. Ruth Kirk reviewed every line of the manuscript, asking good questions. Charles LeWarne shared clippings about Washington cities that he has been gathering for decades. The list of others who contributed is long and star studded: Jean Akers, Elliott Barnett, John Baule, Larry Cebula, Gail Chism, Daniel Clark, David Dilgard, Ed Echtle, Colin Fogarty, Kathryn Franks, Sarah Frederick, Chris Friday, Jeff Jewell, Ron Karabaich, Lisa Labovitch, Ron Magden, Kelly McAllister, Lorraine McConaghy, Chuck Morrison, Randy Nelson, Jack O'Donnell, Lawrence O'Donnell, Ray and Susan Paolella, Lethene Parks, Jim Price, Jerry Ramsey, Bradley Richardson, Richard Sims, Shanna Stevenson, Michael Sullivan, Heather Trescases, Mike Twist, Terry Walker, Diane Wiatr, David Williams, Antoinette Wills, Dale Wirsing, and Courtney Yilk.

It also depended on field testers who tried out the walks. Thanks to Allen Bentley, Anne Bentley, Ashley Gossens, Gretchen Hawley, Amy Hines, Phyllis Johnson, Jackie Kallay, Kelly McAllister, Susan Morris, Peder and Carlynn Nelson, Randy and Karen Nelson, Jim

Price, Darlyne Reiter, Jim Ruble, Shirley Ruble, Tom and Kristi Weir, and, of course, to the intrepid Tuesday Trekkers willing to venture almost anywhere: Lynn Hall, Juli Hill, Sherry Katsuhisa, Arlyn Kerr, Lucia McDonald, Joy Neuzil, Linda Paros, and Marlee Richard. In both history and geography, the errors are mine, but they were much diminished by this cadre of walkers.

Most of all, I would like to thank the supportive and creative folks at the University of Washington Press: Pat Soden, Marianne Keddington-Lang, Nicole Mitchell, Emily Park, and especially Regan Huff, who walked this book through its challenging course.

Index

Campbell, John, 146

canneries, 78, 157, 162–63, 174, 175, 177–79, 181, 192

Carlson, Oscar, 151

Carnegie, Andrew, 146, 180; libraries, 146, 180

Carr, Job, 72, 73, 74, 81, 82

Carter, Dudley, 253, 254

Caruana, Joseph, 202

Carver, Jack, 159, 184

Carver, Raymond, 192, 194, 209, 257

Cascade Lumber Company, 208

Cascade Mountains, 4, 47, 71, 73, 130, 187

Casino (of the Chinook), 21

Cathlapotle, 9

Catholics, 5, 163, 183, 218, 223–24, 234

Cayuse Indians, 47–49, 61–62; war, 54

Celilo Falls, viii

Chambers of Commerce, 91, 100, 155, 230, 234, 235

Chavez, Cesar, 193

Cha-wit-zit, 158, 166

Chehalis River, 23

Cherry Point, 165, 175

Cheshiahud, 115, 118, 119, 122, 127

Chicago, viii, 92, 102, 112, 115, 133, 161, 173, 178, 188, 226

Chicago, Milwaukee, St. Paul, and Pacific Railroad. *See* Milwaukee Road

Chinese Exclusion Acts of 1882 and 1892, 78, 162

Chinese immigrants, 38, 66, 72, 77, 78, 81, 91, 102, 108, 110, 162, 177, 179, 218

Chinook Indians, 3, 4, 5, 9, 12, 20, 21

Chinook jargon, 14, 31, 34, 98, 115

Chittenden, Hiram, 101

churches, xvi, 40, 52, 53, 64, 190, 192, 205; Baptist, 145; Catholic, 17, 54, 55, 66, 163, 181, 182, 202, 203, 234; Christian, 66; Church of Christ Scientist, 202; Church of England, 5; Community, 136; Congregational, 52, 66; Episcopal, 82, 201; Methodist, 32, 41; Methodist Episcopal, 66; Presbyterian, 41, 146

Civilian Conservation Corps, 16

Civil War, 15, 26, 38, 71, 72, 82, 99, 168, 240, 249

Clark, Daniel, 65

Clark, F. Lewis, 230, 233

Clark, John Judson, 147

Clark, Margaret, 153

Clark, Norman H., 150, 152, 257

Clark, William. *See* Lewis and Clark

Clark County, 8, 17

Clark County Historical Museum, 17, 22

Clemmer, Howard, 233

Cleveland, Grover, 227

Clough, David Marston, 132, 153

Clough-Hartley mill, 132*fig.*, 153

coal, vii, 71, 74, 86, 98, 99, 108, 118, 120, 157, 159–61, 163–64, 165, 167, 171–75, 177, 180–81, 239

coal trains, 8, 18, 155, 175

Great Northern Railway, 18, 75–76,
   98, 130, 135, 139, 142, 144, 150, 161,
   169, 171, 175, 214, 237
Greek immigrants, 91, 218
Griggs, Chauncey, 74

Hansen, Cecile, vii
Hanson, Anna, 254
Hanson, Charles, 81
Harris, Daniel Jefferson, 161, 177,
   178, 179, 180
Harte, Bret, 50
Hartley, Roland, 126, 132, 153
Hayes, Rutherford B., 213
Heide, August, 144, 146, 154
Herman, Fred, 239, 243, 258
Hewitt, Clara, 247
Hewitt, Henry, 245
Hewitt, Henry, Jr., 74, 129–30, 143,
   144, 147, 247
Hewitt, John, 245
Higginson, Ella, 157, 163, 181, 183
Higginson, Russell, 180, 181, 183
highways, ix, xiv, 11, 92, 242; 1956
   Federal-Aid Highway Act, 32;
   Highway 99, 112, 179; Highway
   520, 243. See also I-5; I-90
Hill, James J., 75, 130, 139, 141,
   153
Hillaire, Joseph, 166
historic preservation, xv, 113
Hitchcock, Henry-Russell, 28
hoboes, 194, 208, 212, 236
Homestead Act of 1862, 239
Hoquiam, xiv

hospitals, 9, 16, 17, 62, 67, 131, 144,
   146, 163, 180, 183, 242
hotels, xvi, 73, 87, 89, 134, 136, 180,
   195, 225, 232, 242; Bellingham
   Bay Hotel, 179–80; Blackwell
   Hotel, 88; Cadillac Hotel, 111;
   Chinook Hotel, 201; Coeur
   d'Alene Hotel, 222*map*, 224,
   226; Dacres Hotel, 68; Daven-
   port, 222*map*, 232; Fairhaven
   Hotel, 174*map*, 180, 182; Grand
   Central Hotel, 107*map*, 110;
   Grand Hotel, 200; Grand View
   Hotel, 172; Hotel Lusso, 232;
   Marcus Whitman Hotel, 53,
   56*map*, 68; Mitchell Hotel, 146;
   Monte Cristo Hotel, 140*map*,
   144, 146; Morrison Hotel, 112;
   Occidental Hotel, 107*map*, 113;
   Olympus Hotel, 89–90; Pacific
   House, 37–38; single-room occu-
   pancy, 216, 226, 227, 229; the
   Tacoma, 87, 87*fig.*; Washington
   Hotel, 36
houseboats, 121
Hove, Charles, 144
Howard, Rebecca, 38
Hudson's Bay Company, 4, 6–7, 12,
   14, 17, 21, 26, 31, 53, 213
Hutton, Levi "Al" and May Ark-
   wright, 214, 230–31, 232
Huxley College of Environmental
   Studies, 164
Hyde, Eugene, Martha, Rollin, and
   Samuel, 226

Museum of History and Industry, 115, 116*map*, 118, 127

Nabisco, 228
Naches River, 187, 208, 209
National Environmental Policy Act, 154, 155, 219
Native Americans, 25; reservations, 26, 36, 49, 77, 85, 94, 122, 168, 188, 192, 213. *See also individual groups, treaties*
Newell, Gordon, 37, 258
New Market, 31, 36
newspapers, 24, 40, 50, 59, 89, 91, 131, 192, 216, 219, 231, 233, 235
New York, viii, 51, 74, 98, 104, 129, 144
Nez Perce Indians, 47–50, 54, 57, 60*fig.*, 61–62; war, 57
Nez Perce Trail, 47, 53, 58, 61, 62, 63
Nisqually Indians, 25–26, 31, 39
Nisqually River and delta, 25
Nixon, Richard, 154, 220
Nooksack River, 158
Nordstrom, John, 101, 114
Northern Pacific Railway, 7, 18, 23, 27, 31, 51, 53, 63, 73–76, 77, 79, 81, 86–88, 94–96, 109, 129, 161, 175, 188, 189, 197, 201, 208, 209, 213, 214, 224, 247; headquarters, 73, 84*map*, 89, 92–93; land grants and timber sale, 74, 75, 88, 130, 189; terminus, 27, 38–39, 71–72, 78, 82–83, 85, 98, 160
Northwest Company, 5, 14
Northwest Museum of Arts and Culture, 215, 220, 237

Norton, Matthew, 142
Norwegian immigrants, 88, 147, 218. *See also* Scandinavians

Oakes, Thomas Fletcher, 144
Odd Fellows, 36, 64, 125
O'Donnell, Larry, 148
oil trains and tankers, 8, 18, 19, 94, 165, 175
Old Town Pioneer Walk, 79, 80–83; Chinese Reconciliation Park, 81; Job Carr's cabin, 82; Shubahlup, 81; Slavonian Hall, 82; St. Peter's Church, 82
Olmsted Brothers, viii, 179, 120, 122, 211, 219, 234, 258; Frederick Law Olmsted, Jr., 28; John Charles Olmsted, 28, 65, 101, 126–27, 234
Olympia, vi, x, xiii, xv, xvi, 7, 14, 23–45, 30*map*, 47, 60, 72, 97, 112, 125, 143, 203; capital, 23, 25–28, 34, 37, 39, 42, 44, 189; Indian wars, 26–27, 39, 42; legislature, 26, 27, 29, 35, 37, 39, 40–42; loop, 30*map*, 33–44; oysters, 33, 34, 36; port, 35; railroads, 38–39; resources, 45; sources, 258
Olympia Brewing Company, 31, 44, 90
Olympia sites: Barnes Bank Building, 36; Bigelow House, 30*map*, 35, 45; capitol building, 43*fig.*, 44; Capitol Campus, 42–44; Capitol Lake, xvi, 32, 33, 44; Cheet-woot, 34; Percival Landing, 34; Parker &

136, 139, 141–42, 159, 161, 162–63, 165, 187–88, 214, 240, 247, 259

Pugnetti, Don, 96

Puyallup Indians, 25, 72, 76, 77, 78, 81, 83, 85, 86*fig.*

Puyallup River, 73, 76, 77, 86, 88, 93, 94

Quiemuth, 39

railroads, viii, ix, x, 7, 52, 75, 76, 188

railroads, local and regional: in Bellingham, 157, 160, 165, 171–73; Bellingham Bay and British Columbia Railroad (BB & BC), 160, 172–74; Bellingham Bay and Eastern Railroad, 160, 172; in Everett, 130, 135; Fairhaven and Southern Railroad, 161; in Olympia, 31, 38–39; in Seattle, 98, 101; Seattle, Lake Shore and Eastern Railroad, 118, 242; in Spokane, 211, 214, 218, 224, 226, 236; Walla Walla and Columbia River Railroad Company, 51–52, 59, 62, 63; in Yakima, 208–9

railroads, transcontinental: x, 13, 23, 26, 27, 71, 73–78, 95, 139, 171, 212, 214, 217, 227, 228, 232, 239; Burlington Northern Santa Fe, 175; Canadian, 160. *See also* Great Northern; Milwaukee Road; Northern Pacific; Union Pacific

Rainier, Mount, 44, 72, 85, 122, 124, 126, 172, 192, 208

ranching, viii; cattle, 31, 51, 65, 187, 188; sheep, 43, 51, 188

Reclamation Act of 1902, 189, 202

Renton, xiii, 121, 243

Ricard, Pascal, 36

Ridgefield National Wildlife Refuge, 9

Rimrock Dam, 190, 205

Rockefeller, John D., 129, 130, 144, 154

Rockwell, Kate, 91

Roeder, Henry and Elizabeth, 158–59, 166–70

Roeder, Victor A., 172

Rogers, John, 40, 131

Roosevelt, Eleanor, 22

Roosevelt, Franklin, 192

Roosevelt, Theodore, 76, 143, 189, 201, 202, 228

Rucker, Bethel, Jane, and Wyatt, 142, 144

Russell, Ella M., 145

Rust, William R., 92

Ruston, 83, 92; smelter, 79–80

salmon, viii, 9, 12, 13, 33, 34, 143, 161–62, 170, 176–77, 211, 221

saloons, 52–53, 59, 61, 63, 73, 89, 99–100, 110, 145, 172, 179–80, 225, 228, 240

Salvation Army, 111, 148, 229

San Francisco, 24, 34, 51, 59, 66, 71, 73, 81, 97, 98, 103, 108, 158, 160, 169, 257

San Juan Islands, 158

sawmills, viii, 28, 74, 88, 157, 163, 170, 173, 182, 213

Scandinavians, vii, 82, 147, 162, 192. *See also* Finns; Norwegians; Swedes

Schmidt, Leopold, 30*map*, 31, 44, 90

Schupp, William, 251

Schwabacher family, 59, 106, 109

Scott Paper Company, 152

Seale, William, 28

Seattle, vi, vii, viii, ix, xiii, 8, 27, 53, 74, 97–127, 107*map*, 116–17*maps*, 133, 150, 170, 172, 189, 192, 226; Arctic Club, 101, 112, 113; Battle of, 26, 39; bicycles, 114, 115, 122; Chinese in, 77, 102, 108, 110; Eastside connections, 239, 242–45, 251, 254; fire, 90, 99, 107*map*, 108, 110; founding, 97–98, 103–4; gold rush, x, 90, 99–103, 107, 109–14, 119; houseboats, 121; interurban, 106, 111, 112, 148, 149; loop, 106–14; Native Americans in, vii, 97, 98, 104, 106, 111, 115, 118, 122; neighborhoods, 242; parks, 101, 119–20, 121, 122; planning, ix, 258; port, 76, 101; railroads, 72, 95, 98, 101, 118, 122, 141, 161, 214, 217, 242, 247; regrades, 101, 118; resources, 127; Seattle City Light, 120; ship canal, 117*map*, 118, 122, 240; skid road, 98, 108; skyscrapers, 112, 113; sources, 258; South Lake Union to University of Washing-

ton extended walk, xvi, 115–27; trade, 98, 99, 101; twentieth century, 102; university, location of, 26–27, 98–99, 102, 122; world's fairs, ix, 102, 103, 115, 118, 122. *See also* AYPE; Duwamish River

Seattle sites: Alaska Building, 113; Alki pioneer walk, xv, 103–5; Arctic Building, 113; assay office, 112; bathhouse, 104; Burke-Gilman Trail, 117*map*, 122, 127; Cadillac Hotel building, 11; Center for Wooden Boats, 116*map*, 118, 119, 127; Cheshiahud trail, 119–22; Delmar Building, 110; Duwamish Longhouse, 106; Fairview Park, 116*map*, 122; Ford Motor Company, 119; Grand Central Hotel, 110; Herrings House, vii; Interurban Building, 111; Jack Block Park, 105; J. &. M Café, 110; Klondike Gold Rush National Historical Park, 111; Lake Union Drydock, 116*map*, 120; Lake Union Steam Plant, 116*map*, 120; landing monument, 104; Lippy Building, 109; Lynn Street Park, 116*map*, 121; Maud Building, 110; Maynard Building, 110; Merchant's Café, 113; Metropole Building, 113; Morrison Hotel, 112; Mutual Life Building, 109; North Wind's Fish Weir, 106; Occidental Park, 111; Olympic Block, 109; Pioneer Building,

port, 7–8, 18–19; resources, 22; settlement, 4, 6–7, 12; shipyards, 7–8, 9, 19, 20, 21*fig.*, 22, 192; trade, 3–5, 7, 12, 14, 15, 21; transportation routes, 7, 11, 18; wartime, 7–8, 15, 18–19, 21

Vancouver, Wash., sites: Academy, 17; apple tree, 12; balm of Gilead tree, 19; Boat of Discovery, 19; Esther Short Park, 17; George Vancouver statue, 18; Hidden House, 17; Ilchee statue, 20–21; Kaiser Viewing Tower, 22; land bridge, 11–12; Pioneer Mother statue, 17; St. James Cathedral, 17; wall of murals, 18; Wendy Rose monument, 21–22. *See also* Columbia River Renaissance Trail; Fort Vancouver

Vancouver National Historic Reserve, 15. *See also* Fort Vancouver

Vanport, 8

Verona, 150–51, 151*fig.*

veterans, 57, 72, 82, 91, 164, 240, 241, 249, 250; memorials, 18, 201

Victoria, B.C., 26, 38, 158

Victory Ships, 8

Vietnam War, 18, 92, 164, 220

voyageurs, 3, 5

Wade, Richard C., 3

Wadin, Marguerite, 14

Waiilatpu, 48, 51, 52, 54, 62

Wainwright, Jonathan M., 57

walking, viii, ix, x, xiii, xv, xvi

Walla Walla, vi, viii, x, xiii, 27, 36, 47–69, 56*map*, 97, 107, 125, 189, 203, 213; cattle ranching, 51, 65; Chinese community, 66; churches, 52, 53, 54, 64, 66; constitutional convention, 47, 60, 65; frontier aspect, 47, 50, 52, 53, 62, 67, 67*fig.*, 68; gold rush, 50, 58, 66; Italian immigrants, 67; loop, 55–68; parks, 53, 55, 56*map*, 57, 62, 65; railroad, 51–52, 59, 62, 63, 65; resources, 69; sources, 258; treaty council, 49, 60*fig.*, 61, 63, 66; wheat farming, 51–52, 57, 59, 64, 65, 68

Walla Walla Indians, 55

Walla Walla River, 47, 48, 50, 53, 58

Walla Walla sites: Baker-Boyer Bank, 59; Barrett Building, 60; Baumeister Building, 59; Brechtel Building, 59; Christopher Columbus statue, 67; Dacres Hotel, 68; First National Bank Building, 59; Die Brucke Building, 61; Drumheller building, home, 65, 66; Fort Walla Walla, 57; Heritage Park, 55, 62, 64; Isaacs home, 64; Marcus Whitman Hotel, 68; Marcus Whitman statue, 62; Mill Creek, 55, 57; Nez Perce Trail, 47, 53, 58, 61, 62; Odd Fellows Home, 64; Paine Building, 59; Peo Peo Mox Mox statue, 55; Pioneer Park, 57, 65; Reynolds-Day Building, 60; Sayer Building, 60; Schwabacher

Wilson, Otis, 135

wine, 53, 61, 67, 68, 189, 193, 197

Wobblies. *See* Industrial Workers of the World

Wodnik, Bob, 155

women's clubs, 125, 203–4

women's suffrage, 37, 64, 124, 125, 145, 149, 204, 231

Work Projects Administration, 134, 197

Works Progress Administration, 252, 259

world's fairs and expositions, ix, 212, 219; Chicago, 102, 115, 226; Portland, 15, 102; Seattle (1962), 102, 118; Spokane (1890), 219; St. Louis, 147. *See also* AYPE; Expo '74

World War I, 3, 7, 15, 18, 102, 133, 175, 217, 230, 252

World War II, xiii, xiv, 3, 7–8, 16, 18, 21, 22, 57, 78, 102, 164, 193, 198, 218, 228, 239, 241

Wright, Charles, 73, 85

Wyoming, 24, 27, 28, 49, 165

Yakama Indians, 26, 39, 49, 61, 62, 187–88, 189, 190, 191, 192, 202, 203

Yakima, vi, viii, x, xiii, xv, 187–209, 195*map*, 226; Congdon Orchards, 191, 204, 205, 209; farmworkers, 190–93, 204, 205; fruit row, 190, 194, 195*map*, 197, 198*fig.*, 202; Great Depression, 190, 199, 204, 205; Hispanics in,

193; irrigation, 187–90, 193, 199, 200, 201, 203, 205; loop, 194–205; move, 188; North Yakima, 28, 188, 196; public services, 193; railroads, 188–89, 194–99, 203, 206*map*, 208–9; resources, 209; schools, 190, 192–94, 197, 207; sources, 258; state fair, 189–90; stockade, 191, 204*fig.*, 205; water systems, 193, 201, 203*fig.*, 209; wine, 189, 193, 197; Yakima City, 188, 195, 203

Yakima Firing Center, 192

Yakima Greenway, 194, 205–8

Yakima Project, 189–90

Yakima River, viii, ix, 187–90, 192, 208

Yakima sites: Capitol Theatre, 200; City Hall, 196; federal building, 200; Fire Station No. 1, 200; First Church of Christ Scientist, 202; Fruit Exchange Building, 197; Grand Hotel, 200; historic district, 195; JEM Building, 201; Larson Building, 199; Lund Building, 197; Millennium Plaza, 199; Naches Ave., 199, 201, 203*fig.*; Naches River railroad bridge, 208; Northern Pacific depot, 195–96; Opera House, 196; Rotary Lake, 206*map*, 208; St. Joseph's Catholic Church, 202; St. Michael's Episcopal Church, 201; The Tower, 201; Union Pacific buildings, 197; Weisenberger monument, 201;